POSTCARD HISTORY SERIES

Richmond
ON THE JAMES

POSTCARD HISTORY SERIES

Richmond ON THE JAMES

Louis H. Manarin

ARCADIA
PUBLISHING

ISBN 978-0-7385-1384-3

Published by Arcadia Publishing
Charleston, South Carolina

Printed in the United States of America

Library of Congress Catalog Card Number: 2001092147

For all general information contact Arcadia Publishing at:
Telephone 843-853-2070
Fax 843-853-0044
E-mail sales@arcadiapublishing.com
For customer service and orders:
Toll-Free 1-888-313-2665

Visit us on the Internet at www.arcadiapublishing.com

Contents

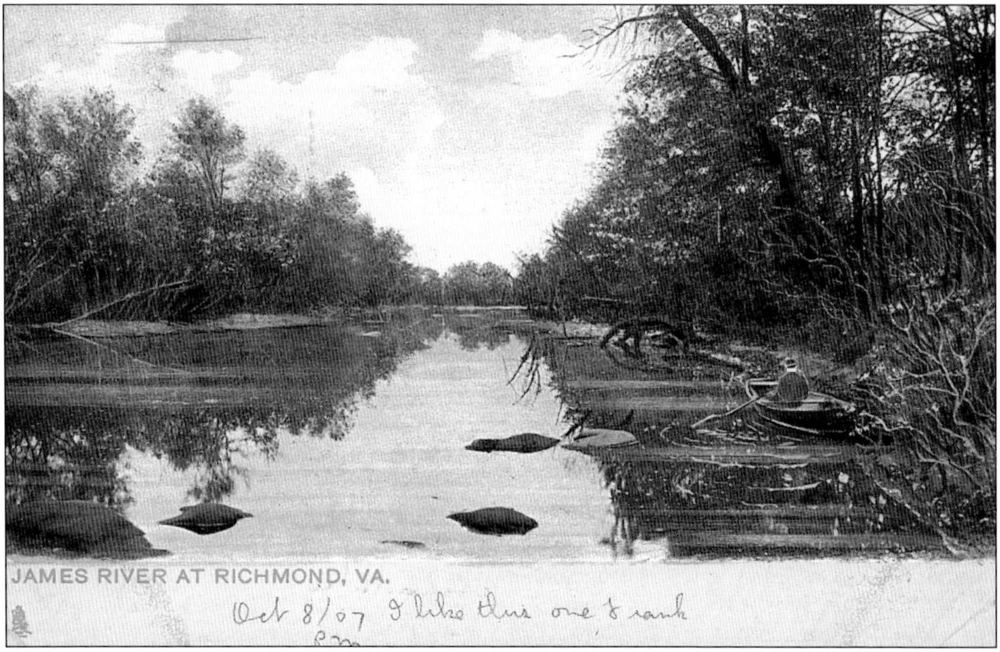

ACKNOWLEDGMENTS

A work of this nature is truly the product of several minds. My interest in the history of Richmond sparked interest in collecting Richmond postcards. Numerous reference people in the city's archival and historical research institutions assisted in identifying sources of historical data. A special note of thanks is due to Terisa Roan, the reference librarian at the Valentine Museum, for her tireless efforts on my behalf. A debt of gratitude is also owed to Fran Costin for her help in providing facts about the Chesterfield Apartments on Grace Street.

As a collector and historian I wish to thank those collectors and dealers who willingly shared their knowledge about the history of postcards. To John Knowles Lorraine Jr., a special thanks for encouraging my interest some 20 years ago and for allowing me to examine his extensive collection. Also, to Richard W. "Dusty" Rhodes, a fellow Kiwanian, who graciously presented his personal collection to the author.

To my wife, Jo Ann, I owe a special debt of gratitude. You dealt with my collecting habits and assisted in preparing this work for publication. Together we dedicate this book to our granddaughters, Grace and Kerry Cavanaugh.

Louis H. Manarin
Richmond, Virginia

Introduction

English explorers under Capt. Christopher Newport first visited the falls of the James River in May 1607. After finding the site of the present city of Richmond inhabited by Indians of the Powhatan Confederation, Captain Newport erected a cross on one of the islands in the river and claimed the land for King James I. In August 1609, Capt. Francis West was sent up to the falls to establish a fort near Shockoe Creek and Powhatan's village. Purchasing land from the Indians, Captain West erected West's Fort. As president of the governing council, Capt. John Smith referred to the falls area as "Non such" and "World's end." After losing several men to Indian attacks, Captain West abandoned the fort and returned to Jamestown.

Not until 1611 did the governing council authorize a second attempt to establish a fort at the falls of the James. Sir Thomas Dale decided to plant a settlement to command the falls and the islands below them. Although initially tenuous, the colony began to grow and land along the falls was granted to wealthy influential colonists. Thomas Stegge Jr. amassed a considerable estate on the south side of the falls and established a trading post. In 1670 his lands and the trading post passed to his nephew William Byrd I. In March 1676, Byrd received a grant of land on the north side of the James. Expanding trade with the Indians, Byrd became the leading Indian trader in Virginia. The volume of trade soon necessitated the establishment of a warehouse at the falls. William Byrd II, Byrd's son, inherited the land; and in 1730 the General Assembly authorized a public warehouse on William Byrd II's land at Shockoe Creek. In 1733 Byrd decided to establish a "city" at the mouth of Shockoe Creek to be call Richmond in honor of Richmond on the Thames River in England. The area at the falls of the James, once referred to as "world's end," was intended by nature and trade routes to become a market center.

Maj. William Mayo agreed to lay out the proposed "city" into lots. In April 1737 the town lots were offered for sale for seven pounds each. On June 19, 1742, the General Assembly passed an Act "establishing the Town of Richmond." The town grew as the frontier expanded to the west and farmers began sending their crops down river. As an inland port the city experienced increased growth and prosperity. In June 1779 the General Assembly decided to move the seat of government from Williamsburg to Richmond. The move was not completed until May 1780. On May 1 the assembly resolved that the public building would be located on Shockoe Hill.

During the Revolution the city was visited by British troops under Benedict Arnold in January 1781 and by Lord Cornwallis in June 1781. The torch was liberally applied to magazines, workshops, and public buildings during both periods of occupation.

After the war, in May 1782, the Town of Richmond was incorporated under the name of the City of Richmond, and on July 1, 1782, the citizens elected 12 men to the city's first Common

Hall. The incorporating act defined the powers of the city and transferred all property, real and personal, formerly vested in the trustees of the Town of Richmond to "the corporation for the benefit of the said city."

The City of Richmond continued to grow as a commercial center, and its population increased from 3,761 in 1790 to 16,060 in 1830. Thirty years later, in 1860, Richmond opened the decade with a population of 37,968. By 1860 the city's economic base rested on banking, flour mills, tobacco factories, coal and iron works, and numerous supportive industries. During the first five years of the 1860s it served as the capital of the Confederate states. At the end of the war, in April 1865, Richmonders once again found their business district in ashes and the manufacturing interests in ruin. Although under occupation until 1870, Richmonders increased to 51,000 and began to rebuild their city. During the last 30 years of the century the city experienced economic and population growth even though local and national depressions tended to stunt that growth. By 1900 the city's population increased by 34,000 over 1870's number to 85,000. After 1900 the city's population increased by 50 percent during the first decade of the new century. The city grew in size by annexation of land from neighboring counties, and by 1920, there were over 171,000 inhabitants. Nearly 35,000 Richmonders were employed in manufacturing firms. Tobacco related products accounted for 20 percent of the total production valued at $157 million. Foundry, machine shop, and agricultural implements, fertilizers, and chemicals helped make up the balance. However, the stock market crash of 1929 halted Richmond's great leap forward. Like many other Americans, Richmonders maintained a determination and commitment to overcome adversity during the Depression. Prosperity returned during the 1940s, and Richmond became a vibrant urban center.

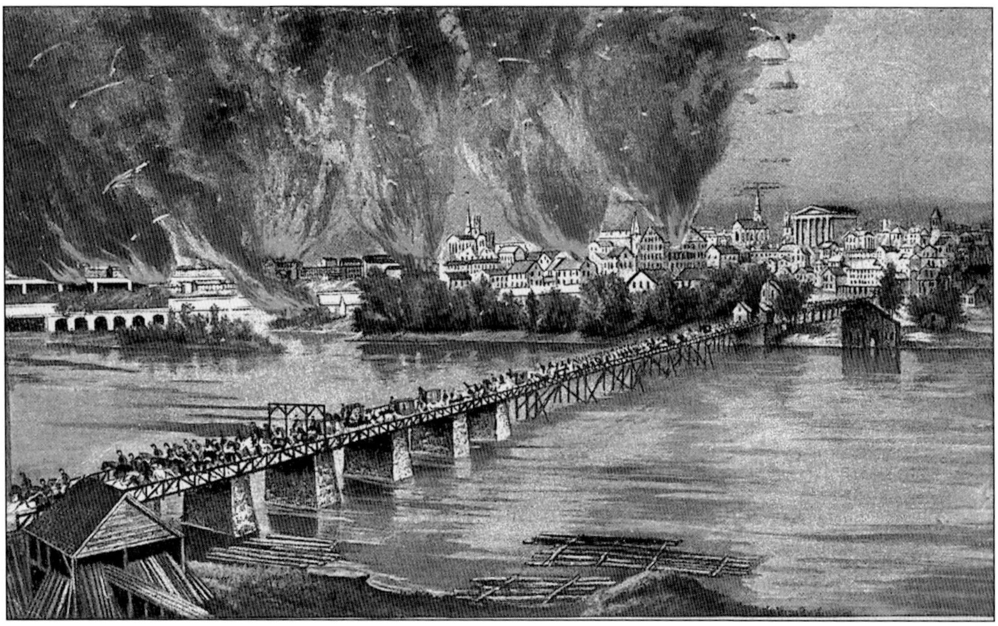

Confederate leaders and troops in Richmond were evacuated on the night of April 2, 1865 when the city was threatened by the impending Federal occupation. Departing troops destroyed commodities such as tobacco and cotton so that they would not fall into Union hands.

One

The James River

When Capt. Christopher Newport led a party of 22 men up the river to the present site of the City of Richmond in May 1607, the members of the Algonquian tribes referred to the river as Chief Powhatan's river. At the future site of the city, Newport encountered large rocks in the river. Capt. John Smith, a member of the expedition, described the area of the falls thusly: "We were intercepted with great craggy stones in the midst of the river, where the water falleth so rudely, and with such a violence, as not any boat can possible passe."[1] Unable to continue above the falls, Captain Newport landed on one of the islands in the river and erected a cross with the inscription "Jacobus, Rex, 1607." By doing so he claimed the river and the land for King James I and renamed the river James River.

During the city's early years the lack of water depth prevented the docking of larger vessels until the Richmond Dock Company opened navigation from the upper wharf at Rockett's Landing by constructing docking facilities. Above the city, the James River Canal Company constructed a canal along the north bank of the river from the city to bypass the falls. Eventually a canal connecting the James River Canal Company's basin with the port at Rockett's opened navigation from up river to tidewater. The docking facilities were enlarged to accommodate larger vessels, and Richmond developed a thriving maritime industry.

The James River has always been a vital part of the life of Richmond. First, it was the principal means of transportation down river. Later, as the frontier expanded westward and a canal was constructed around the falls, the city became a bustling port for trans-shipping products shipped from up river. Formed by the confluence of the Jackson and Cowpasture Rivers in Botetourt County, the James flows east some 340 miles into the Chesapeake Bay through a broad estuary at Hampton Roads. Navigable up to Richmond, a deep-water terminal for ocean-going vessels serves the city.

1. John Smith, *True Relations, 1608,* ed. Albert Bushnell Hart and Edward Channing (New York: 1896), 3.

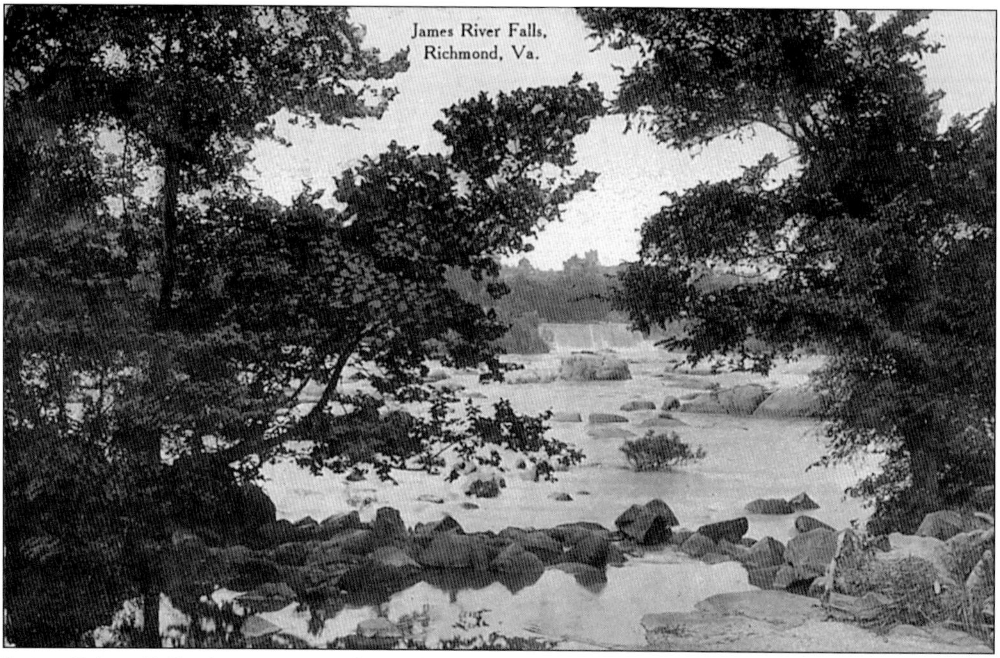

James River Falls, just up river from the center of the city, is shown in this postcard. The absence of man-made structures provides a glimpse of how the river must have looked when the first settlers visited the falls in 1607.

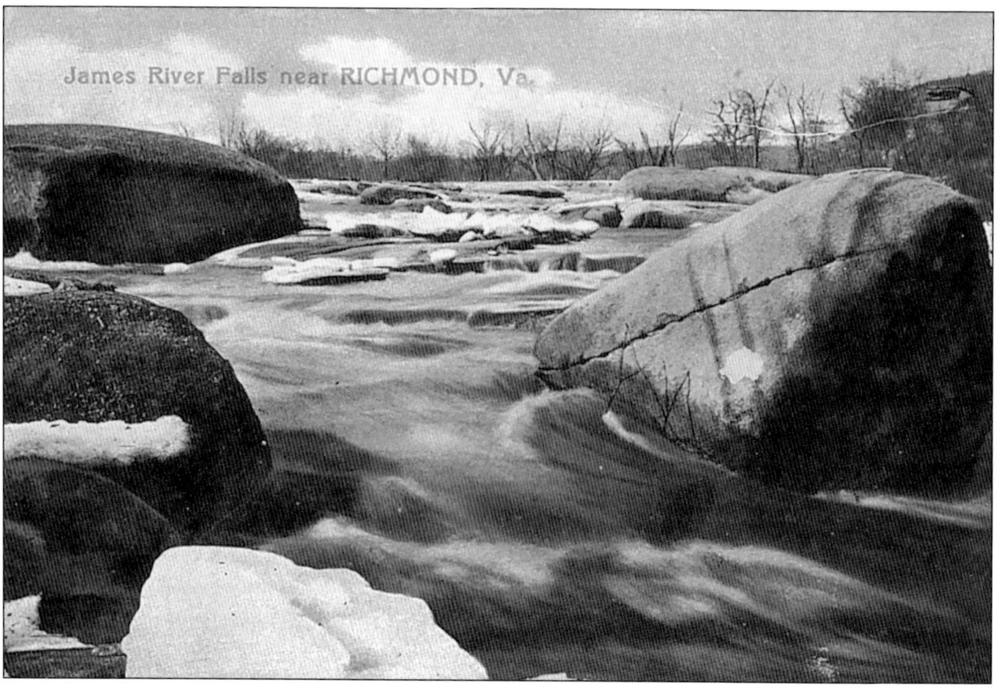

The James River from just above the falls is seen in the postcard above.

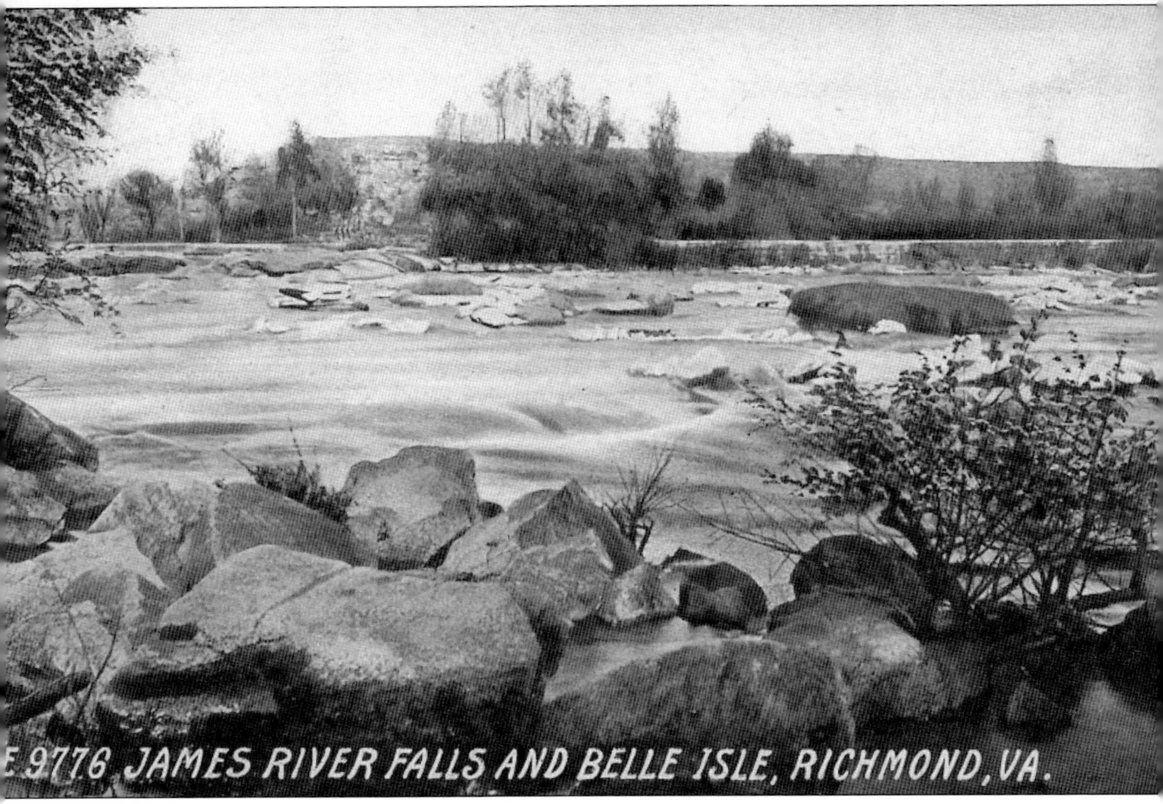

Below the falls there are several islands. The largest of these is Belle Island on which the Confederates established a prisoner of war camp during the Civil War.

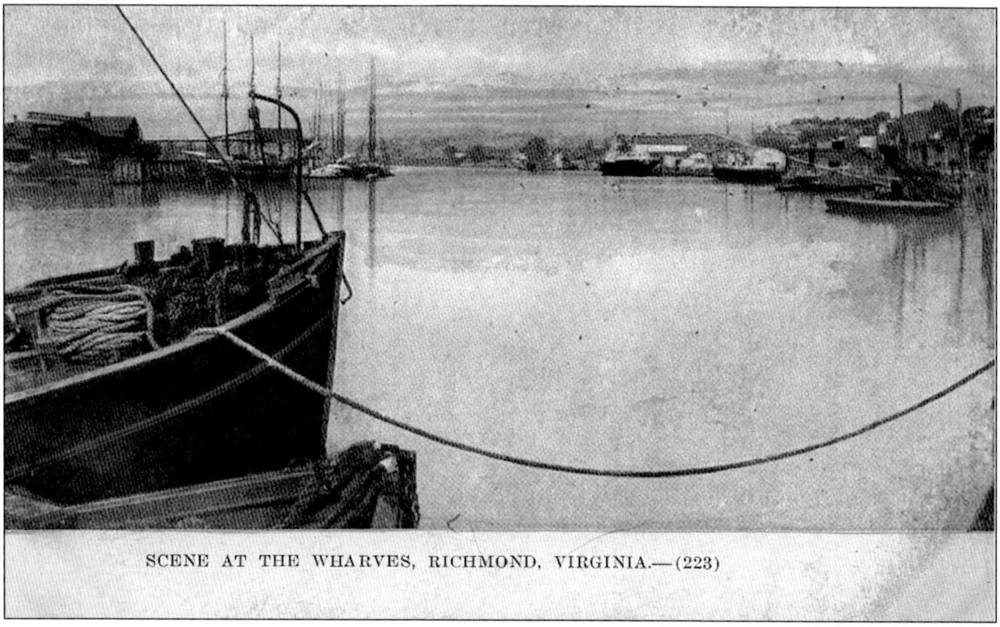

This postcard provides two views of the port at Rockett's on the eastern end of the city. It was so named because Robert Rockett operated a ferry across the river at that point as early as 1730. The spot where his ferry docked was called Rockett's Landing. It was here that the first steamboat arrived in Richmond in 1816. During the Civil War it was part of the Confederate Navy Yard.

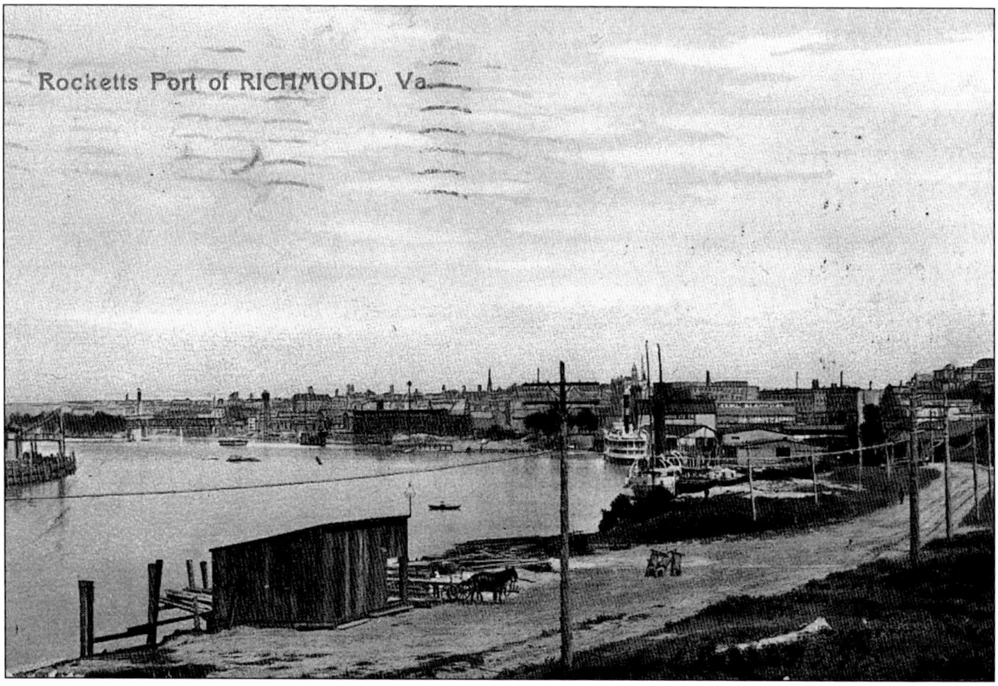

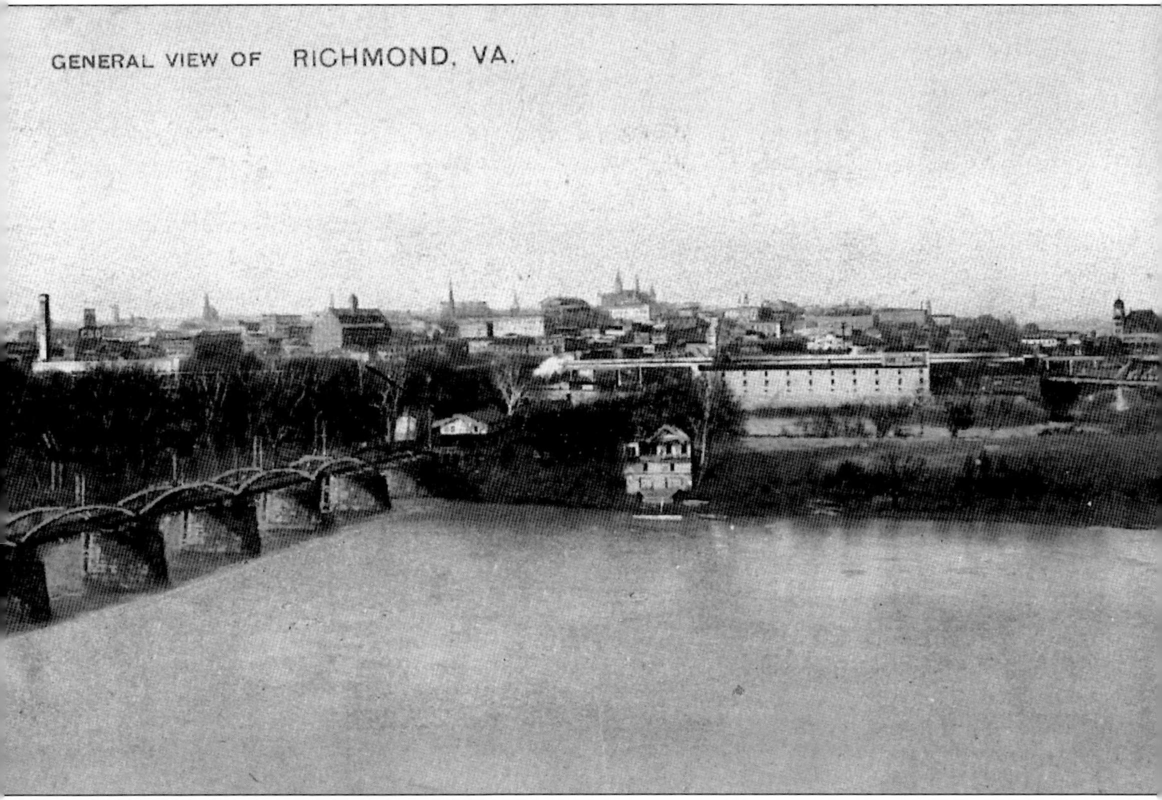

The first bridge across the James River was a plank structure privately built by John Mayo Jr. in 1788. Mayo's original structure extended from the north bank to an island and then crossed to the south bank on pontoons. It was destroyed by river ice, so Mayo replaced it. As the owner of the bridge, Mayo collected tolls, and the bridge became known as Mayo's Bridge. The island also belonged to Mayo; it became Mayo's Island. The bridge washed away a number of times during the 19th century, even after the construction of stone piers. This view of the bridge, captured prior to 1911, was taken from the south bank. Mayo's Island is in the foreground and the Capitol and City Hall are visible on the skyline. The large wooden structure on Mayo's Island was owned by the Virginia Boat Club, which was founded about 1894. The structure burned in December 1930.

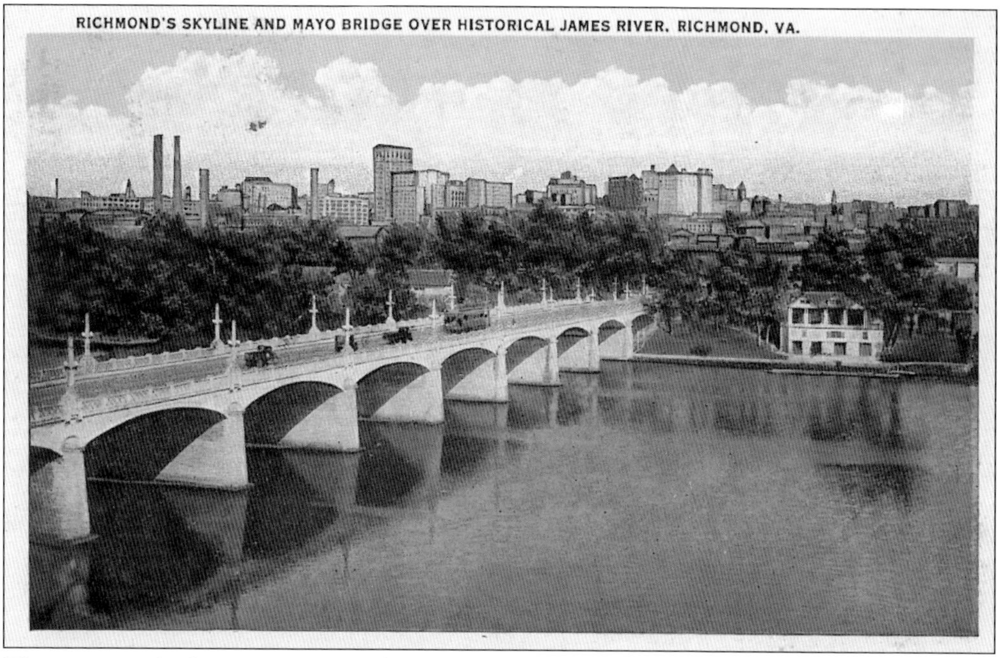

These postcards show two views of the new Mayo Bridge. In 1911 construction started on the concrete and steel span pictured in these views, looking from the south bank of the river. Referred to as the Mayo Bridge and the Fourteenth Street Bridge, it was completed at a cost of $300,000 and opened to traffic in September 1913.

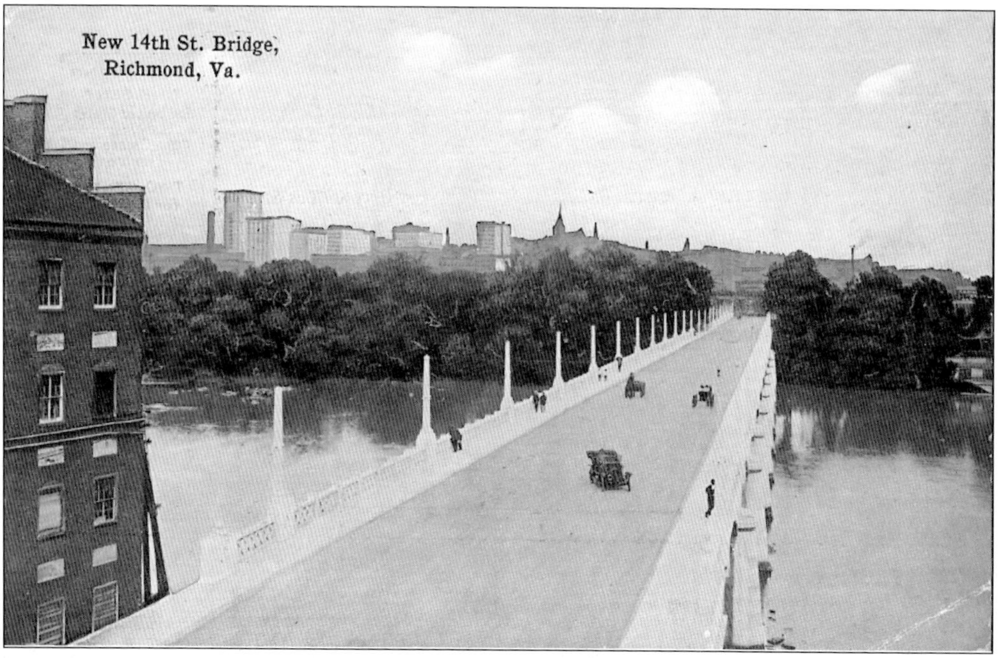

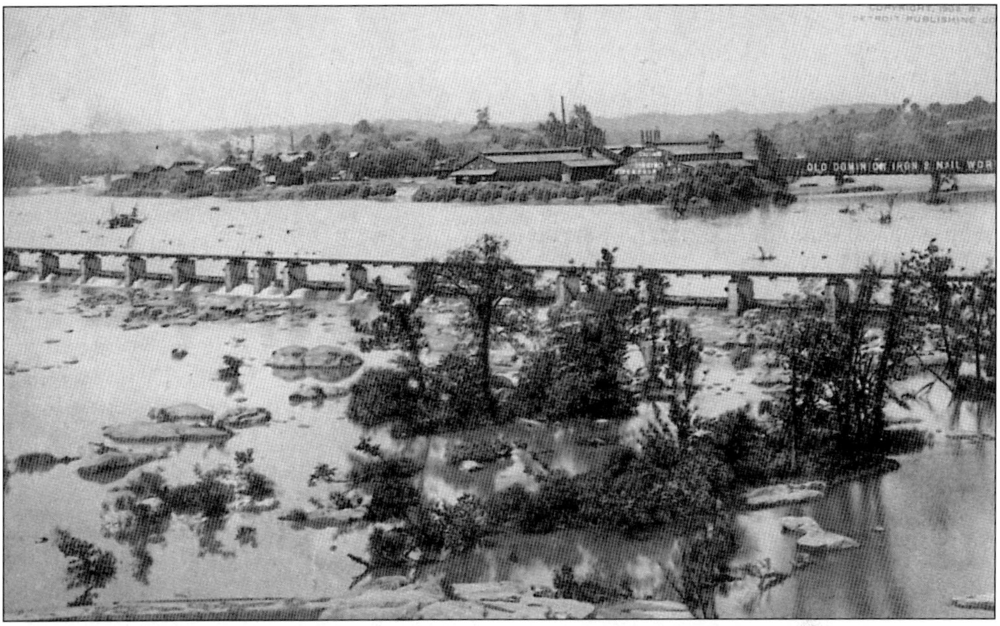

Up the river from Mayo's Island is Belle Island. Seen in the view above is the Old Dominion Iron and Nail Works on the eastern end of the island. The predecessor of this company was the Belle Isle Manufacturing Company, which was founded in 1836. The bridge in the foreground is the Chesapeake & Ohio (C&O) Railroad bridge. The lower view shows Belle Island from the north bank. The granite formation afforded business opportunities for quarries to flourish. Pictured here is a stone-crushing plant. The railroad tracks in the foreground were laid on the towpath of the James River Canal, which appears in the immediate foreground.

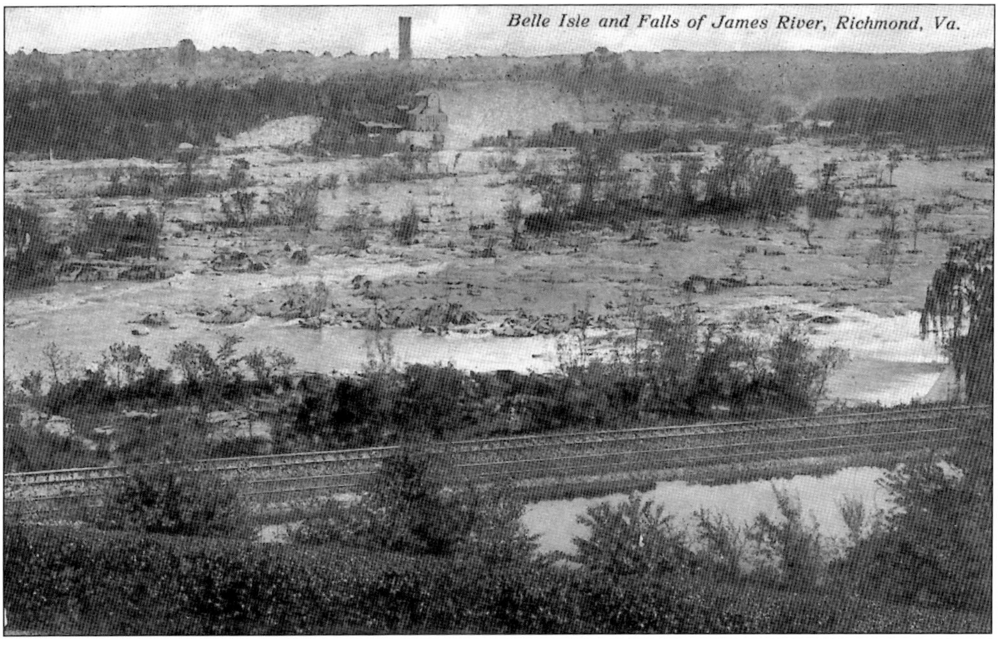

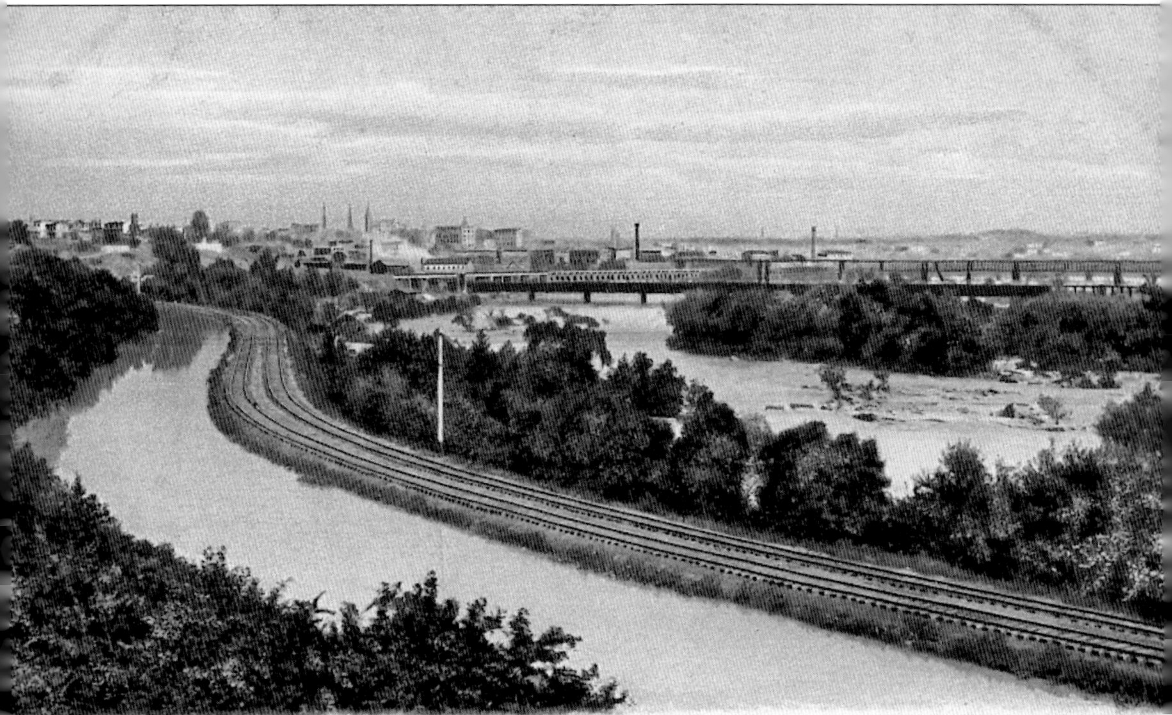

BIRD'S-EYE VIEW OF RICHMOND, VA. and James River from Hollywood Cemetery.

Looking east from Hollywood Cemetery a visitor can view the city's skyline and the river in all its majesty. In the foreground is the James River Canal with the tracks of the Richmond & Allegheny (R&A) Railroad on the towpath. Belle Island can be seen in the river. The numerous railroad bridges spanning the river give testimony to the city's economic strength. The steeples of Broad Street Methodist and St. Paul's Episcopal Churches can be seen on the skyline along with City Hall.

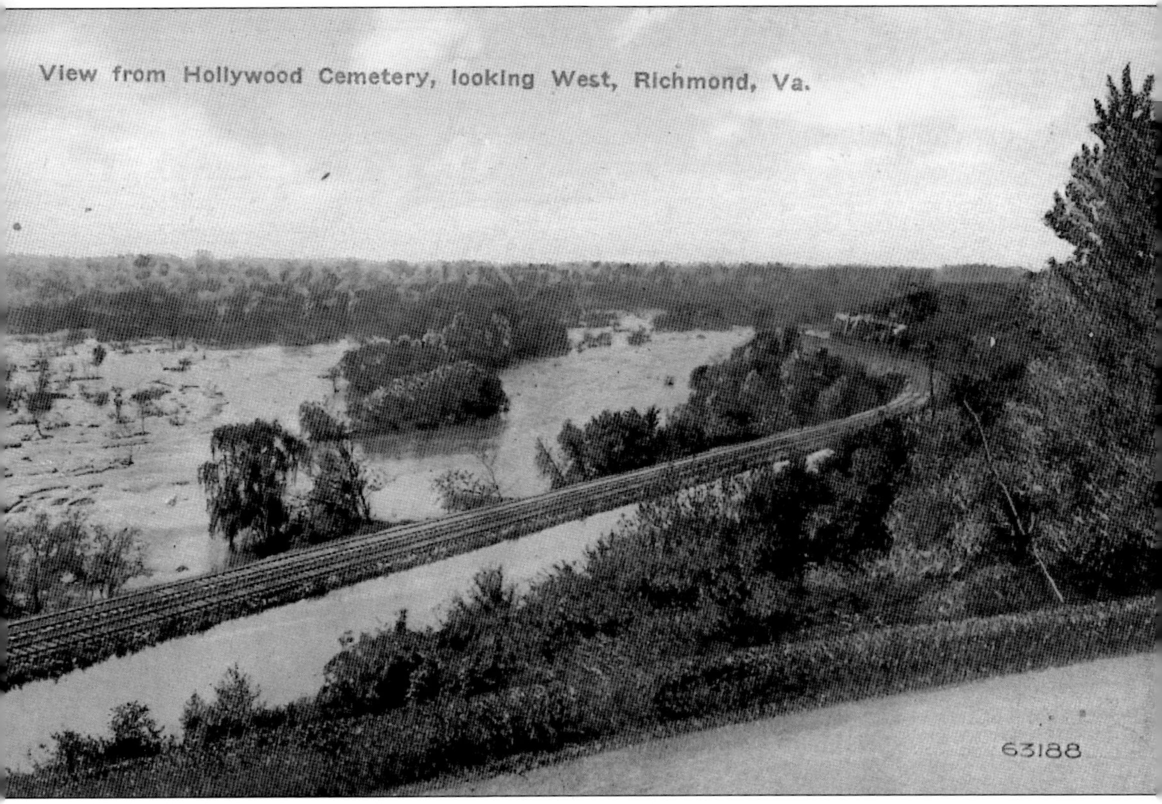

A view of the falls is provided when looking west, up the river, from Hollywood Cemetery. The turbulent waters of the James can be seen cascading over and around the rocks. The James River Canal and the tracks of the Richmond & Allegheny Railroad on the towpath can be seen in the foreground. The Chesapeake & Ohio Railroad acquired the Richmond & Allegheny tracks.

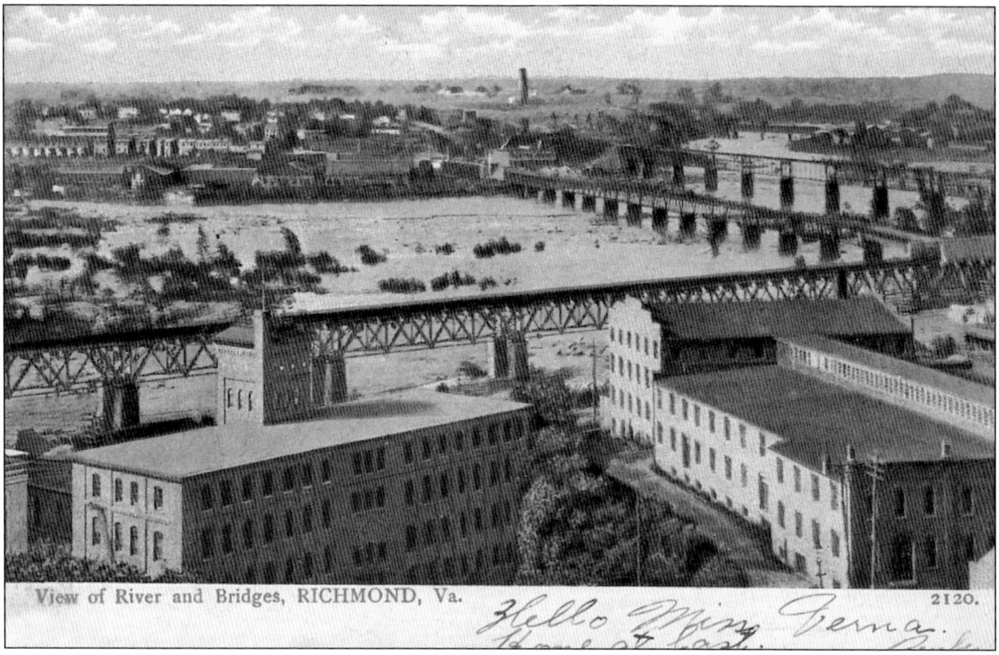

Across the river from Richmond the town of Rocky Ridge grew into the City of Manchester. In 1910 Manchester merged with Richmond and became Washington Ward. Pictured below are the Southern Railroad shops on the south bank of the river.

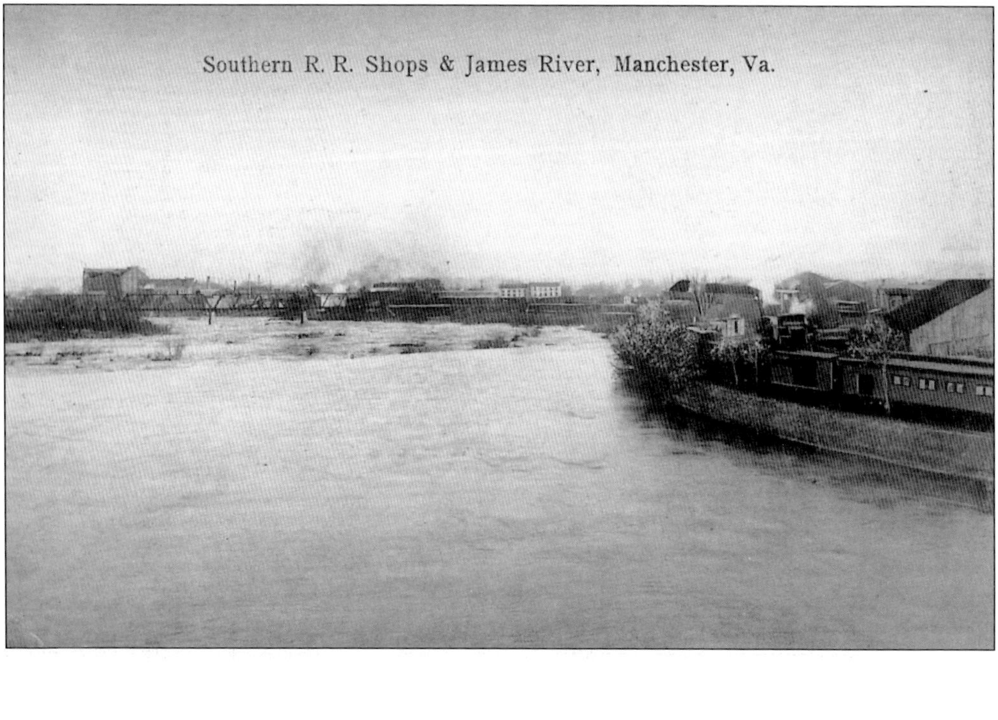

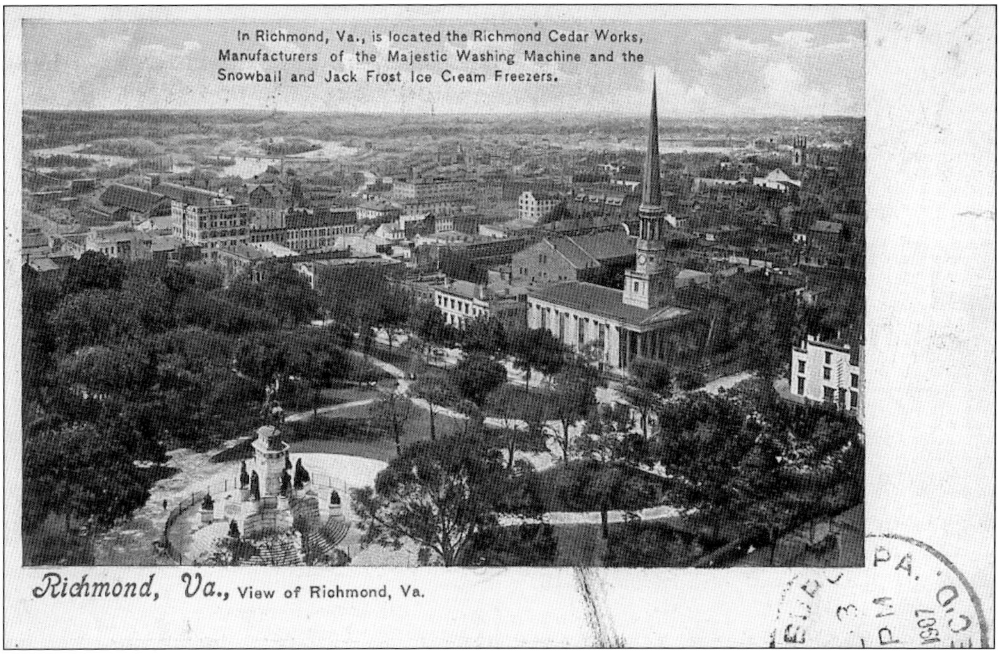

The postcard above shows a bird's-eye view of the James River from Capitol Square. Rocks on the James River, as seen from Belle Island, are pictured below. The loading ramps are all that remain of a quarry.

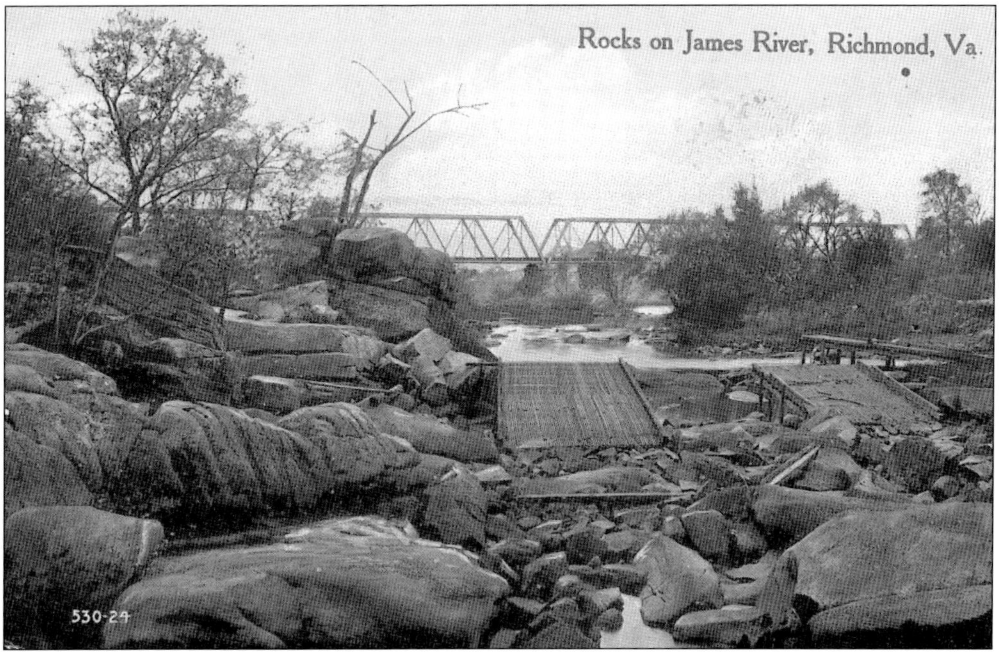

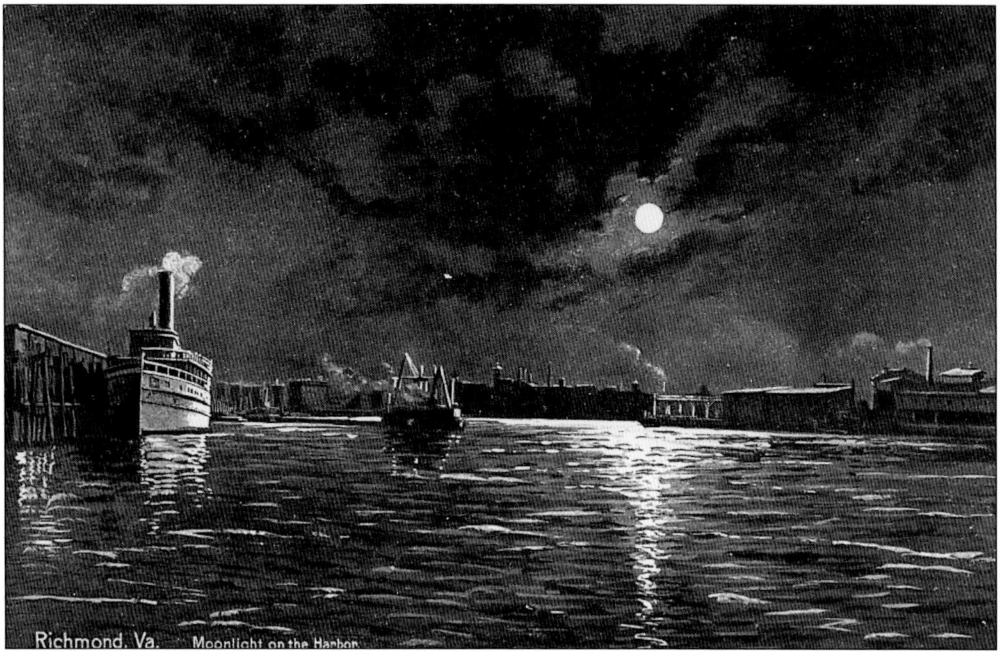

These postcards showcase night scenes on the James River. The top view is entitled "Moonlight on the Harbor" and captures the port at Rockett's at night. The lower image is of the Mayo, or Fourteenth Street, Bridge at night with a streetcar passing over it.

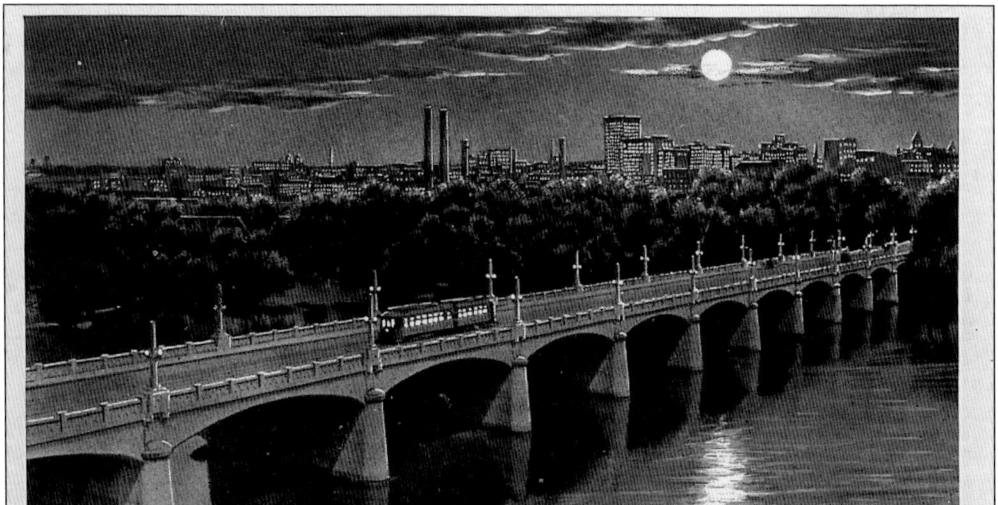

Two

Capitol Square

By an act of the General Assembly passed on June 12, 1779, the seat of government was moved from Williamsburg to Richmond. Under the act, the directors of public buildings were empowered with authority to enlarge the boundaries of the town and to set aside six squares for public buildings. Specifically the act made reference to a capitol, halls of justice, statehouse, and governor's mansion to be located on the six-square parcel. Using the power of condemnation, the directors acquired six squares on Shockoe Hill to create one large tract to be known as Capitol Square.

Originally Capitol Square was a rugged piece of ground with deep ravines on either side of the crest of the hill. Springs of cool water flowed from various spots at the base of the hill, and after a heavy rain, the ravines were filled with raging water. When the land was cleared, only a few of the original trees, oaks and pines, were left standing. Ground cover was limited to a few chinquapin bushes and jimson weed. In 1816 Maximilein Godefroy, a French architect and engineer, was employed to landscape the Square. Godefroy proposed the closing of the streets that ran through the square and enclosing it with an iron fence. He proposed grading the hillside to eliminate the deep ravines and the planting of trees in a formal garden. Godefroy's plan met with opposition both as to design and cost. It was not until 1824, when the city assumed responsibility for caring for the square, that a large number of trees were set out. In the 1850s while laying out Hollywood Cemetery, John Notman was paid $200 by the City Council to prepare a landscape design for Capitol Square. Notman's design incorporated shade trees, grass, winding paths, and open vistas. He also lowered the mound in front of the Capitol and included ornate fountains on either side at the bottom of the hill. By doing so he transformed the rugged hillside into a pleasant oasis in the midst of a bustling city.

Capitol Square has been enhanced by the addition of walkways that follow the contours of the hillside and by the placement of numerous statues on the grounds. As the seat of government, Capitol Square also serves to preserve significant aspects of the city's and the state's history.

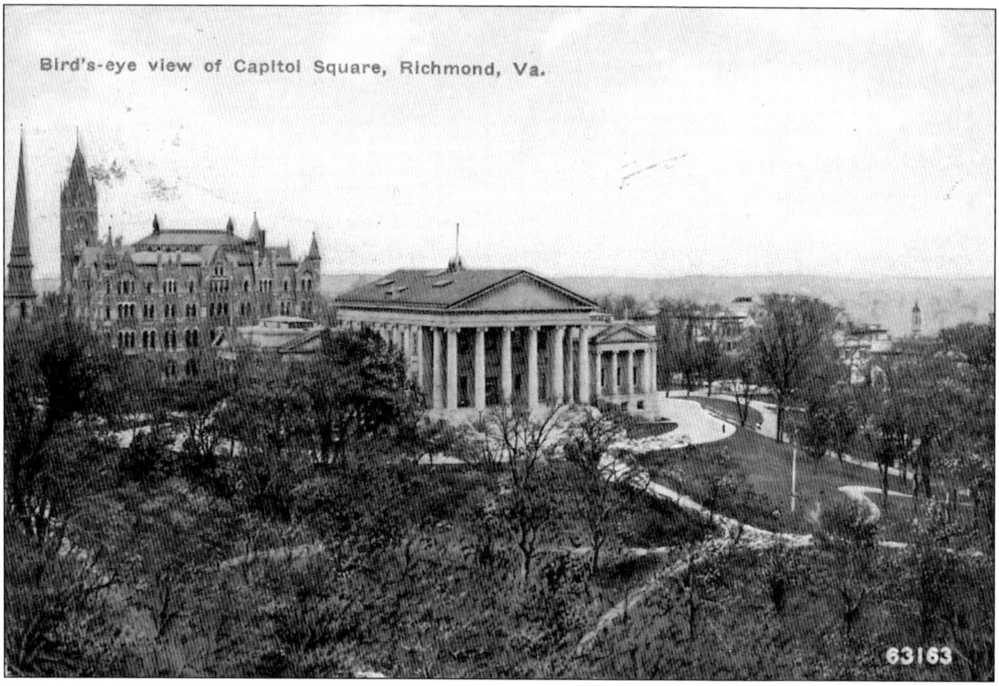

When the cornerstone of Virginia's Capitol was laid on August 18, 1785, the view from Capitol Square was unobstructed by other structures. As the city grew around it, the Square became enclosed by high-rise buildings. The Capitol was also expanded with the addition of two wings shortly after the turn of the 20th century. These two postcards provide views of the Capitol with its two wings. The upper card is a bird's-eye view taken around 1910. Richmond's City Hall stands in the background. The lower view reveals the Senate wing, which is hidden behind the trees in the upper view.

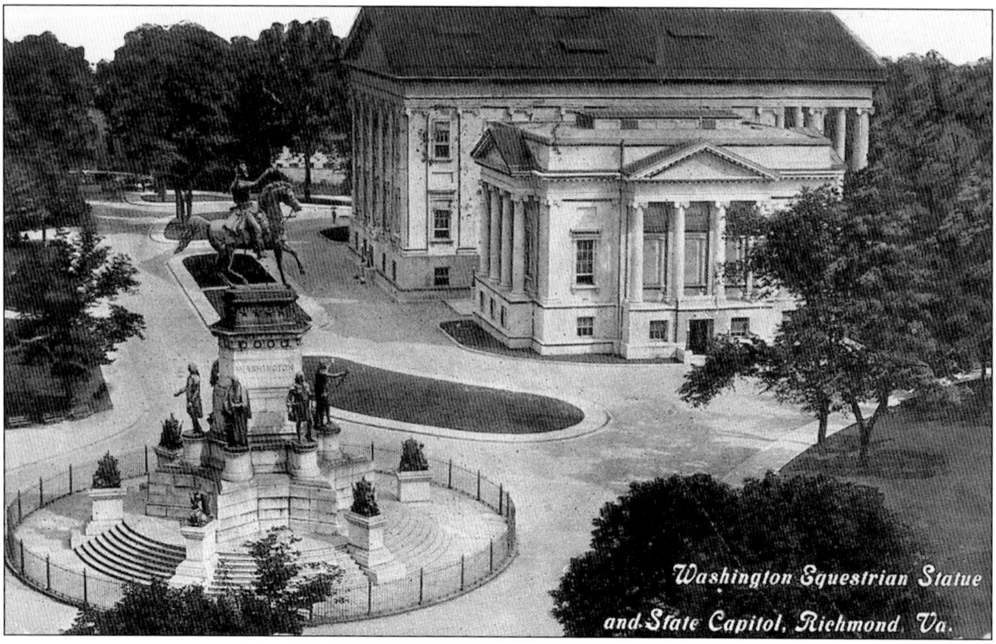

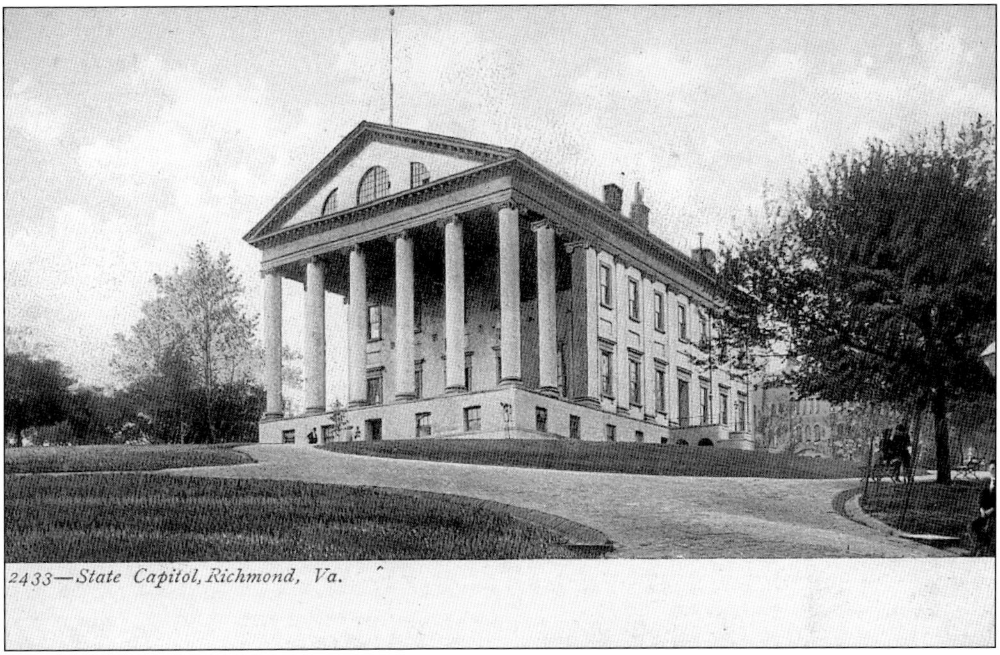

The postcards above and below show views of the Capitol prior to the addition of the wings that would provide new halls for the Senate and House, a project that was completed in January 1906. As one of the directors of public buildings, Thomas Jefferson recommended that the Capitol be modeled after the Maison Carreé, a Roman temple in Nimes, France. The cornerstone was laid on August 18, 1875. Constructed of red brick, the building was not covered with stucco until 1800.

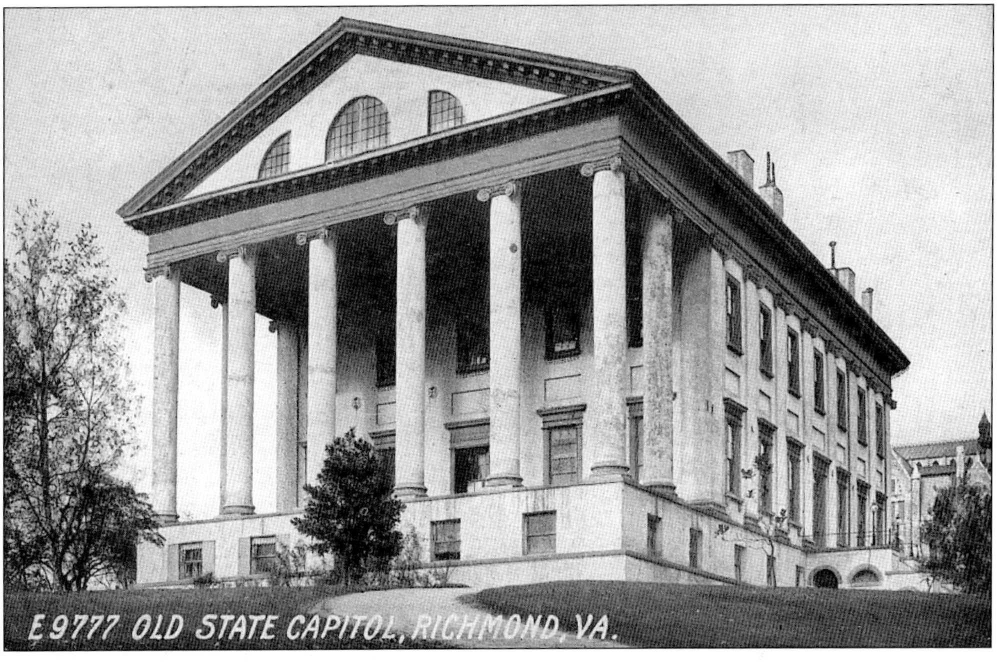

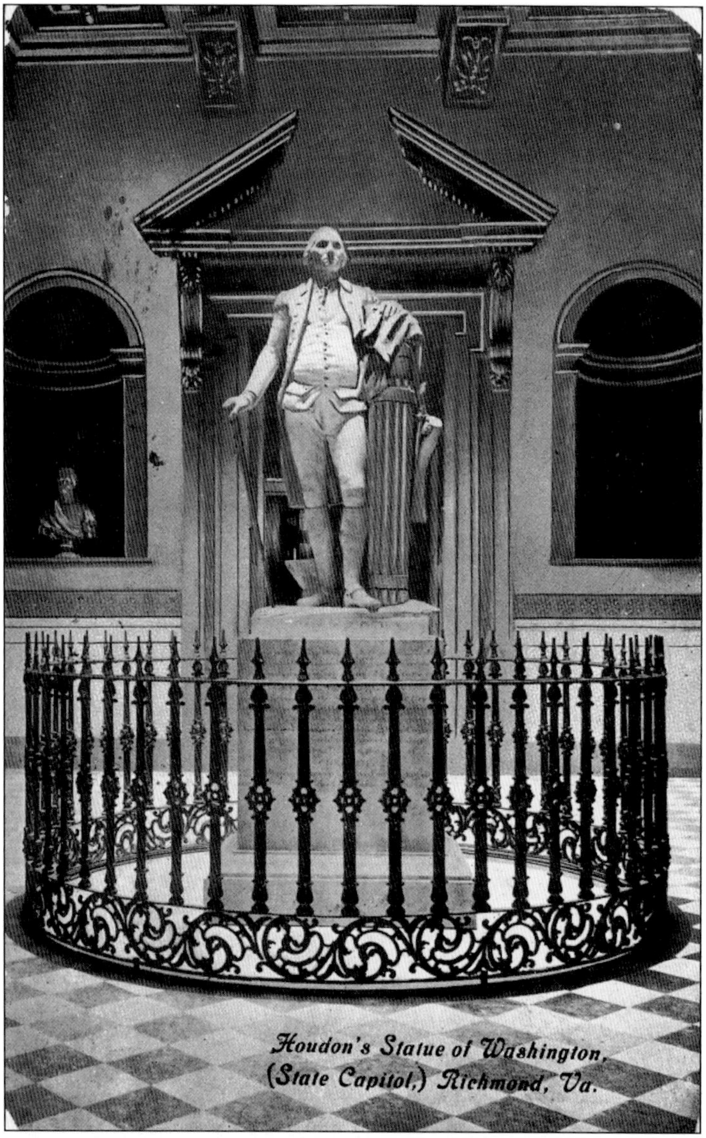

Sculpted by Jean-Antoine Houdon from Carrara marble and located in the Capitol rotunda, this statue of George Washington is based on measurements made by Houdon while on a visit to Mount Vernon in 1785. Taking a plaster model back with him to Paris, Houdon completed the marble statue in his studio in 1789. It remained there until 1796 when it was shipped to Richmond and placed in the completed rotunda. There it was placed on a pedestal. An inscription composed by James Madison was not carved on the pedestal until 1814.

While the General Assembly was in session in January 1866, gunfire erupted in the rotunda. The publishers of the *Enquirer* decided to resort to the use of weapons to respond to critical articles in the *Examiner.* Henry Rives Pollard of the *Examiner* sought refuge behind Houdon's Washington and drew his pistol. Nathaniel Tyler and William D. Coleman of the *Enquirer* pulled out their pistols. Only Pollard and Coleman fired at each other. They missed their targets, but one bullet knocked the marble tassel from Washington's cane. In 1903 a visitor to the Capitol broke off a piece of the ploughshare on the base of the statue. The iron fence surrounding the statue was put in place to protect the statue from vandals.

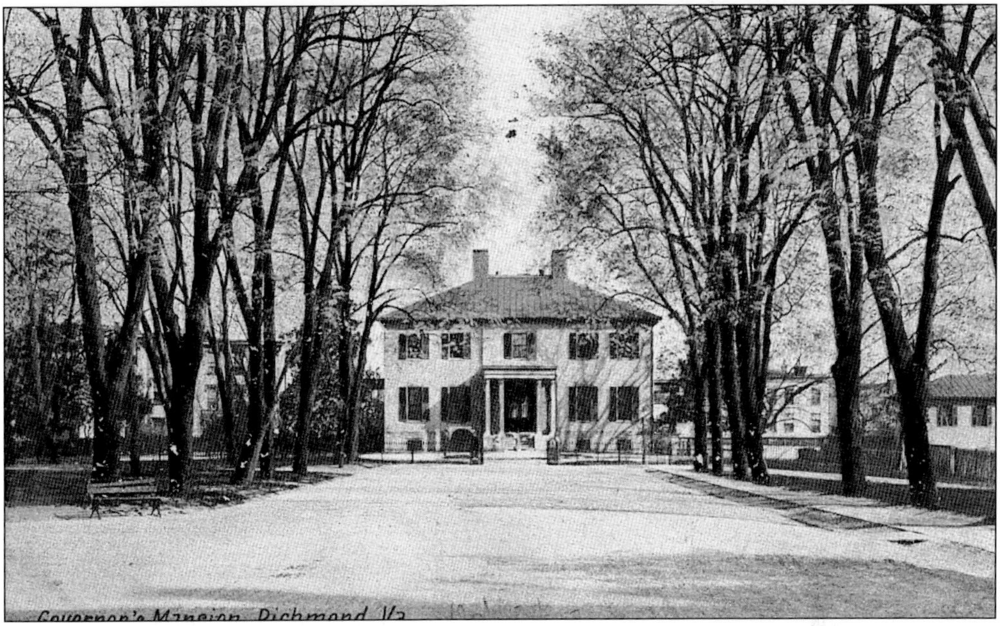

Alexander Parris, a native of Massachusetts, designed the Governor's Mansion. This Federal-style structure was under construction by July 1811 and was completed by January 1813 at a cost of $14,525.53. Outbuildings, fencing, grading, and construction and appraisal fees added an additional $4,346.29 for a total of $18,871.82. Gov. James Barbour first occupied the home in March 1813, and it has served as the home of the Commonwealth's chief executive since that date. Except for alterations to the side porches and the removal of the balustrades between the chimneys and around the main and porch roofs, the general appearance of the building's exterior had not changed between the time of its construction and the printing of these *c.* 1900 postcard views. The iron fence, however, has since given way to a brick serpentine wall.

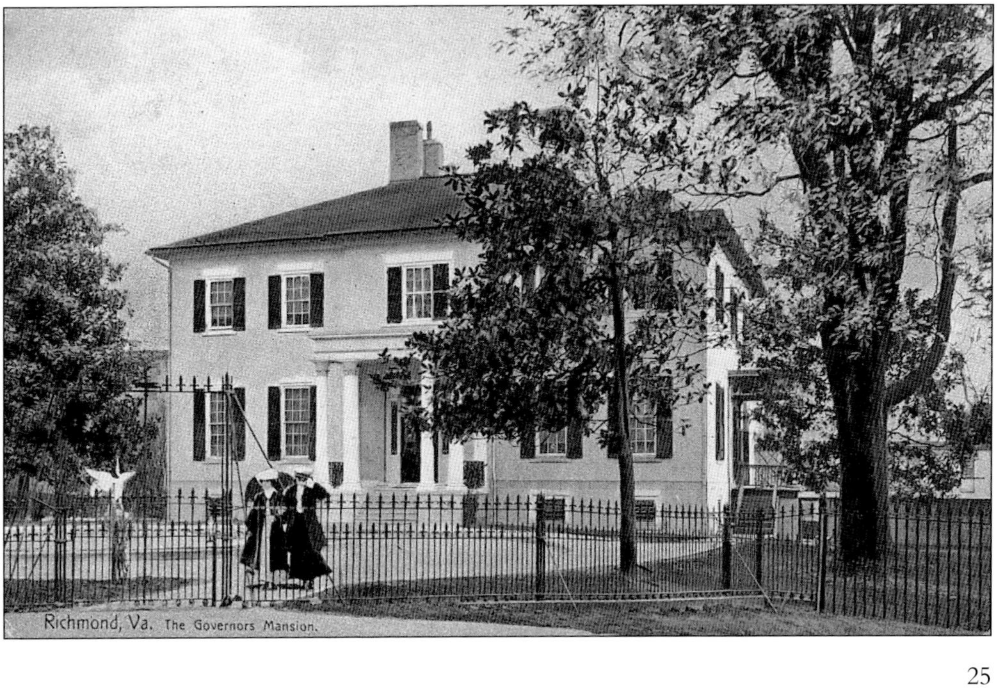

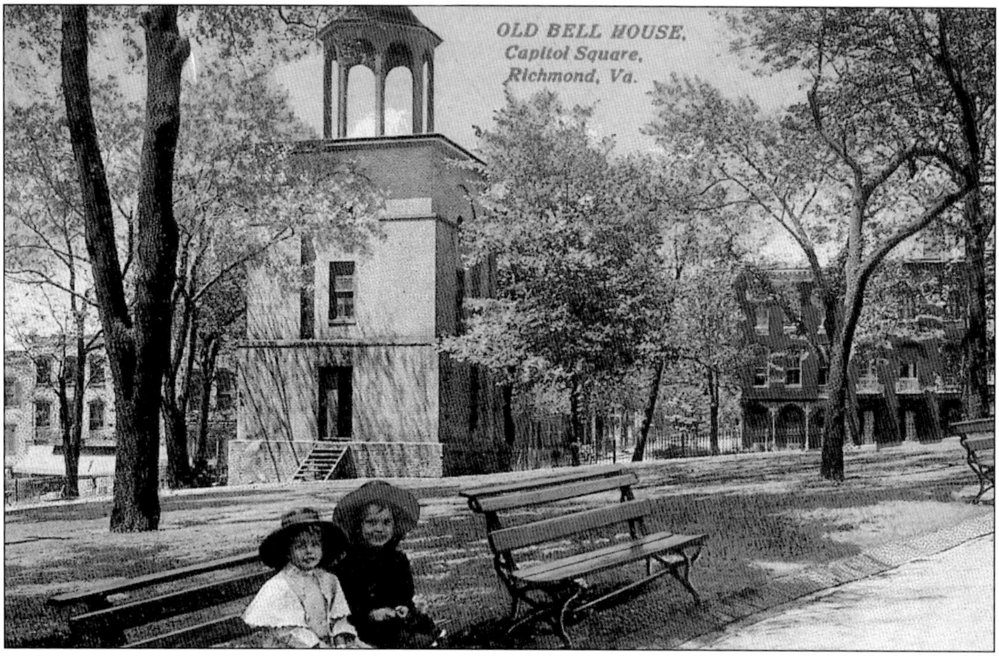

The Bell Tower, built in 1824, stands in the southwest corner of Capitol Square, near the corner of Ninth and Bank Streets. It replaced a wooden building known as The Barracks. The structure was erected for the accommodation of the detachment of the State Guard stationed for the protection of the Capitol, and its lower floors served as a guardhouse and armory. The bell was used during General Assembly sessions to summon legislators, to warn of fires in the city, and to call out the militia and local defense troops during military emergencies.

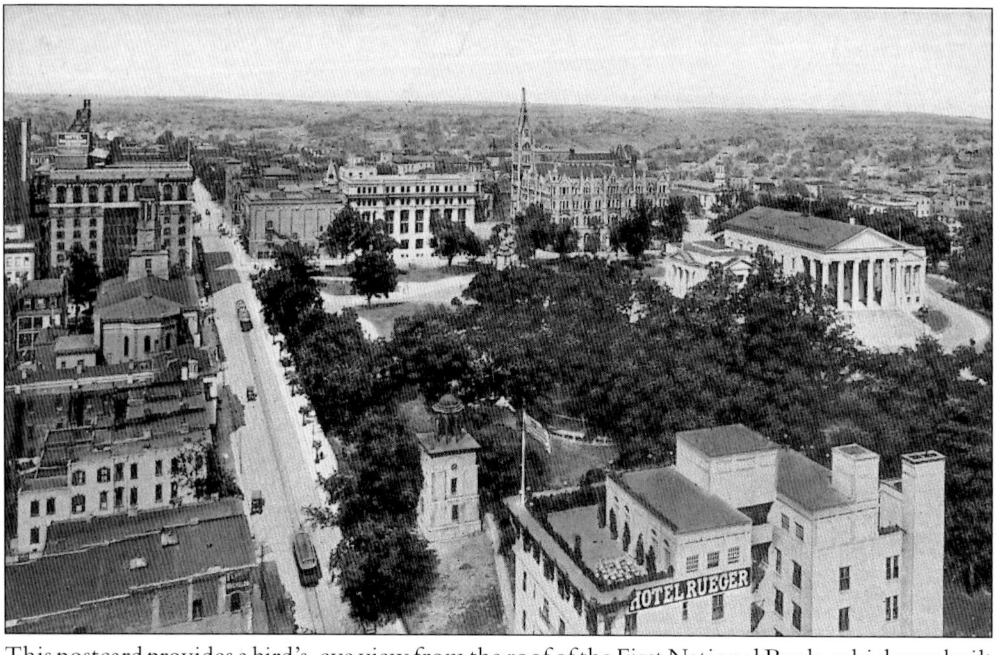

This postcard provides a bird's-eye view from the roof of the First National Bank, which was built in 1913. Note the Bell Tower in the center foreground just across from the Hotel Rueger.

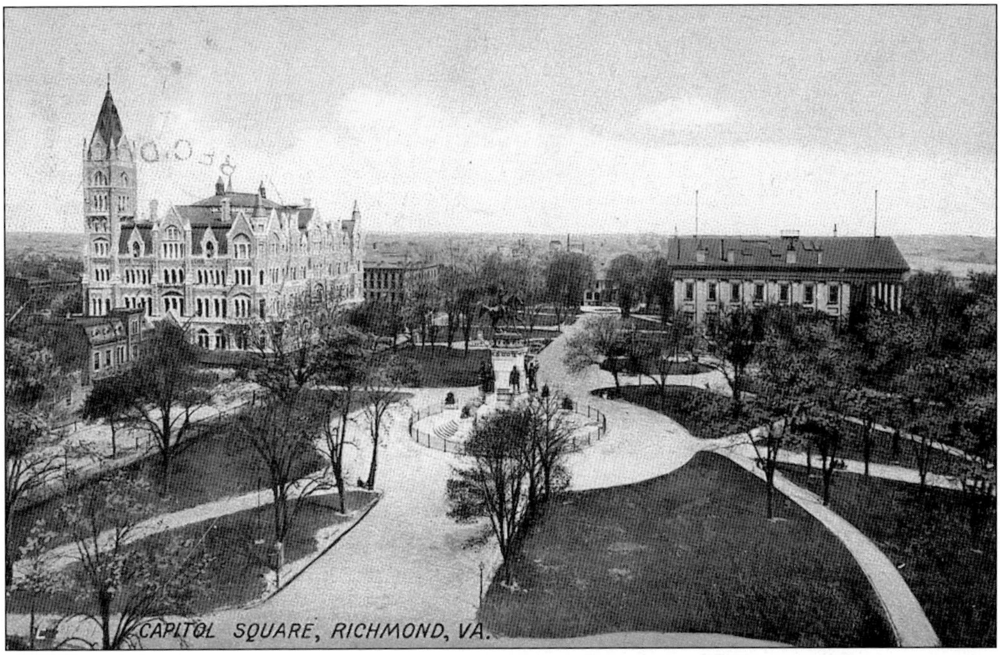

The postcards above and below show two views of the northern half of Capitol Square looking east. The equestrian statue of Washington is in the foreground and the Governor's Mansion is at the far end of the wide gravel roadway. To the right is the State Capitol and to the left is the Richmond City Hall, which was built in 1894. In the upper image the red brick building to the right of city hall is the Ford Hotel. It was demolished to make way for the Supreme Court of Appeals–State Library building. In the lower image the church to the left of City Hall was Broad Street Methodist. Today the new City Hall occupies this site.

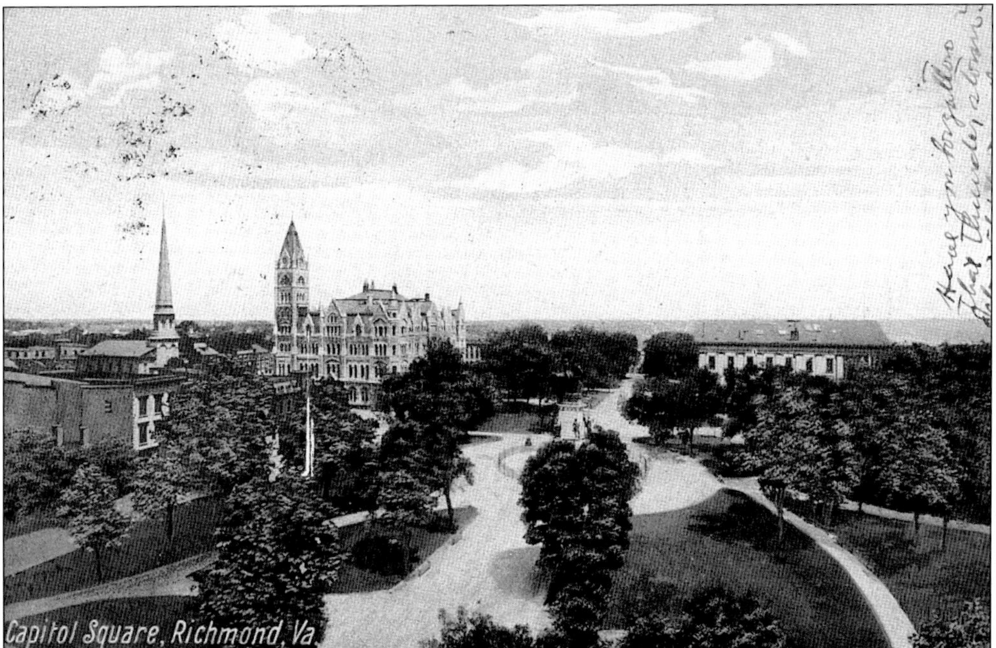

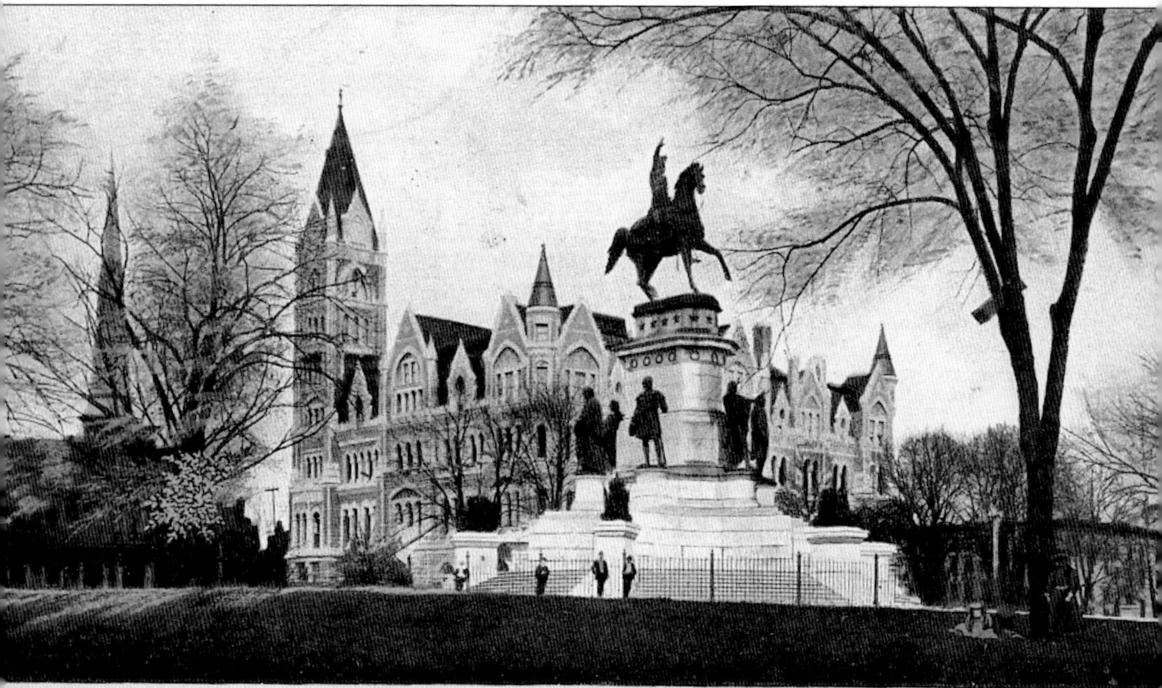

ITY HALL, WASHINGTON MONUMENT, RICHMOND, VA.

The Washington Monument on Capitol Square was designed by Thomas Crawford of New York, and the cornerstone was laid on February 11, 1850. Crawford was living in Rome at the time and he completed the statues of Thomas Jefferson and Patrick Henry by 1855. They were cast in Munich and shipped to Richmond. The equestrian statue of George Washington was also cast in Munich, and it arrived in Richmond in 1857. Weighing 18 tons, it was dragged by horses from the city dock to Main Street. From there, men and boys pulled it up Ninth Street to the entrance of Capitol Square. Under the direction of Capt. Charles Dimmock, an engineer, the horse and rider were raised to the pedestal, and the statue was unveiled on February 22, 1858. Crawford finished the statue of George Mason before his death from a brain tumor. He had also completed the statue of John Marshall, except for the head. The statue of Mason was cast and installed on the monument in 1860. Randolph Rogers contracted to complete the John Marshall statue and to execute statues of Thomas Nelson and Andrew Lewis. These were completed and installed in 1867. Rogers also designed the allegorical figures on the lower tier; the last of these was installed on June 24, 1869.

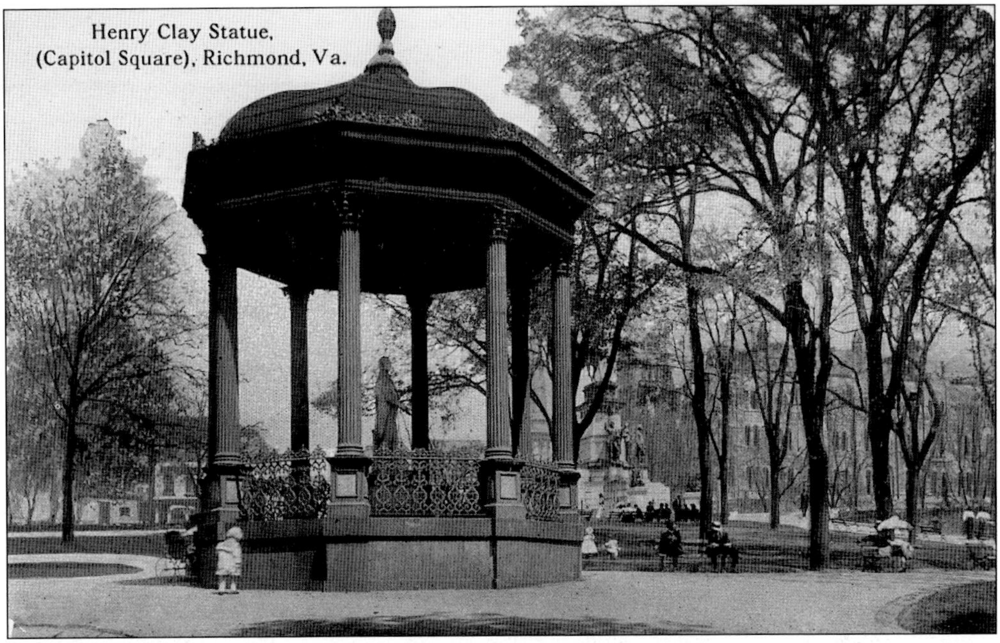

The Henry Clay statue stood on the slope just northeast of the Bell Tower. Joel T. Hart, a native of Kentucky, executed the marble statue of the author of the Missouri Compromise. It was unveiled on April 12, 1860 and later sheltered by an iron pavilion designed by Henry Exall, a local architect. The statue remained in place until 1930 when it was removed and placed in the old hall of the House of Delegates in the State Capitol. The iron pavilion, in need of repair, was torn down in 1932.

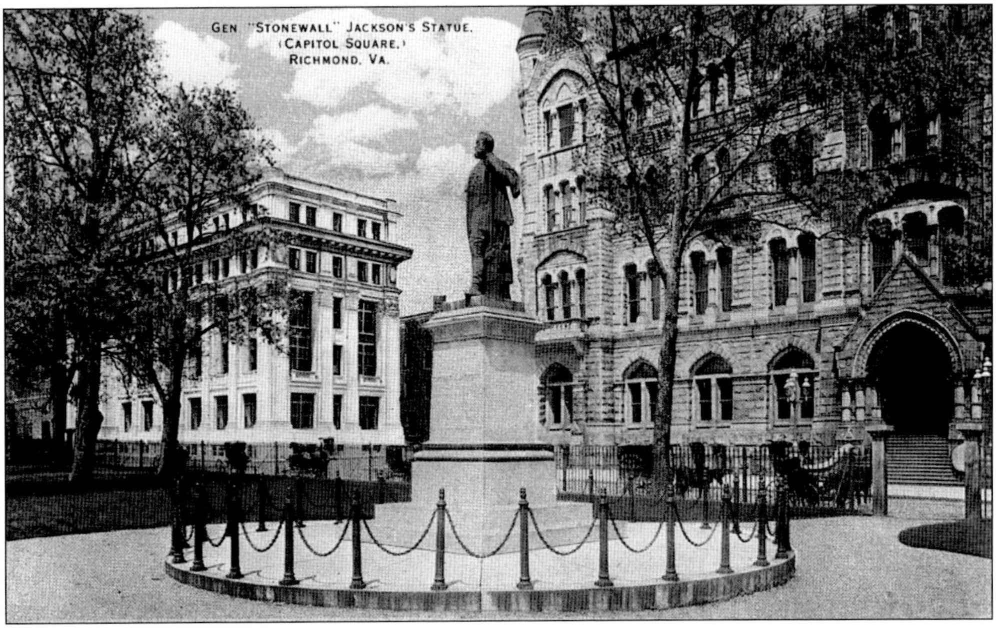

This statue of Thomas Jonathan "Stonewall" Jackson was presented to the Commonwealth by a group of English gentlemen as a tribute to Jackson's military genius. J.H. Foley, an Irish sculptor, created the statue that was unveiled on October 26, 1875.

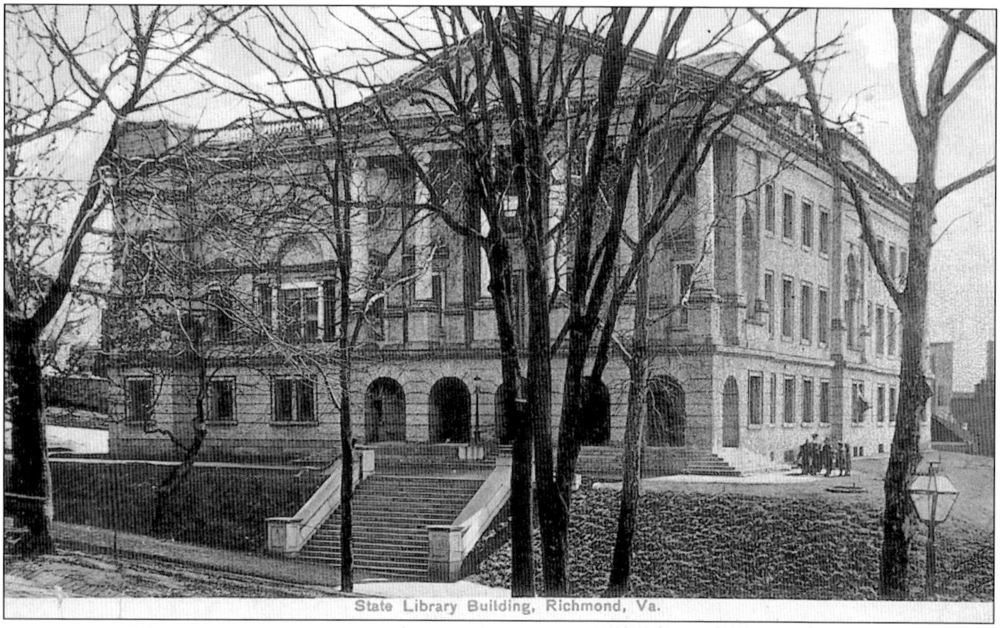

The State Library was built south of the Governor's Mansion in 1895. Designed by W.M. Poindexter, an architect from Washington, D.C., the structure had a lower story built of granite and upper stories of buff-colored brick. The porticoed building was designed to complement the State Capitol. The image above depicts the original building, and the image below includes the south wing addition, which was built in 1909.

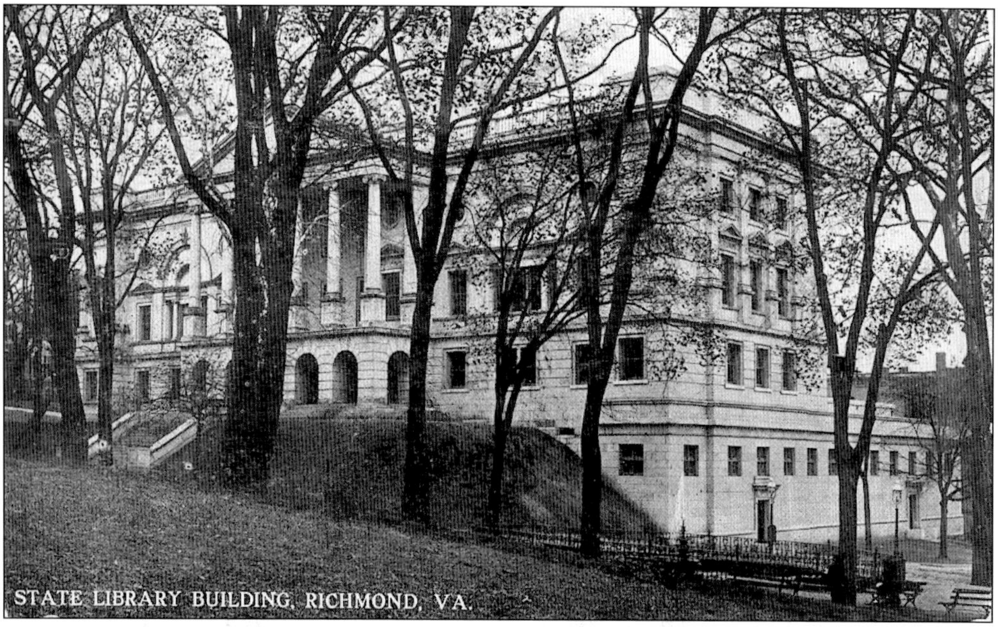

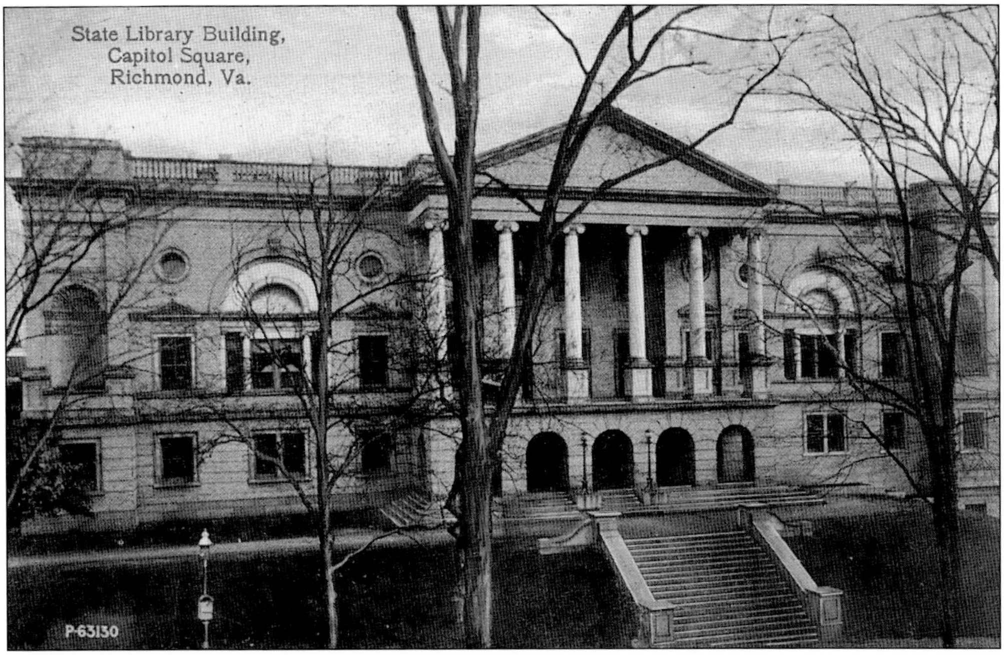

This postcard shows the frontal view of the State Library around 1912. The lower floors contained the courtroom of the Supreme Court of Appeals, the law library, and offices of various officials. The third floor housed the archival and bibliographic collections of the State Library.

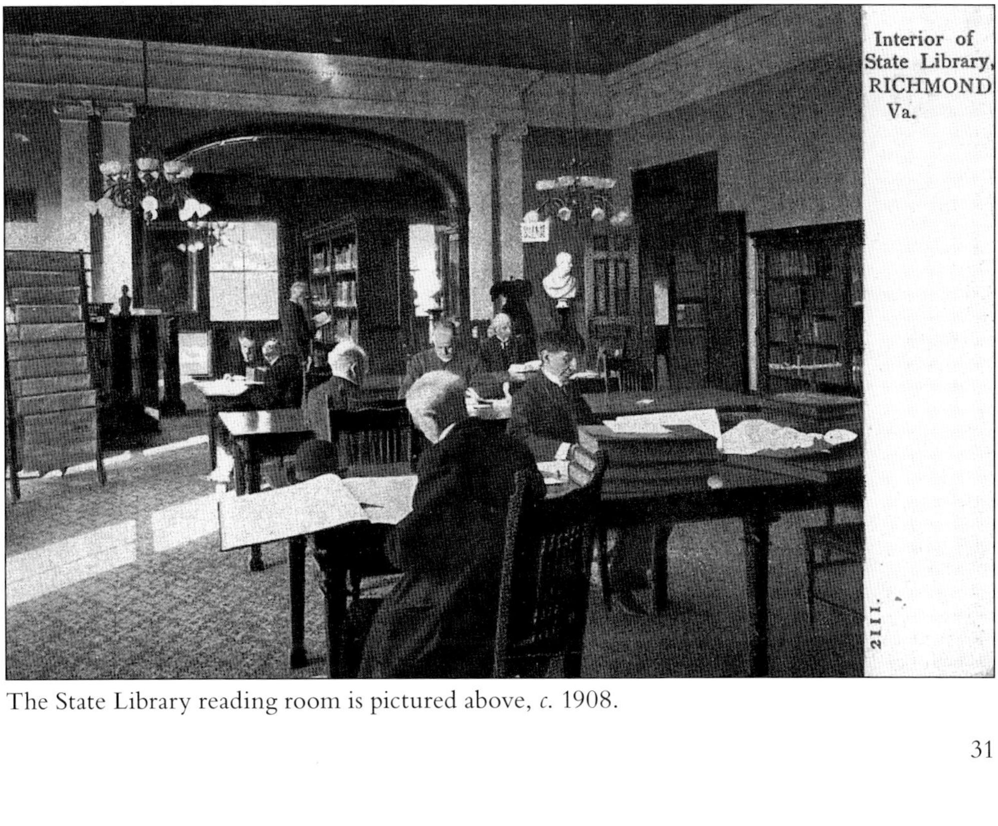

The State Library reading room is pictured above, *c.* 1908.

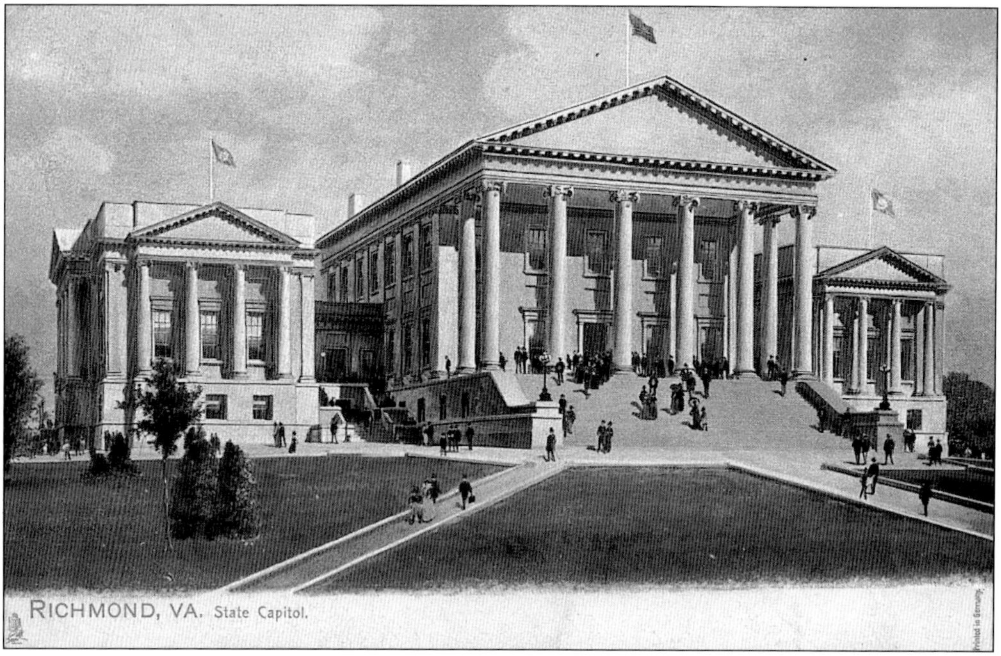

These postcards provide two views of the State Capitol as it appeared after construction of the two wings was completed in 1906. While the construction was in process, alterations were made to some of the details of the original building. Steps were added to the south portico as Thomas Jefferson had intended in his original design. The left wing houses the Senate, and the House of Delegates meets in the right wing.

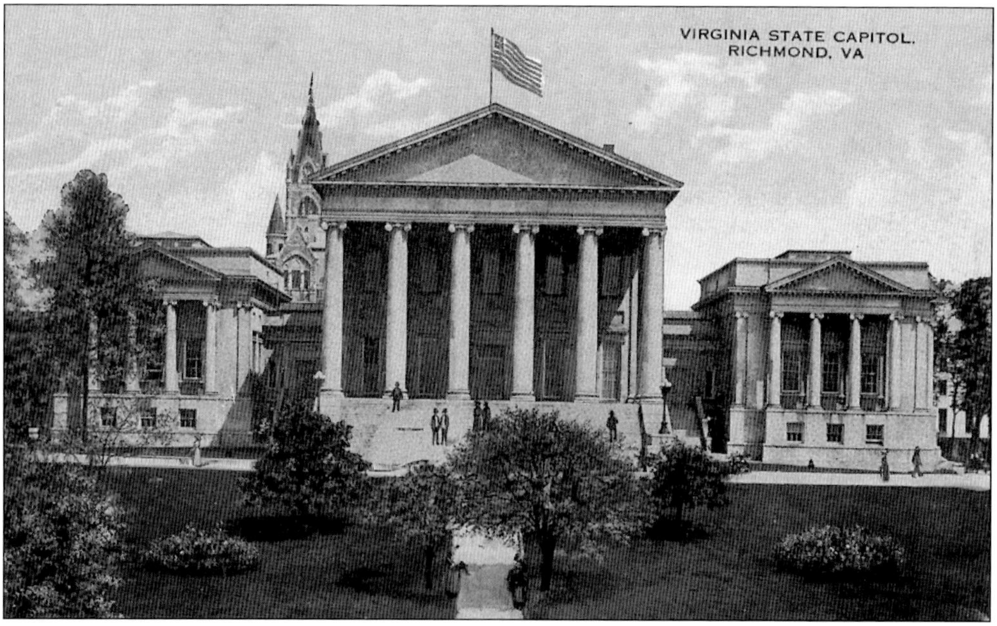

Three

Buildings, Statues, and Monuments

When President William Howard Taft visited Richmond on November 11, 1909, the city virtually shut down to pay tribute to the nation's chief executive. Met at Byrd Street Station, President Taft was escorted to the Governor's Mansion by Richmond dignitaries and military companies. After breakfast with Gov. Claude Swanson, President Taft walked to the State Capitol for a tour and press conference. Later he and the governor led a motorized parade up Franklin Street to Monument Avenue where he reviewed the troops. This was followed by lunch at the Jefferson Hotel, a quick trip to Hollywood Cemetery to visit the graves of James Monroe and John Tyler, and then to the City Auditorium for speeches. President Taft was greatly impressed with Richmond's progress and prosperity. While remarking about the city's growth and development he admitted that he was "charmed with Richmond's historical traditions and associations, and touched with the fidelity with which these traditions are preserved and commemorated, and with the inspiration which must emanate from them."[2]

As residents of the historic capital and gateway to the South, Richmonders have always taken pride in preserving vestiges of their past. In doing so, there is a sense of history inbred into every true Richmonder. There is strength in such a group of people who seek to pay homage to their past by not forgetting the triumphs and the failures that are part of their city's historical fabric. By preserving historic buildings they pass on to future generations a sense of that history, and by erecting monuments and statues they communicate their own sense of pride in their history. The fidelity to this sense of history is incorporated when meeting the challenges of expansion and growth allowing citizens to maintain contact with their past. Some believe this respect for the past has hindered the city's ability to compete in changing times, but it must be recognized that Richmond is Richmond because of its past and that true Richmonders are proud of that past and of the city's future.

2. W. Asbury Christian, *Richmond: Her Past and Present* (Richmond: 1912), 519.

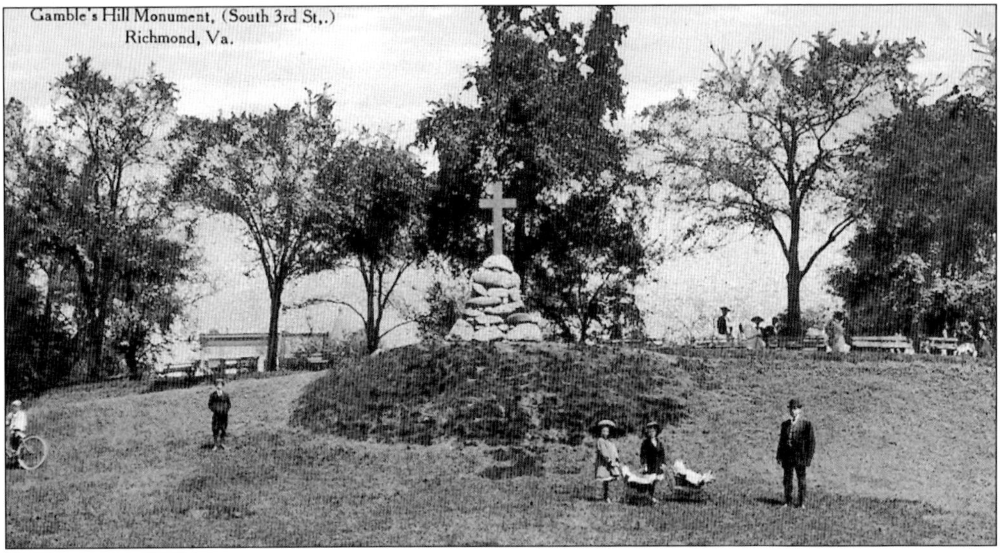

The First Visit Cross monument was placed in Gamble's Hill Park overlooking the James River by the Association for the Preservation of Virginia Antiquities and was dedicated on June 10, 1907. The bronze cross is mounted on boulders taken from the falls of the James River. The monument was erected to commemorate the first visit by Christopher Newport in 1607 when he had a wooden cross constructed on one of the islands and claimed the land and river for King James I.

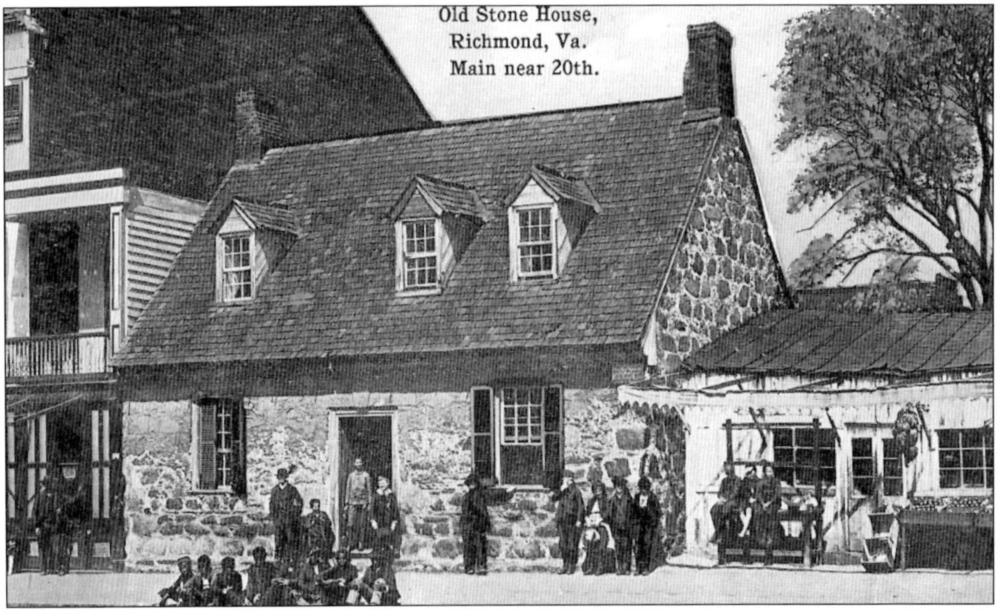

The Jacob Ege house, the oldest house in Richmond, was built between 1738 and 1739. Also known as the Old Stone House, the structure was home to the descendants of Jacob Ege until 1864. After that date it was rented and became a curio shop. Although never used by George Washington, a sign calling it "Washington's Headquarters" attracted many customers and visitors. In 1911 the Association for the Preservation of Virginia Antiquities purchased the house at auction. In 1922 it was opened as a shrine to Edgar Allan Poe and is now under the direction of the Poe Foundation.

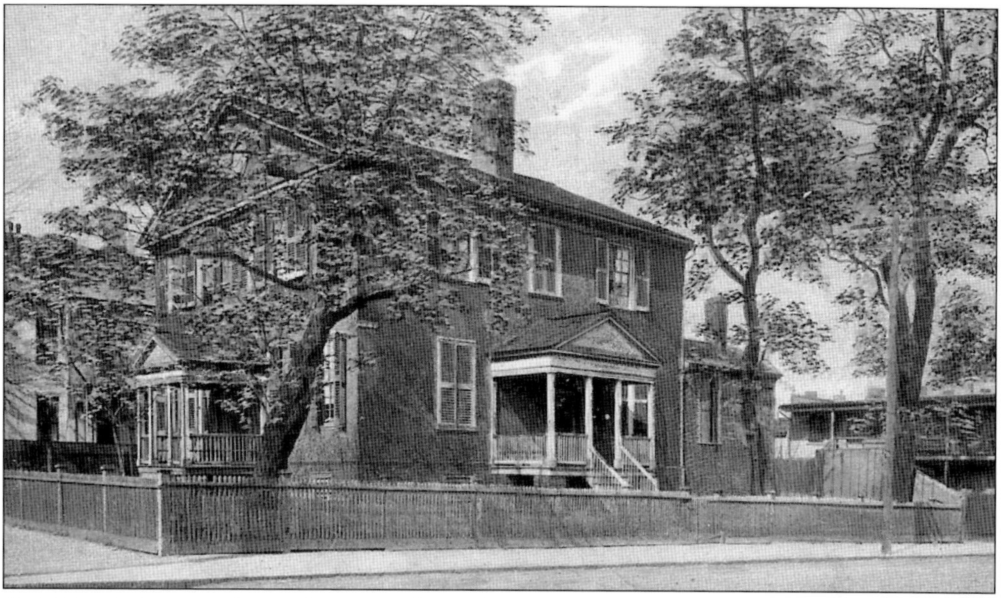

Chief Justice John Marshall's home, located at Ninth and Marshall Streets, was built by Marshall and served as his residence from 1795 until his death in 1835. It was acquired by the Association for the Preservation of Virginia Antiquities in 1913 and is now home to the John Marshall museum.

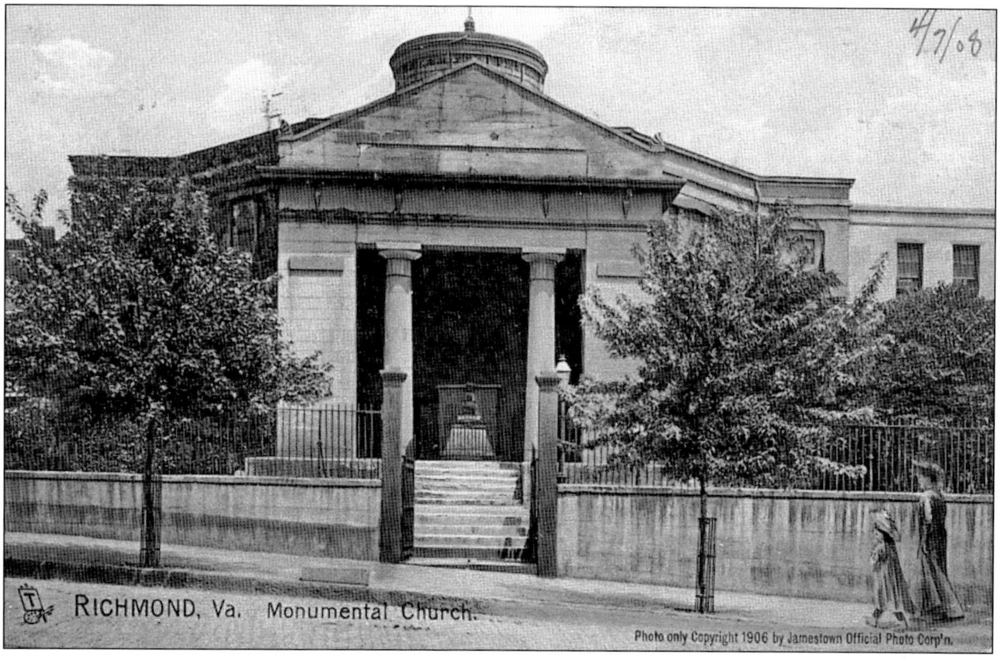

Monumental Church at Twelfth and Broad Streets was built as a memorial on the site of the Richmond Theater. On the night of December 26, 1811, during the performance of *The Bleeding Nun*, one of the backdrops caught fire and 72 patrons, including Gov. George W. Smith, perished in the flames. Grief-stricken Richmonders willingly contributed to the construction of a proper memorial. Architect Robert Mills designed the building and supervised the laying of the cornerstone on August 1, 1812. The first service was held on May 4, 1814.

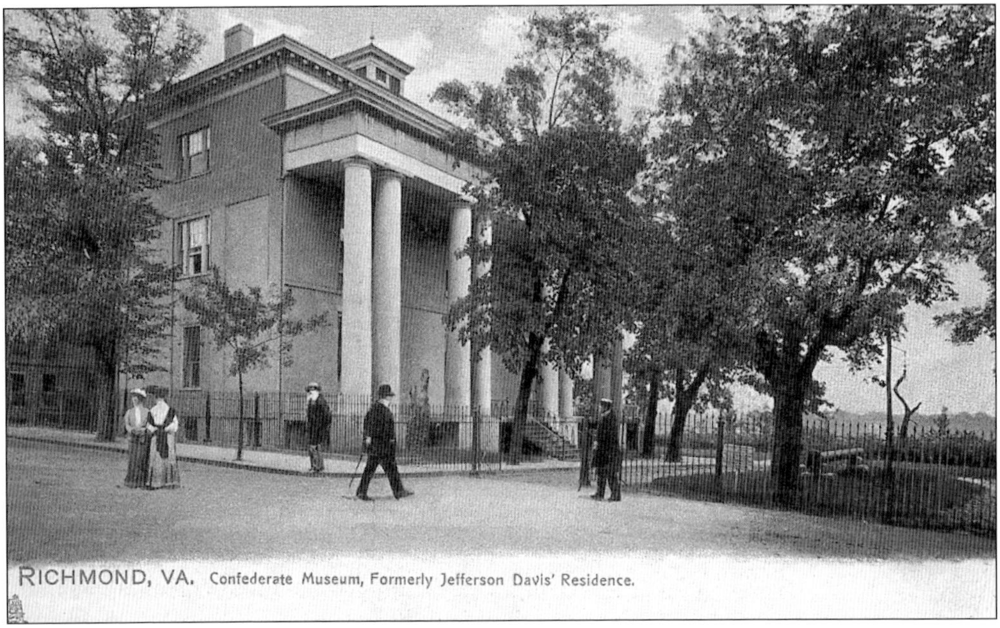

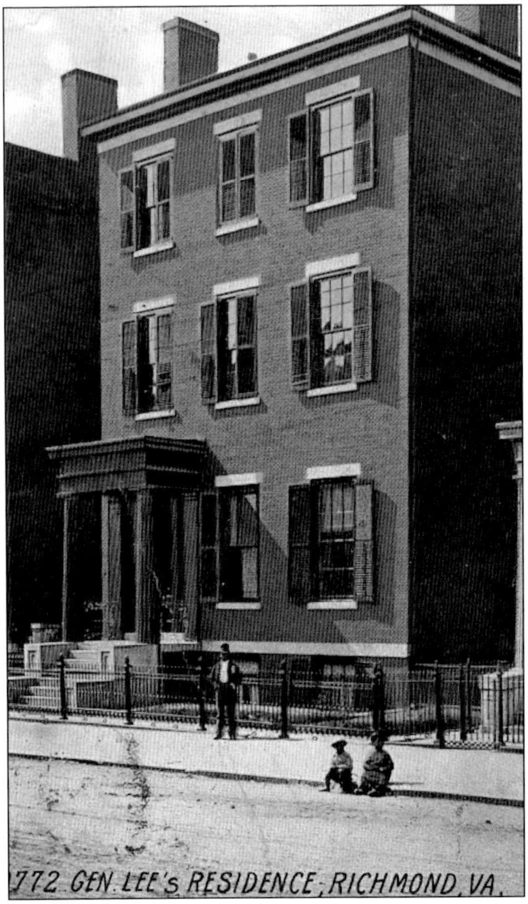

Built by Dr. John Brockenbrough in 1809, this house was purchased for $35,000 by the Richmond City Council in 1861 from Lewis D. Crenshaw for use by Confederate President Jefferson Davis as the Executive Mansion. After Richmond was evacuated on April 3, 1865, President Abraham Lincoln visited the house two days later. On September 5, 1870, the house was restored to the city, and in 1871 it was converted into a public school. On June 3, 1894, the Confederate Memorial Literary Society acquired the building and established a museum in the White House of the Confederacy.

Gen. Robert E. Lee's family resided at 707 East Franklin Street during the Civil War. It was to this house that he returned after surrendering his army at Appomattox Court House on April 9, 1865. Later the Virginia Historical Society acquired the house, and it served to hold the collections of the society until it moved to Battle Abbey in 1959. The house was transferred to the Museum of the Confederacy and remained as one the museum's properties until it was transferred to the Historic Richmond Foundation.

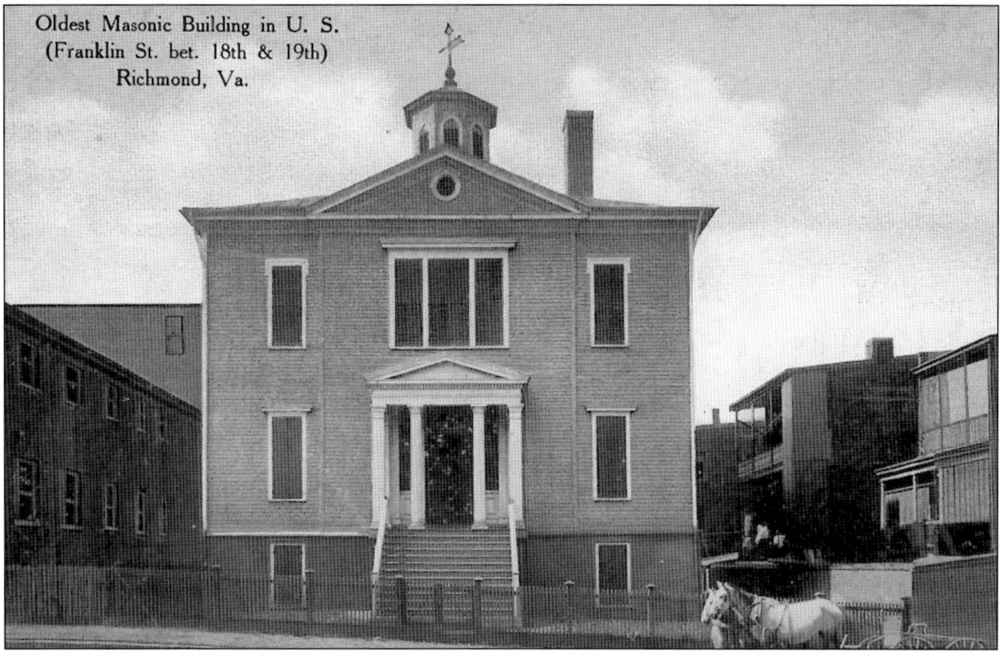

This building, erected in 1785, is owned and occupied by Richmond Randolph Lodge No. 19, A.F. & A.M. and is the first edifice ever built in the United States exclusively for Masonic purposes. Chief Justice John Marshall, General Lafayette, and many other statesmen and soldiers have attended its "stated communications."

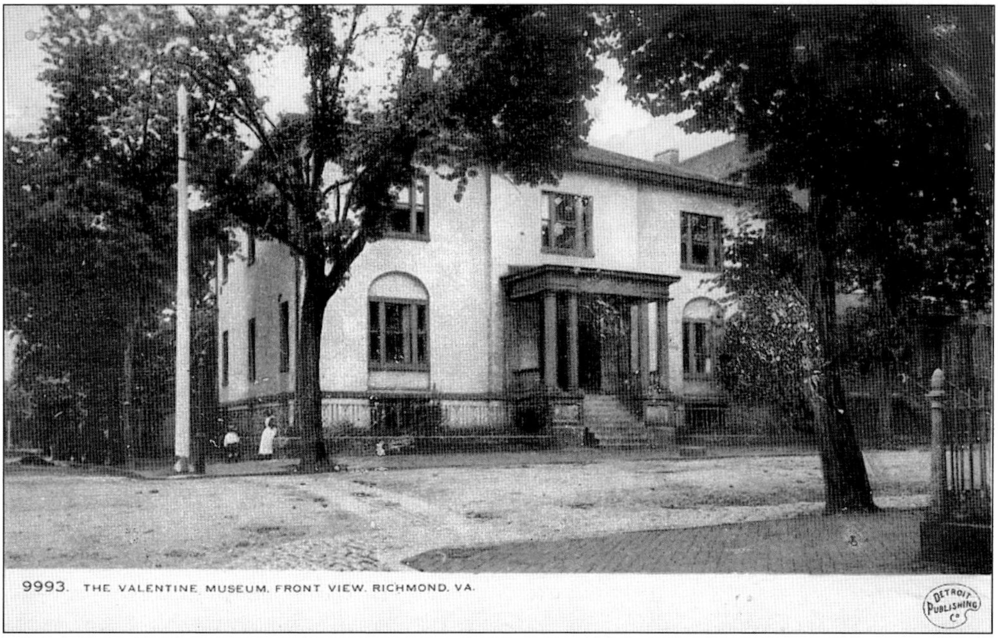

The John Wickham House on the corner of Eleventh and Clay Streets was given to the city by Mann S. Valentine, along with his collection of books, manuscripts, and works of art. On November 21, 1898, the Valentine Museum opened to the public as a museum dedicated to the history of Richmond.

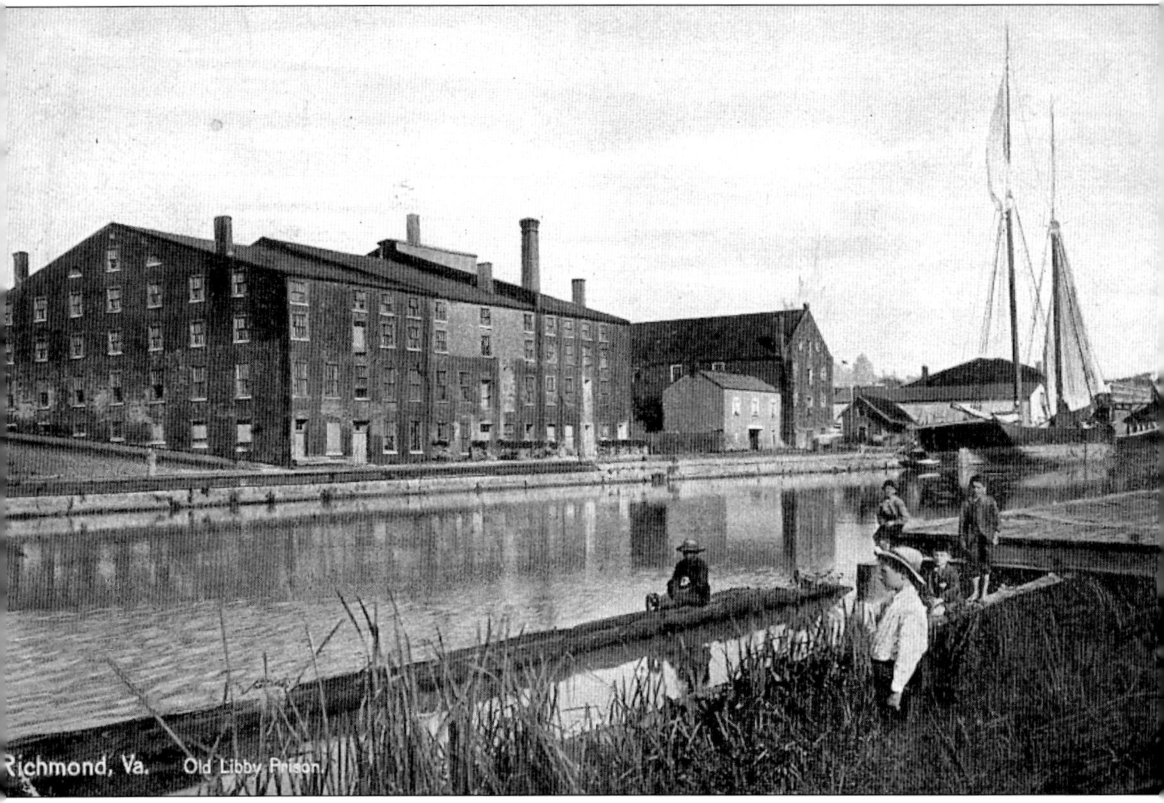

Libby Prison consisted of three, loft-style tenement buildings four stories high and built between 1845 and 1852. Capt. Luther Libby, a native of Maine, leased the west building in 1854. A ship chandler, Libby contracted with northern ships to transport goods and merchandise. He placed a sign on his building: L. Libby & Son, Ship Chandler. Following the Battle of First Manassas in 1861, the Confederate authorities appropriated the buildings to house prisoners, and Libby was given 48 hours to vacate. The sign was not removed and thus originated the name Libby Prison. More than 50,000 Union prisoners of war passed through the prison, which had an estimated capacity of 1,200, during the Civil War. After the war the Union authorities used it until August 3, 1868, to incarcerate former Confederates. It was then returned to its original owners, and in 1888 a Chicago syndicate purchased the buildings for removal to Chicago. It took a total of 132 20-ton boxcars to transport the brick and timbers. Incorporated as the Libby Prison Museum Association the syndicate rebuilt the building by September 1889. The syndicate disbanded in 1899 and the buildings were disassembled. Many bricks were sold as souvenirs and to builders. A large quantity went to the Chicago Historical Society for use in the society's new building. The timbers were sold to Charles J. Danielson, an Indiana farmer. He used the wood to build a massive barn. The original prison site continued to attract the attention of visitors long after the buildings were moved, so entrepreneurs produced this postcard from a contemporary photograph.

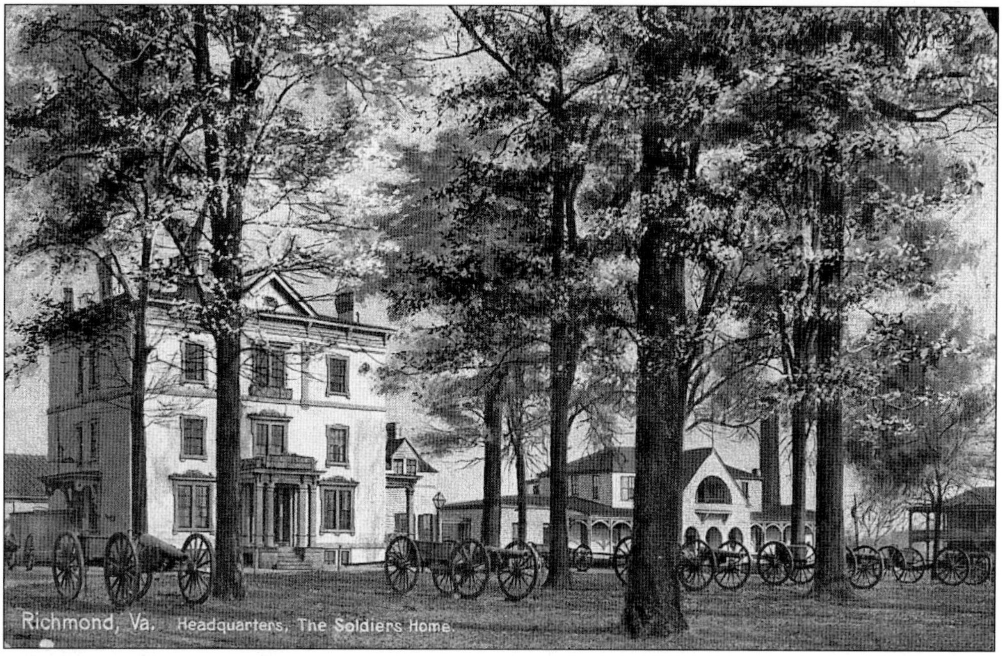

Located at Boulevard and Grove Avenues, the Confederate Veterans Home, which opened on January 1, 1888, is seen in these two views. The Virginia Museum of Art and the United Daughters of the Confederacy Headquarters Building now occupy the site. Only the original camp headquarters building and a small chapel remain standing today.

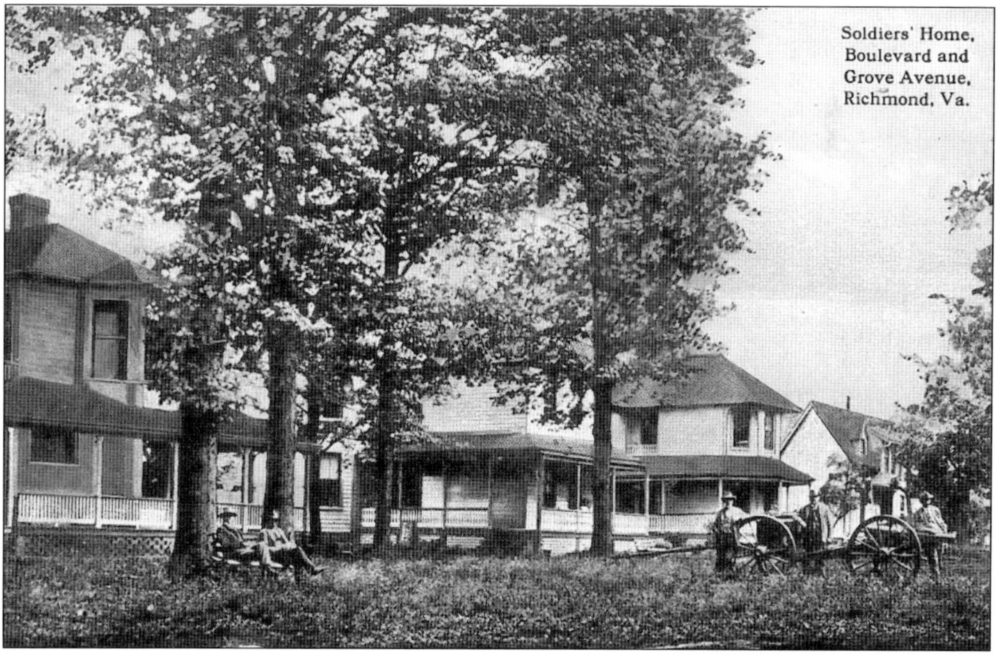

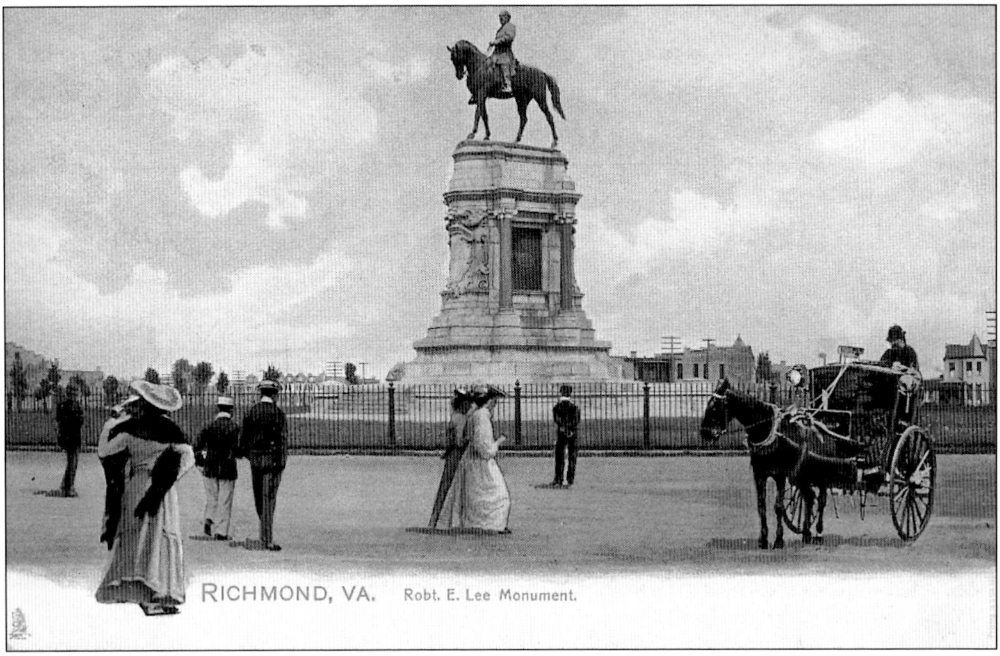

The cornerstone of the Gen. Robert E. Lee Monument was laid October 27, 1887, by the Grand Lodge of Virginia, A.F. & A.M. French sculptor Jean Antoine Mercie finished the castings of the statue by February 1890. The statue was unveiled on May 29, 1890, by Gen. Joseph E. Johnston.

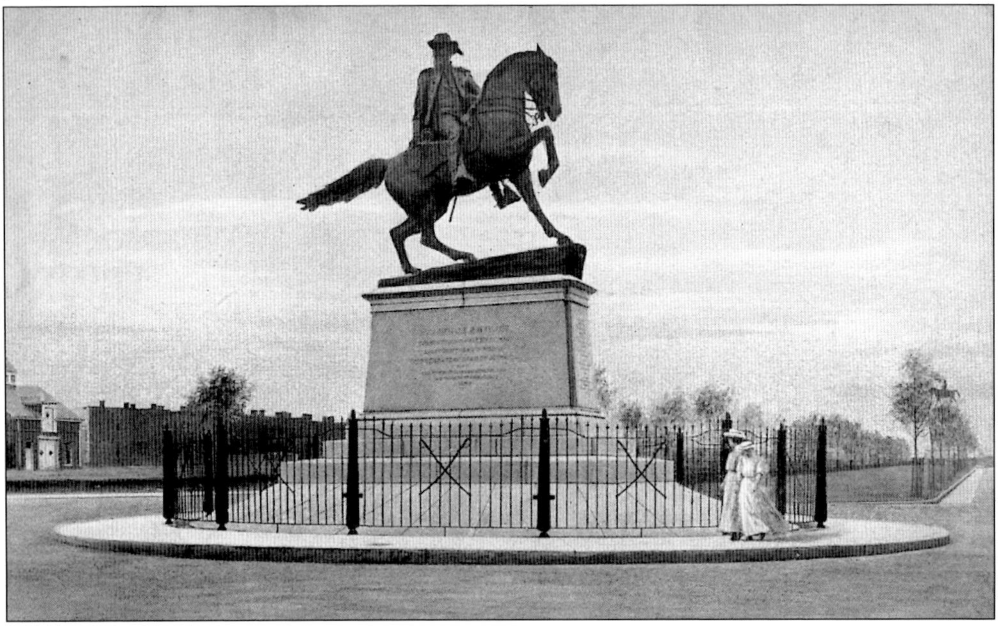

Maj. Gen. James Ewell Brown Stuart's monument, located on Lombardy Street and Monument Avenue, was sculpted by Fred Moynihan of New York City. It was unveiled on May 30, 1907, by Virginia Stuart Waller, the general's granddaughter. Mortally wounded at the Battle of Yellow Tavern on May 11, 1864, Stuart died the next day at his brother-in-law's home on Grace Street just a few blocks east of the monument.

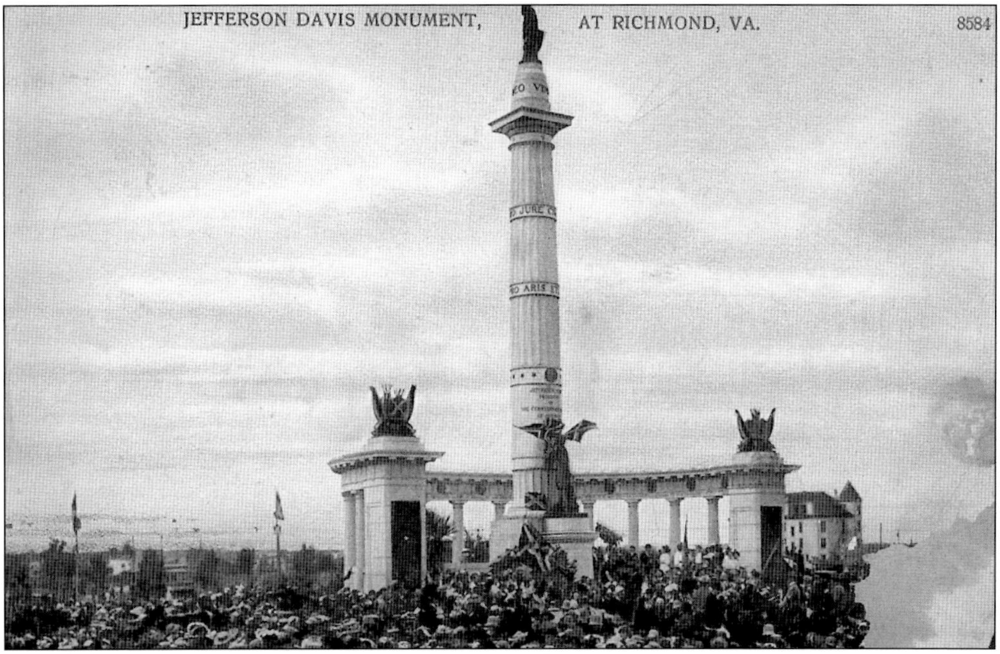

The Jefferson Davis Monument was unveiled on June 3, 1907. Richmond sculptor Edward V. Valentine prepared the statue of Davis. The statue stands at the base of a tall column, which is surmounted by an allegorical figure representing the "Spirit of the South."

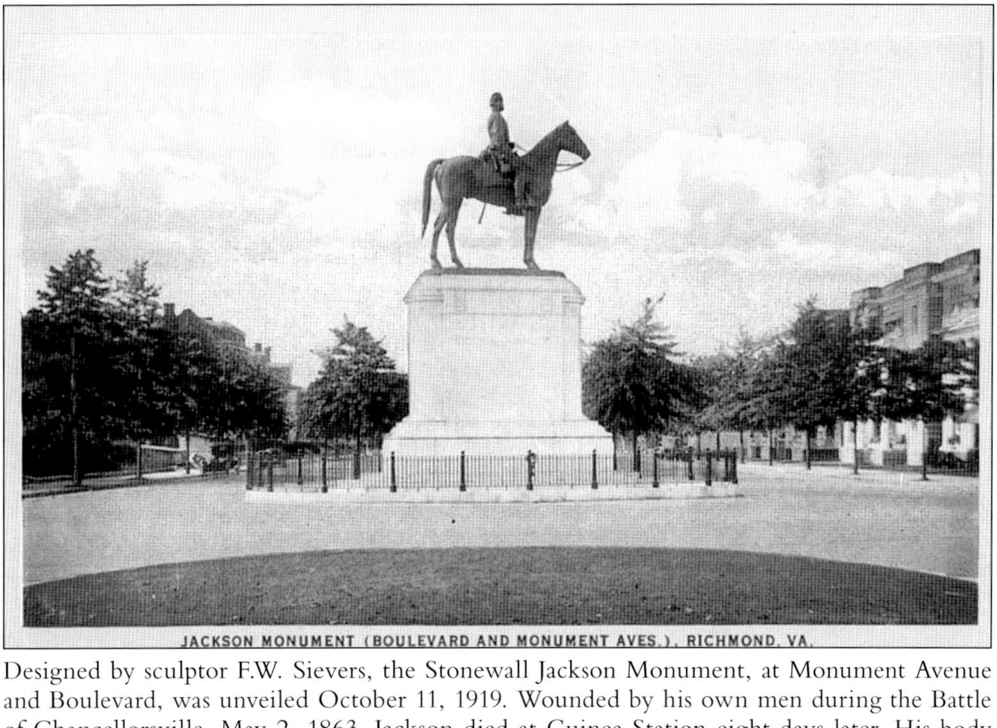

Designed by sculptor F.W. Sievers, the Stonewall Jackson Monument, at Monument Avenue and Boulevard, was unveiled October 11, 1919. Wounded by his own men during the Battle of Chancellorsville, May 2, 1863, Jackson died at Guinea Station eight days later. His body was brought to Richmond to lie in state in the State Capitol before it was taken to Lexington for burial.

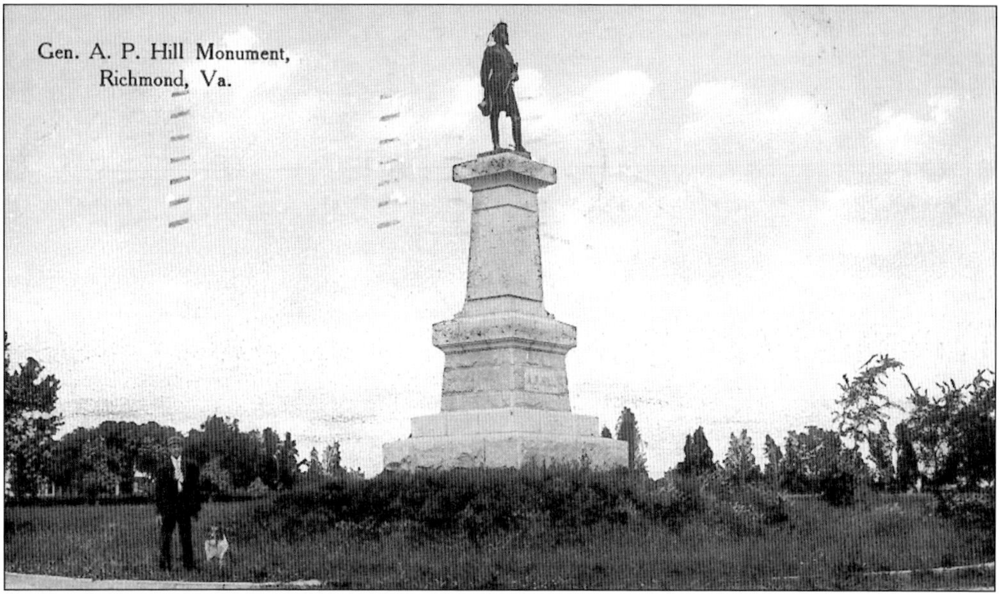

Killed during the Battle of Petersburg on April 1, 1865, Gen. Ambrose Powell Hill's remains were first interred near Coalfield in Chesterfield County. They were later moved to Hollywood Cemetery. When this monument was under construction his remains were again removed and placed under the monument. Located at Laburnum Avenue and Hermitage Road, the monument was unveiled on May 30, 1892.

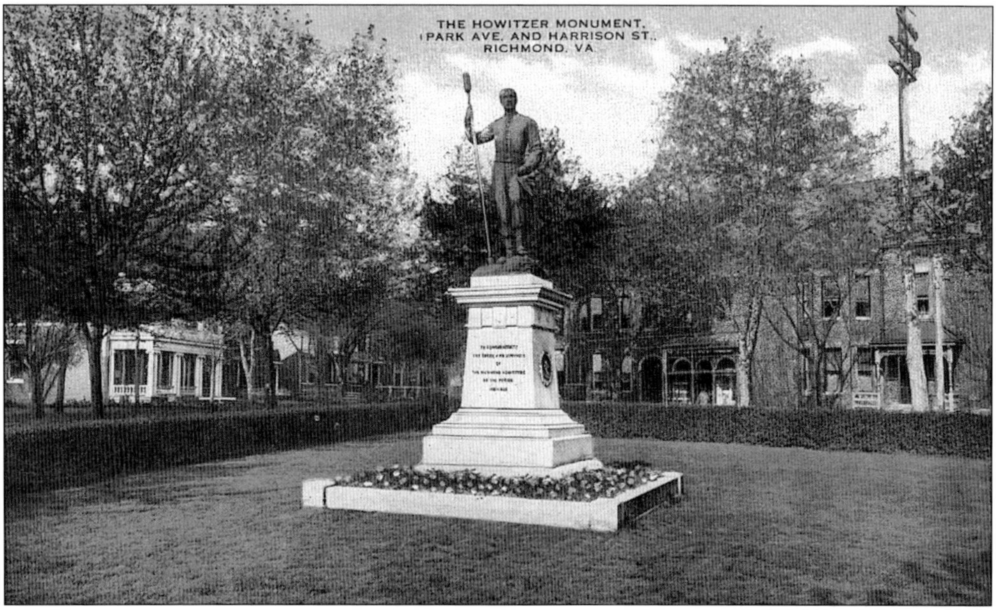

The Howitzer Monument was erected to commemorate Richmond's own Howitzer Battalion. Organized on November 9, 1859, as the Howitzer Battery, it quickly increased to a four-battery battalion. The monument, which stands at Park Avenue and Harrison Street, was sculpted by William L. Sheppard, a gifted Richmond artist and sculptor who served as a 2nd Lieutenant of 2nd Company, Richmond Howitzers. The statue depicts an artilleryman at Position No. 1 and was unveiled December 13, 1892.

The Confederate Soldiers and Sailors Monument was initiated at a mass meeting of citizens on January 9, 1888. City Council granted a site on Libby Hill and approved a gift of $5,000 toward the monument. The ladies of the Confederate Soldiers and Sailors Monument Association held a bazaar and raised $14,939. The Commonwealth contributed $3,500 and individuals gave the balance necessary to meet the cost of $33,018. Col. W.E. Cutshaw, the city engineer, supervised construction, and the monument was unveiled on May 30, 1894. Two children, Edward S. McCarthy and Mary Curtis, drew the veil.

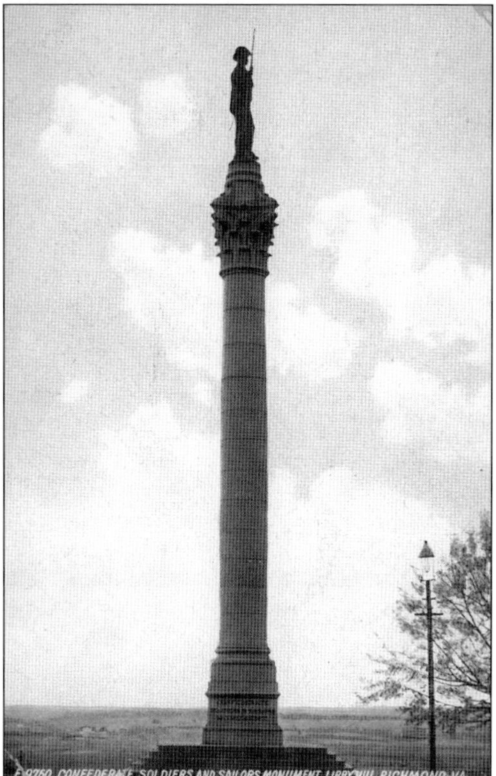

E 9760 CONFEDERATE SOLDIERS AND SAILORS MONUMENT, LIBBY HILL, RICHMOND, VA.

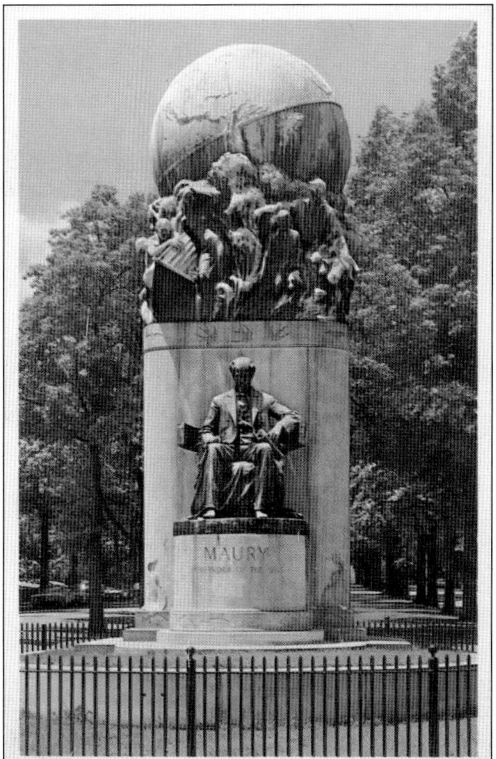

Matthew Fontaine Maury Monument, Richmond, Va.

Matthew Fontaine Maury was born near Fredericksburg and achieved fame for his studies of ocean currents and trade winds, earning him the title "Pathfinder of the Seas." He resigned from the U.S. Navy to join the Confederate service in 1861. Appointed a commander in the Confederate Navy, he supervised Richmond's river defenses before being sent to England. After the war, he served as a professor of physical and astronomical geography at Virginia Military Institute until his death on February 1, 1873. His remains were brought to Richmond for interment in Hollywood Cemetery. This monument to Maury was sculpted by F. William Sievers, a native of Indiana, who had taken residence in the city. It was unveiled in 1929.

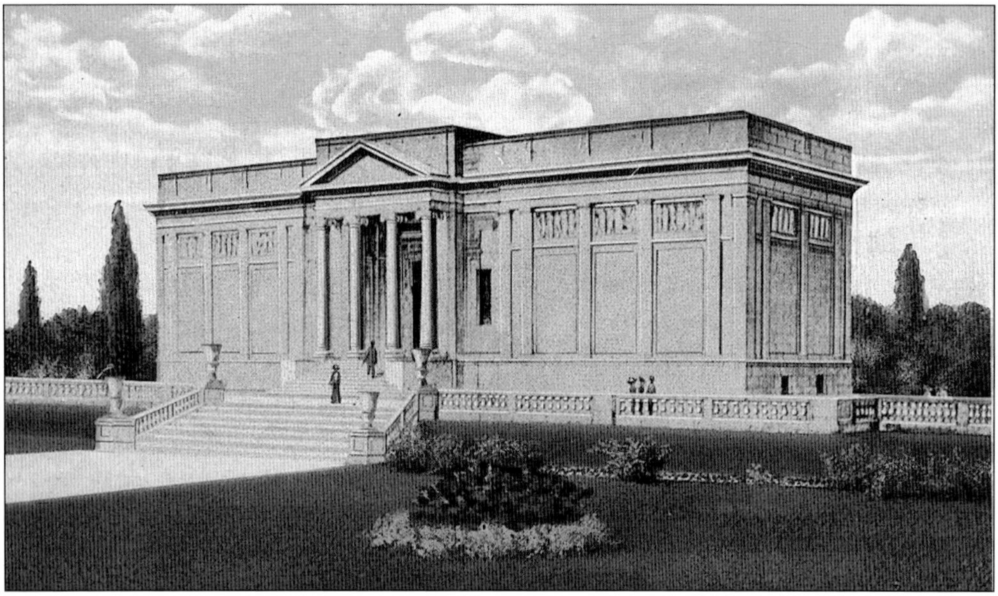

First suggested in 1892 by Sen. John W. Daniel of Lynchburg as a memorial to the men and women of the Confederacy, the cornerstone of the Confederate Memorial Institute was laid on May 29, 1912. Construction was virtually completed in 1914. Called Battle Abbey, the Greek Revival–style building was dedicated in 1921 and opened to the public. Today it is the home of the Virginia Historical Society.

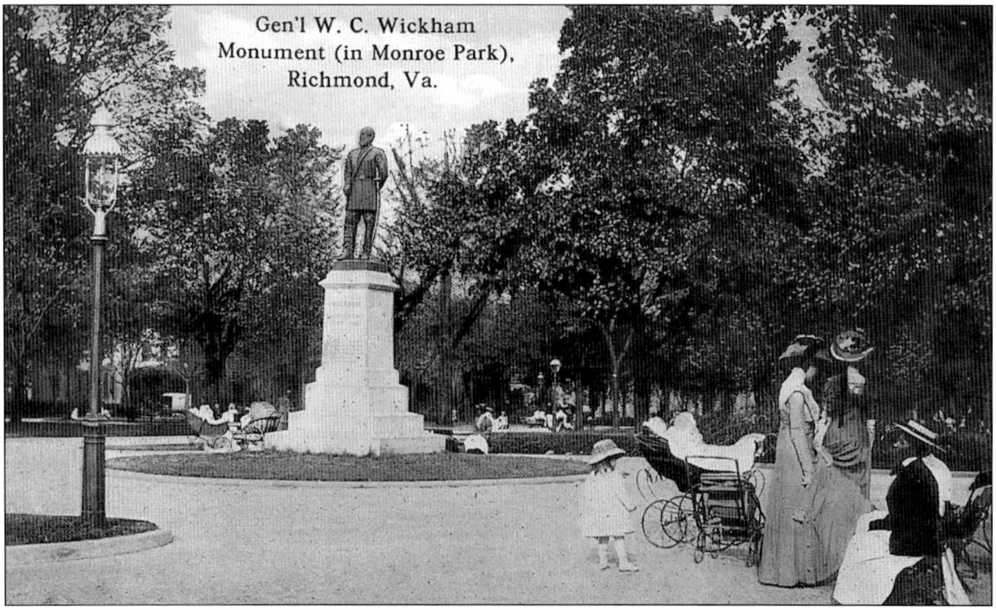

Gen. William C. Wickham, a native Richmonder, was a lawyer by profession. In 1861 he entered Confederate service and later commanded a brigade in Stuart's cavalry. After the war he served in various governmental positions and as president of the Virginia Central Railroad and then as second vice president of the Chesapeake & Ohio. He died in Richmond on July 23, 1888. Survivors of his cavalry brigade and employees of the C&O erected this monument in Monroe Park. The unveiling occurred on October 19, 1891.

Four

Business Districts

The City of Richmond's origins were tied to the river, which was an avenue of commerce. The first commercial enterprise was the establishment of a public warehouse at Shockoe Creek in 1730. The presence of the falls necessitated the warehousing of products for transshipment up and down the river. Situated on the fall line, the site benefited from the increase in economic activity. A town grew up around the warehouse, and eventually with the transfer of the capitol, the town became a city. Business ventures expanded into manufacturing, milling, and transportation. Within the city, residents demanded produce, provisions, and mercantile goods as well as services.

As the city grew, the need for banking and financial services expanded. Business districts evolved over time as similar types of businesses were clustered in particular areas. The ship chandlers were around the wharves on Rockett's. Manufacturing and milling was situated along the river from the east end up to and including the islands in the river. The markets were located in the bottom area along the valley between Church and Shockoe Hills. The mercantile and business area was along Main Street at first, but in time the mercantile center shifted to Broad and Grace Streets and the banking and financial interests congregated along Main Street west of the bottom area.

With the coming of the railroad business, districts grew up around the various railroad terminals on Broad and Main Streets and in Rockett's. At one time no less than five railroad companies served the city and a thriving freight hauling business evolved to carry materials and merchandise between the stations. Eventually, as railroad companies consolidated, the tracks were rerouted around the downtown business district.

Originally the residential area was on Church Hill, but as the city extended westward new ground was broken for residential development beyond the business districts. Actually, the city's resident population began expanding to the north and west with African Americans moving into the north side of Broad Street and affluent whites moving into the new western suburbs. Eventually the city would annex the western suburbs and bring them into the city.

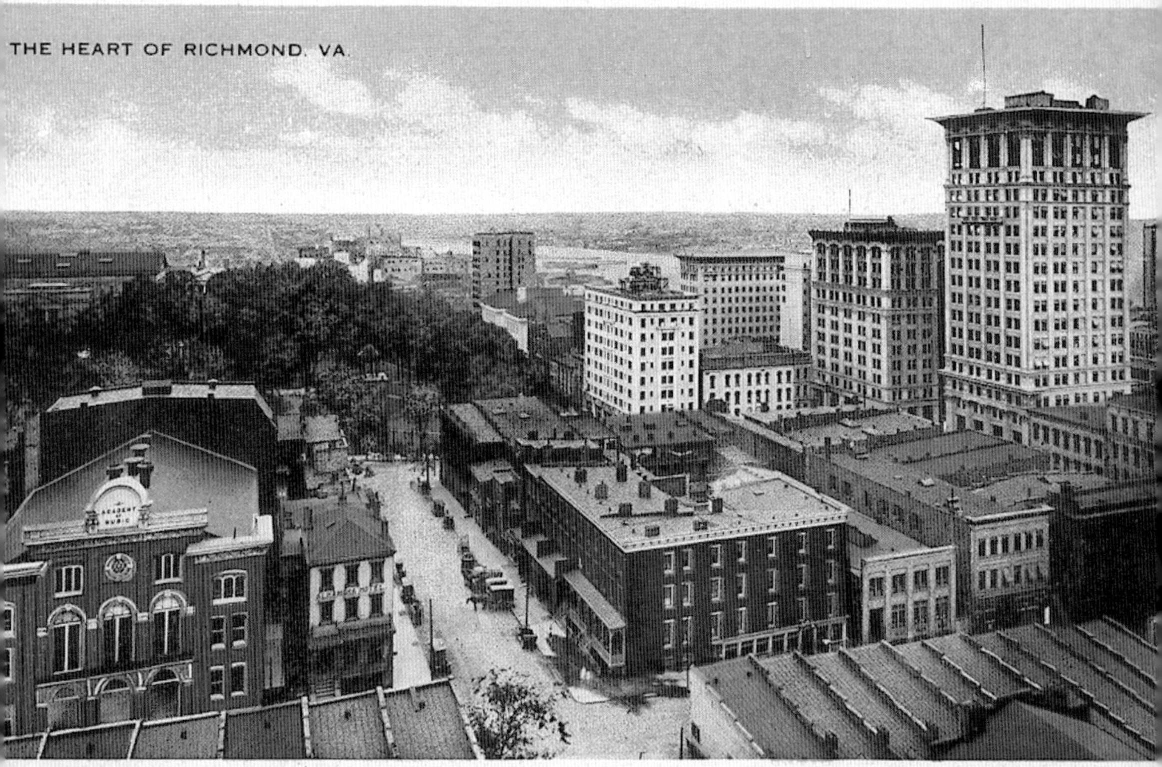

This view of the heart of Richmond captures the cultural crosscurrents that contributed to the city's vibrant growth. Looking east on Franklin Street one sees the Bell Tower on Capitol Square, the political and governmental center. To the left is the Academy of Music on Eighth Street, built in 1884 and one of the city's leading theaters until it burned in 1925. To the right is the city's financial and business district along Main Street. The building with the flag on its roof is the First National Bank Building, which was constructed in 1913. The Mutual Building to its left was built in 1904 and was the city's first skyscraper.

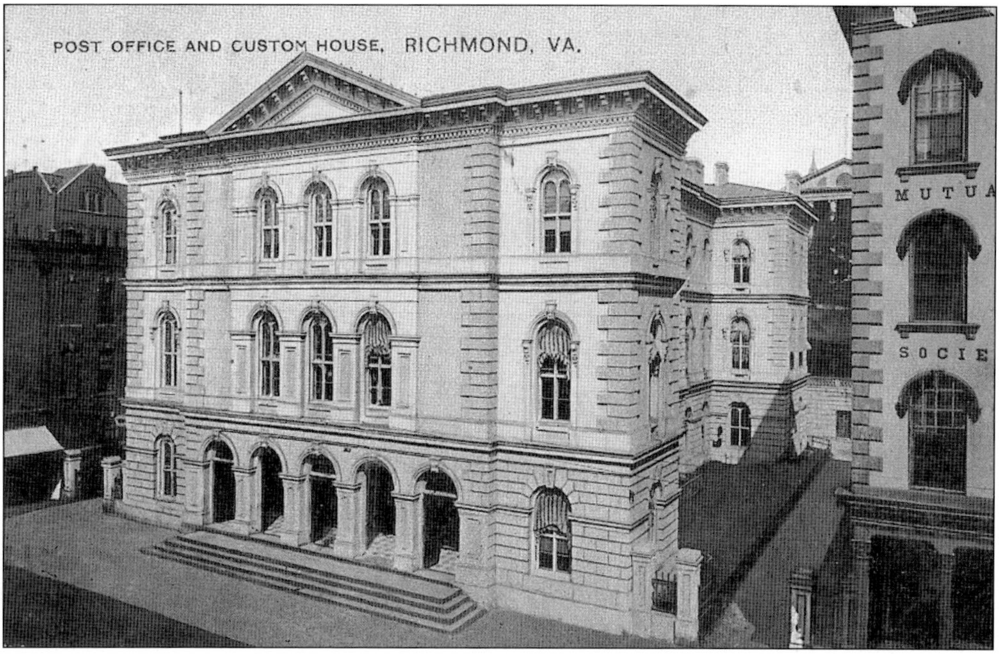

The heart of the financial and business district on Main Street extended from Eighth to Fourteenth Streets. Construction of the original part of the U.S. Post Office and Custom House started in 1855, and it was completed in 1858. During the Civil War, President Jefferson Davis's office was in this building. This view, taken about 1900, shows the building after it was enlarged and renovated in 1889. To the right of the Post Office and Custom House is the Mutual Assurance Society of Virginia Building. The Shafer Building is to the left.

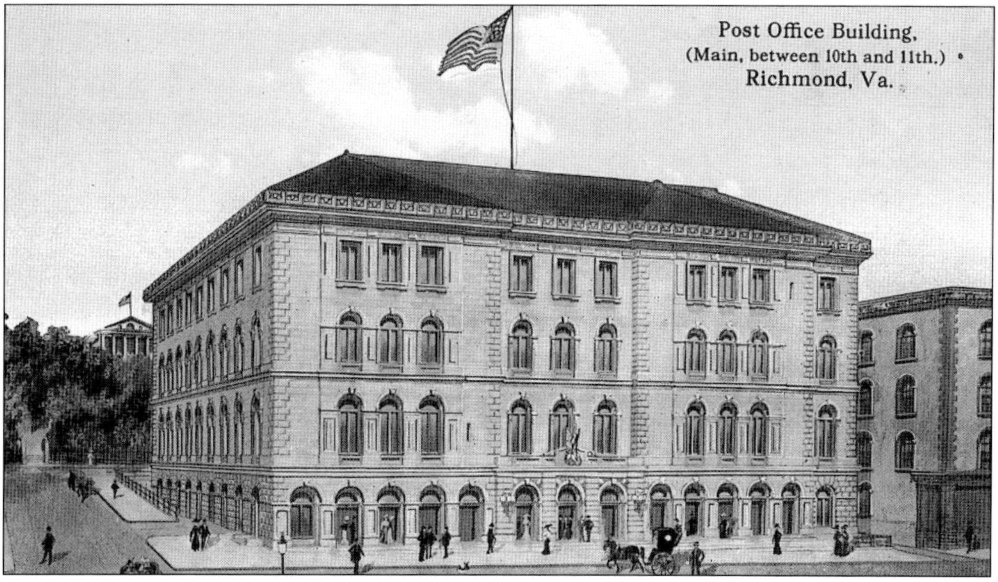

This postcard shows the Post Office and Federal Court of Appeals Building as it appeared after the original Post Office and Custom House was enlarged. The government purchased and demolished the Shafer Building. On December 17, 1910, the cornerstone was laid for the new addition, and the $800,000 structure was completed in 1912.

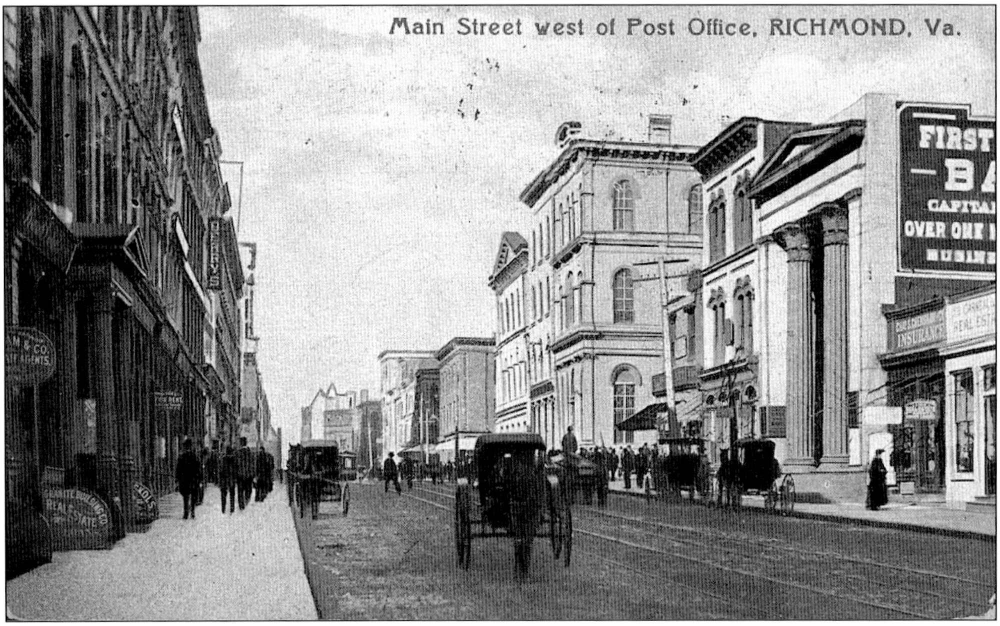

The triangular roof-cap of the federal post office can be seen midway up on the right side of this view of Main Street looking west from Twelfth Street. In the right foreground are the two 30-foot granite columns of the old Exchange Bank of Virginia, built in 1841. These columns were all that survived when the building burned during the evacuation fire in April 1865. When the National Exchange Bank was constructed, the two columns were incorporated into the front façade. Across Main Street on the south side is the National Bank of Virginia and next to it is the City Bank of Richmond.

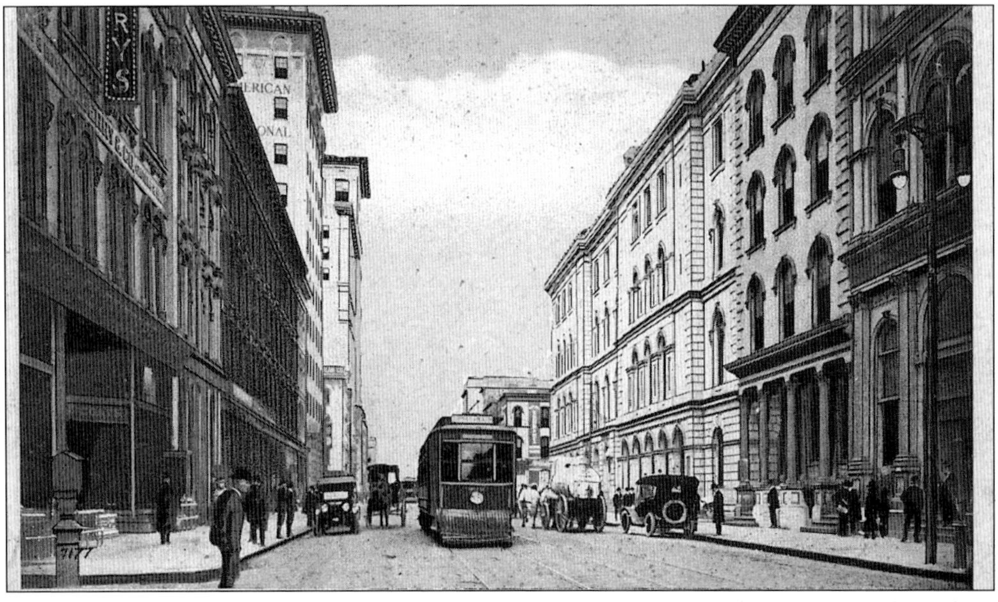

In this view, looking west up Main Street around 1905, the Merchants National Bank at 1101 East Main Street appears on the south side in the foreground. On the north side are the National Bank of Virginia, the Mutual Assurance Society of Virginia, and the Post Office–Custom House.

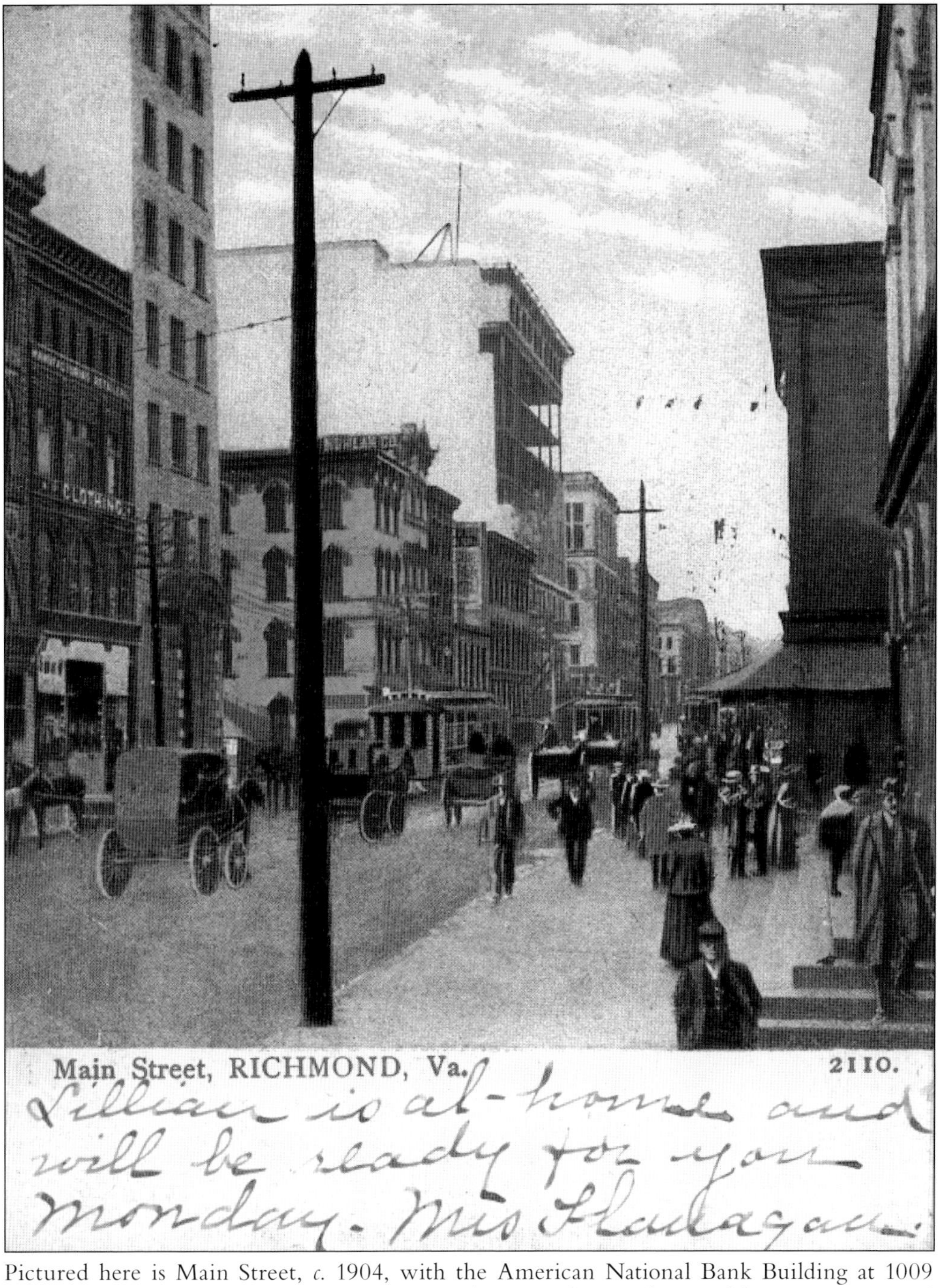

Pictured here is Main Street, *c.* 1904, with the American National Bank Building at 1009 East Main, which was completed in 1904. Up the street the new home of the Virginia Mutual Assurance Society of Virginia is under construction. Located on the southeast corner of Ninth and Main Streets, the Mutual Building, as it was called, would rise nine stories before it was completed in 1905. It was the tallest building in the Old Dominion at that time. In the right foreground is the Post Office–Custom House. Beyond it the Shafer Building can be seen. This red brick structure housed lawyers' offices.

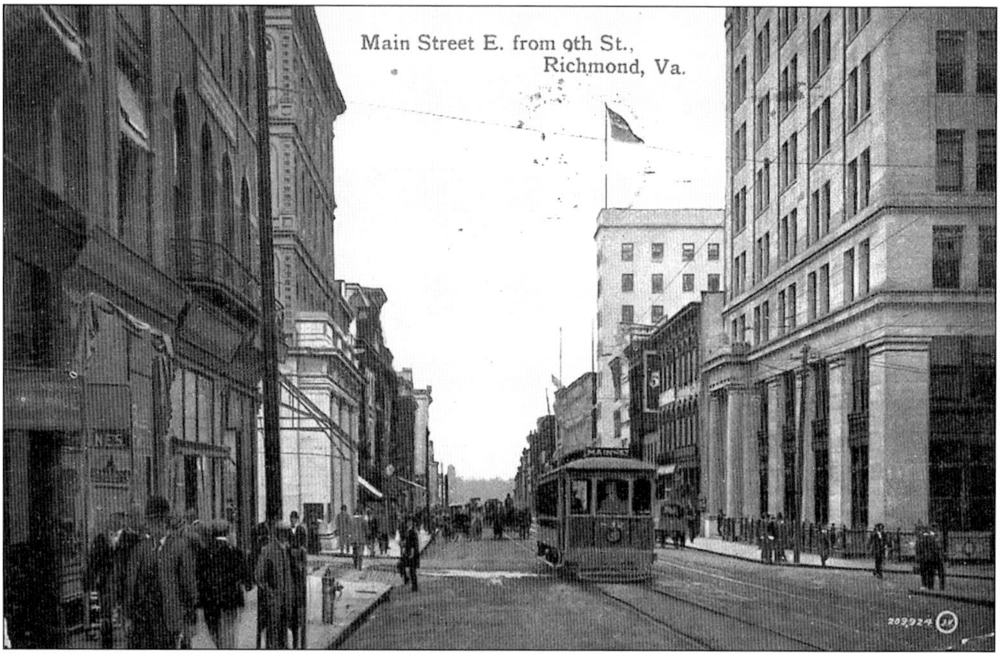

The view in this postcard shows the intersection of Main and Ninth Streets around 1910. The Mutual Building is on the southeast corner and the Bank of Richmond is on the northeast corner. The building with the flag on top is the American National Bank Building at 1009 East Main.

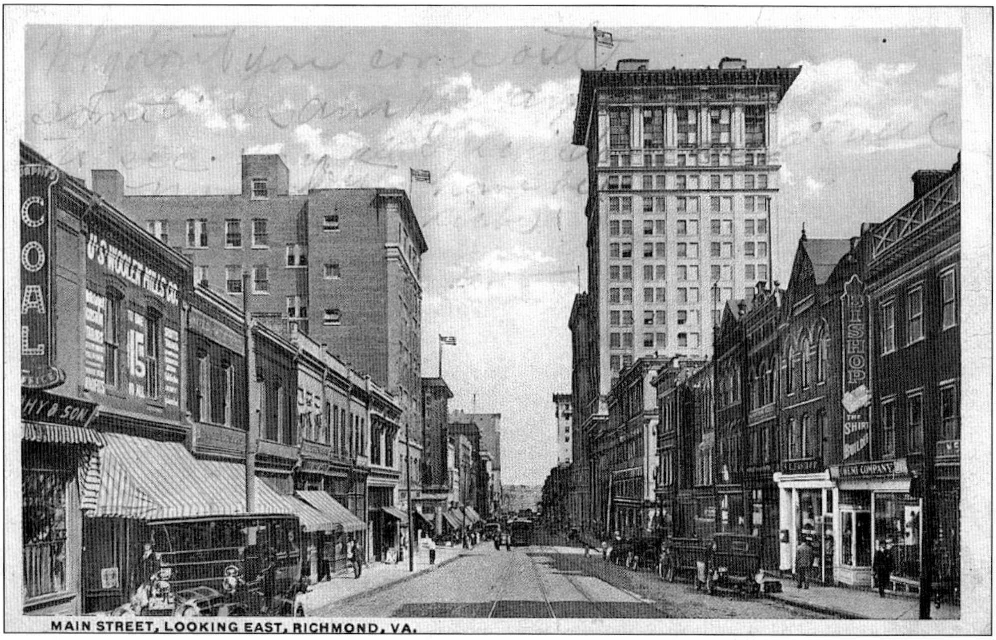

Looking east on Main from Eighth Street, one can see the Hanewinckel Building on the northeast corner of Ninth and Main in this view. The flag is flying atop the Post Office at Tenth and Main. Across from the Hanewinckel Building is the First National Bank Building.

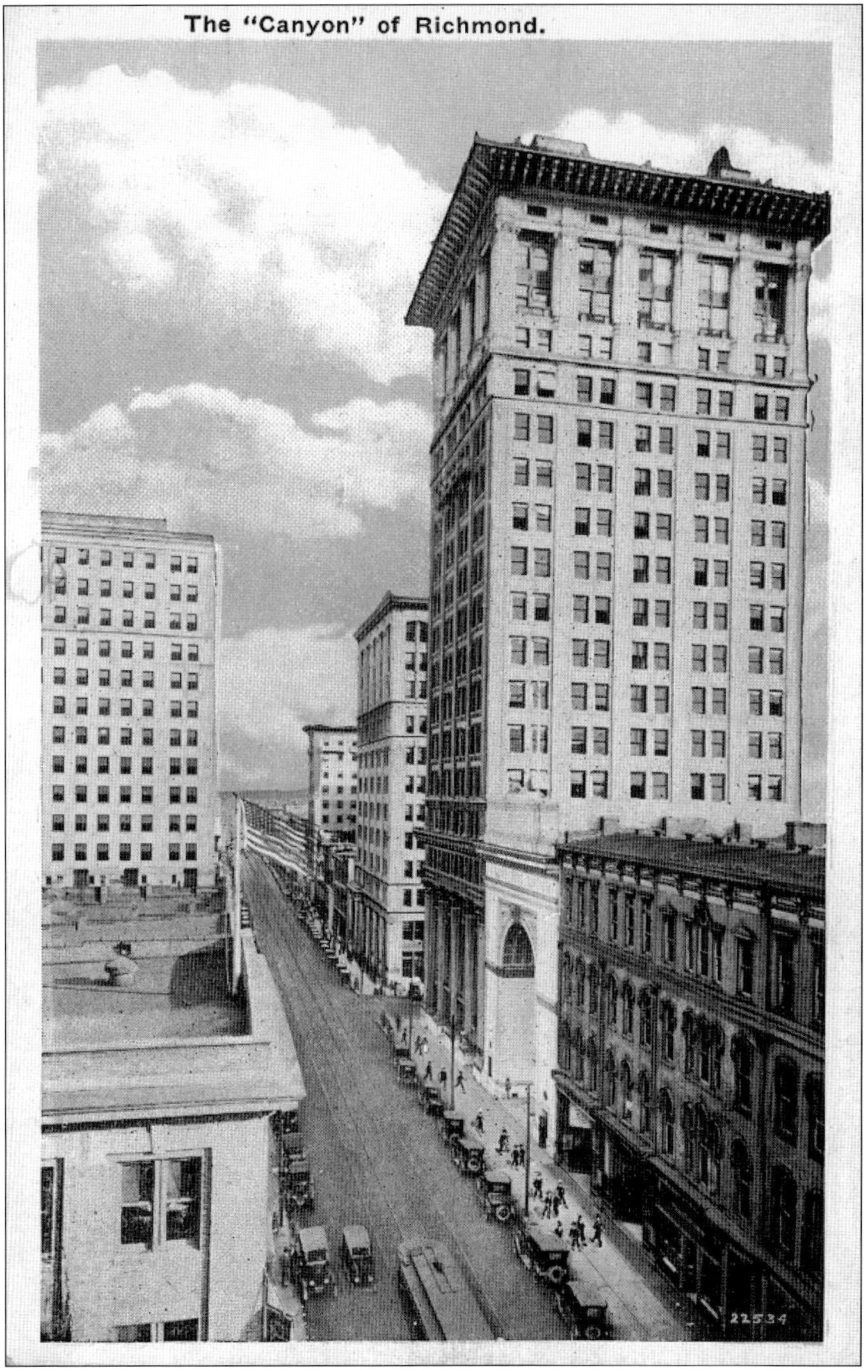

With the construction of high-rise buildings on Main Street, the street became known as the "Canyon" of Richmond. Seen here in the right foreground is the First National Bank Building on the southwest corner of Ninth and Main. Behind it is the Mutual Assurance Society of Virginia Building, and the Mutual Building on the southeast corner of the intersection. Beyond the Mutual Building the next tall structure is the American National Bank. The tall building on the north side of Main is the State and City Bank and Trust Company.

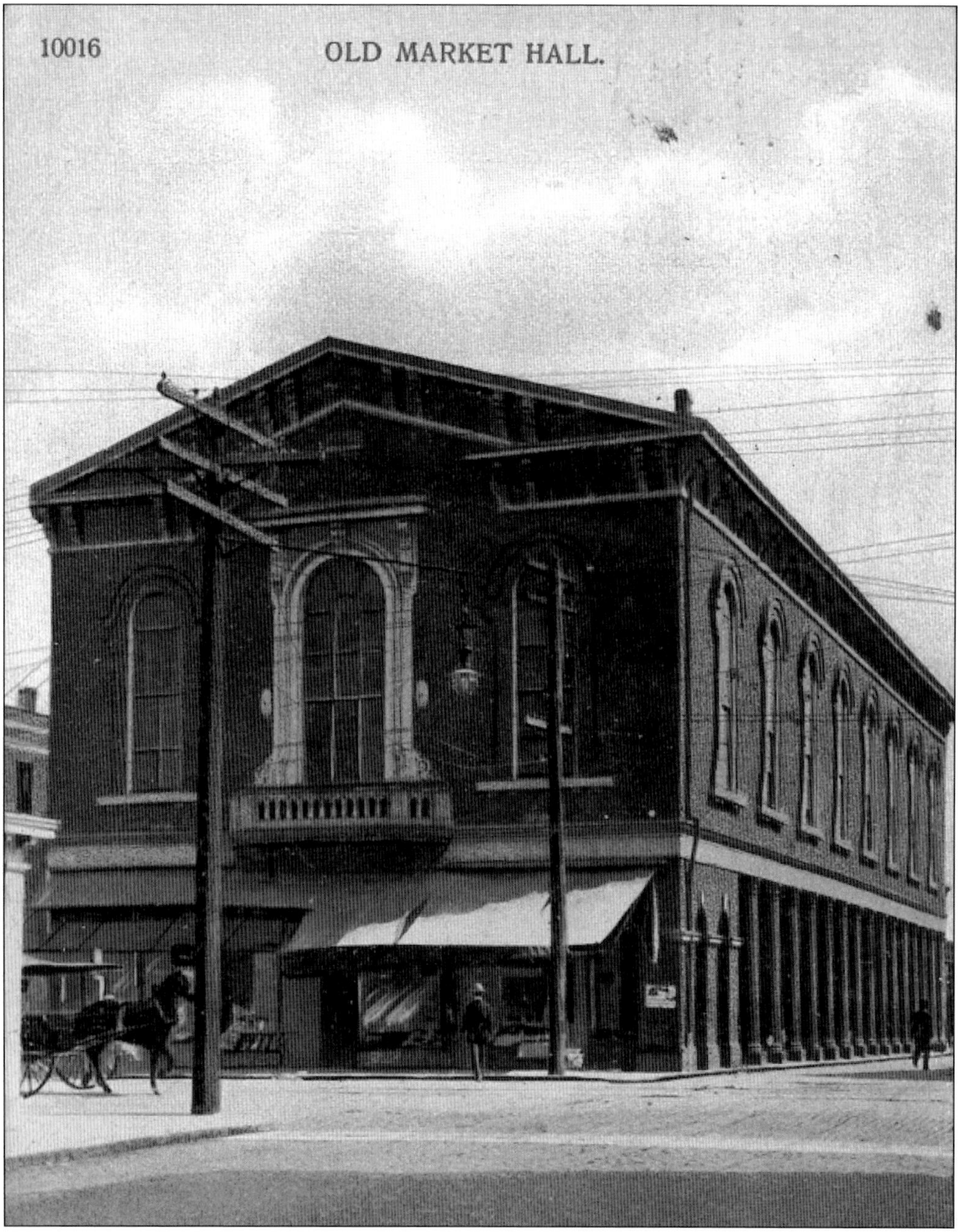

Just beyond the financial and business district on Main Street a public marketplace had been established on the western side of Shockoe Creek as early as the 1780s. A wooden shed supported by locust posts was provided for protection from the elements. In 1794 a brick building replaced the wooden shed. Individual vender stalls lined the first floor. The second floor was used for public meetings. In 1854 a larger market was constructed and stood until 1913, when a new "Old" or First Market was built. By then Shockoe Creek had been diverted into underground pipes and paved over by Eighteenth Street. The image above is of the pre-1913 building. In addition to serving as a marketplace, the upper floor was used for church services in the 1890s.

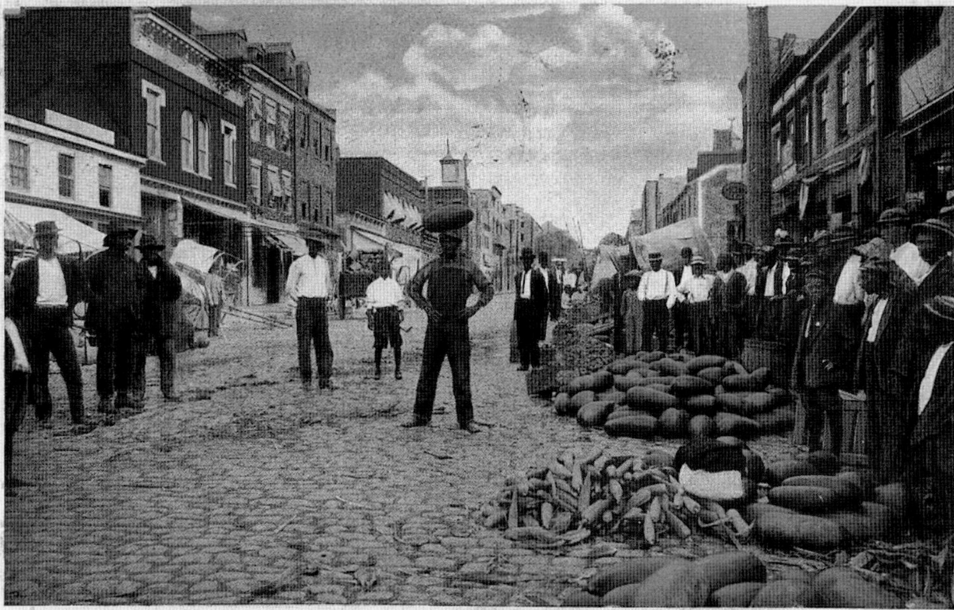

OPEN AIR MARKET SCENE (FRANKLIN STREET, EAST FROM 17TH STREET), RICHMOND, VA.

The area along Main and both Seventeenth and Eighteenth Streets became one large open-air market during the summer and fall each year. It was here that many local farmers from the surrounding counties brought in produce for sale. The two-wheeled carts were referred to as Hanover Carts.

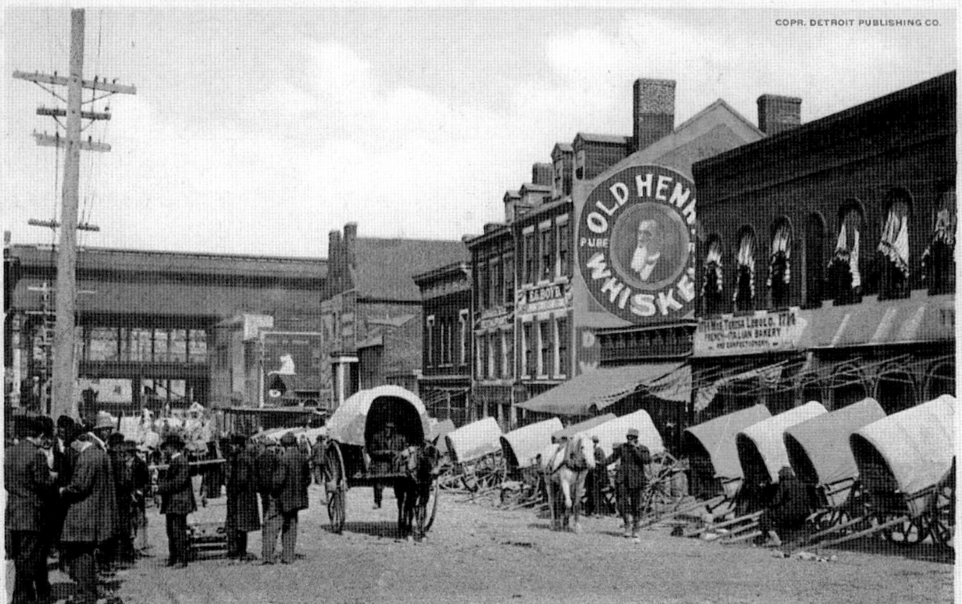

70276 MAIN STREET MARKETS, RICHMOND, VA.

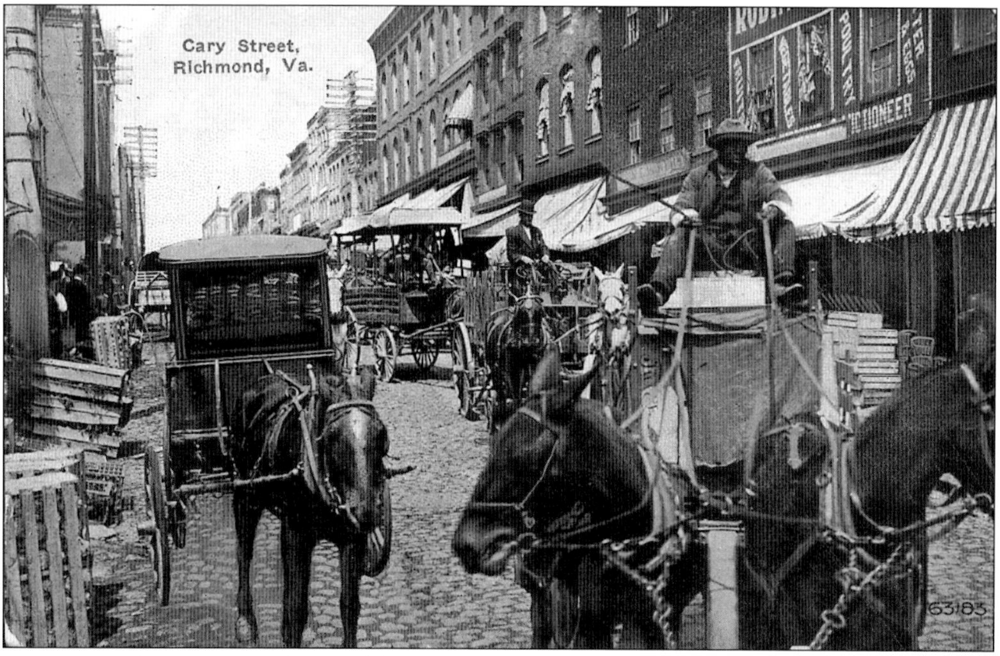

Between Main Street and the canal basin there were numerous small factories, workshops, and produce wholesalers along Gary Street. The street was always congested with wagons and carts as seen in this postcard view taken *c.* 1910.

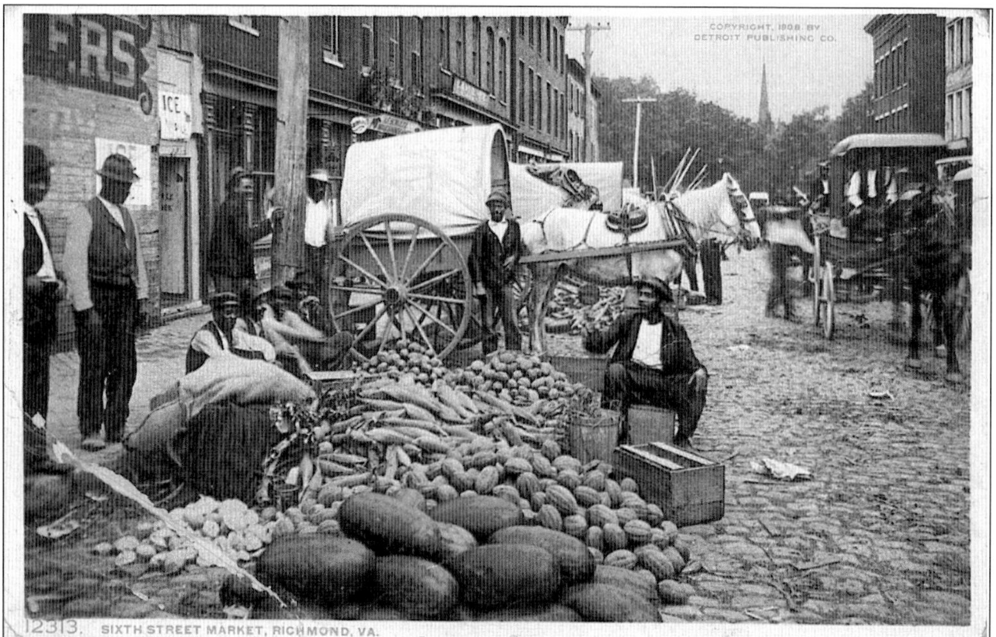

The city's Second Market was located on Sixth Street just north of Broad Street. During the harvest season, vendors displayed their produce along the sidewalks around the market building. This view along Sixth Street was taken around 1909.

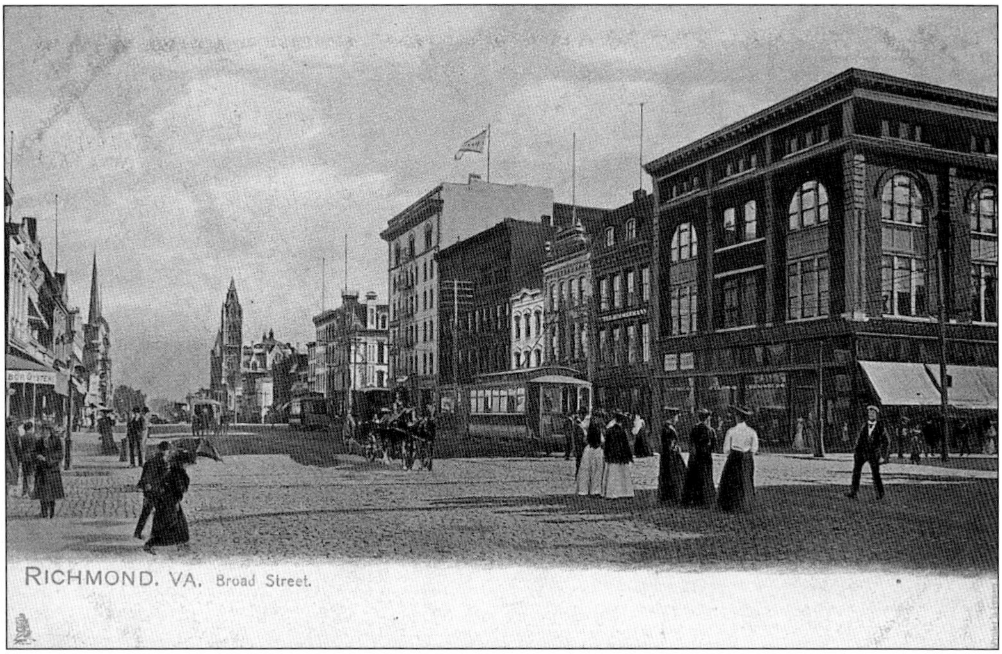

These postcard views of Broad Street, looking east, were taken around 1907. The upper view is from Eighth Street and the lower image is from Seventh Street. The Murphy's Hotel, built in 1902, appears on the south side of the street. In the distance the steeple on the north side is Broad Street Methodist Church. The tower of City Hall can be seen on the south side. City Hall occupied the square between Tenth and Eleventh Streets.

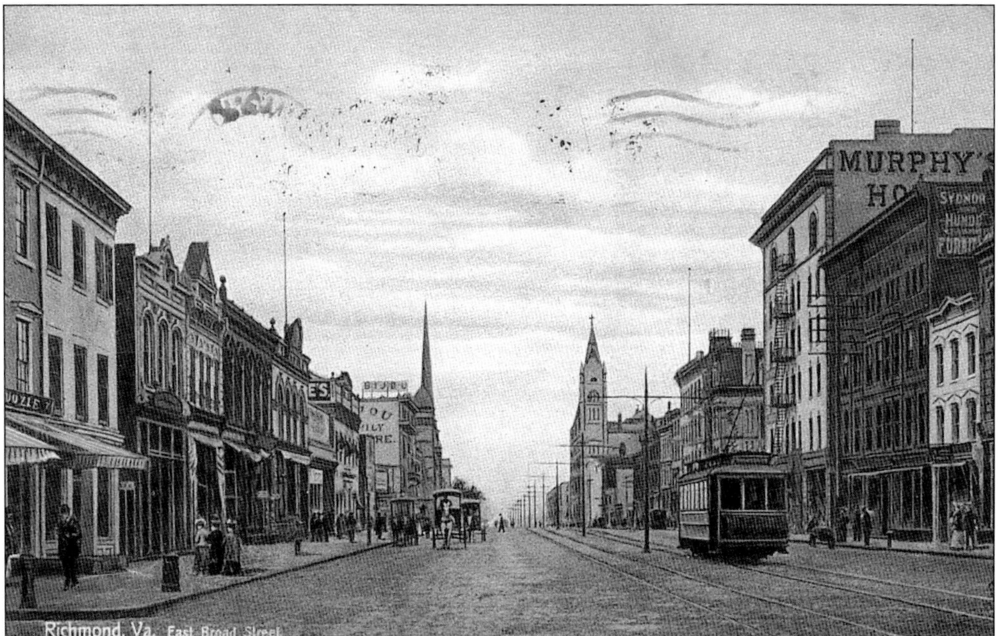

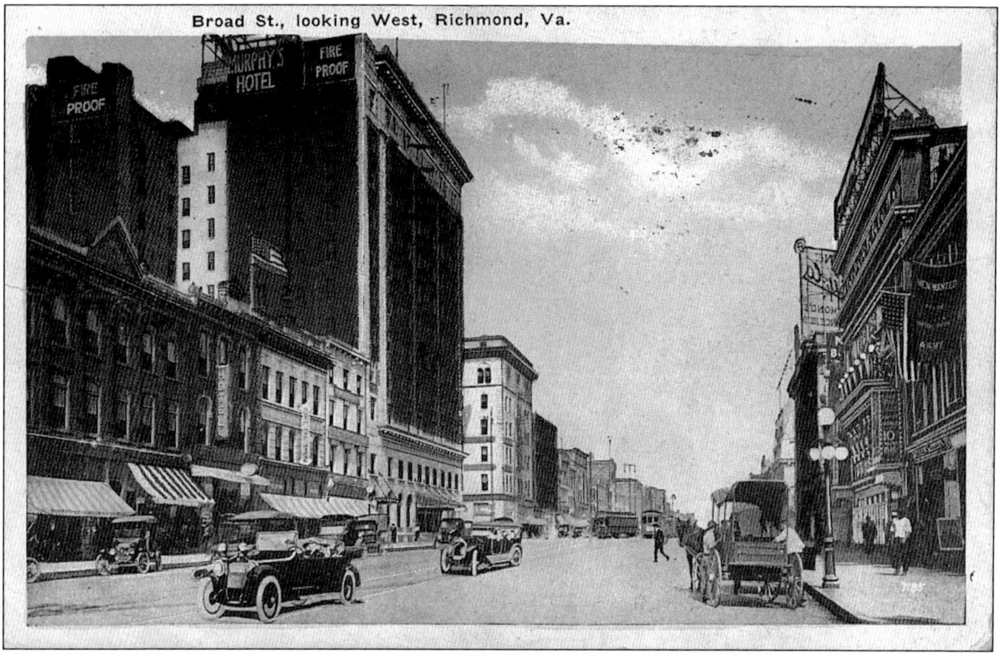

In this view, looking west on Broad Street, new Murphy's Hotel, which was built after the original hotel was torn down in 1913, stands on the southeast corner at Eighth and Broad Streets. The lower white annex on the southwest corner was sold in 1939 and the street-level floor was converted to retail shops. The new Murphy's became the King Carter Hotel in 1949, and 20 years later it was purchased by the Commonwealth and became the Eighth Street Office Building.

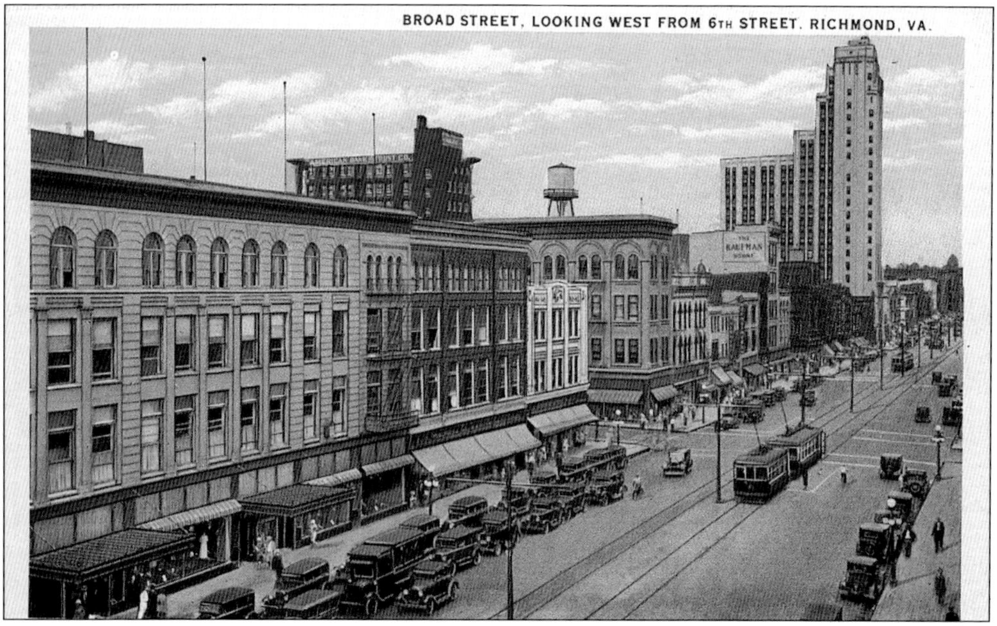

Miller & Rhoads appears in the left foreground of this view looking west on Broad from Fifth Street. Further down the street is the Central National Bank Building in the 300 block. Built between 1929 and 1930, this 22-story structure was Richmond's first skyscraper.

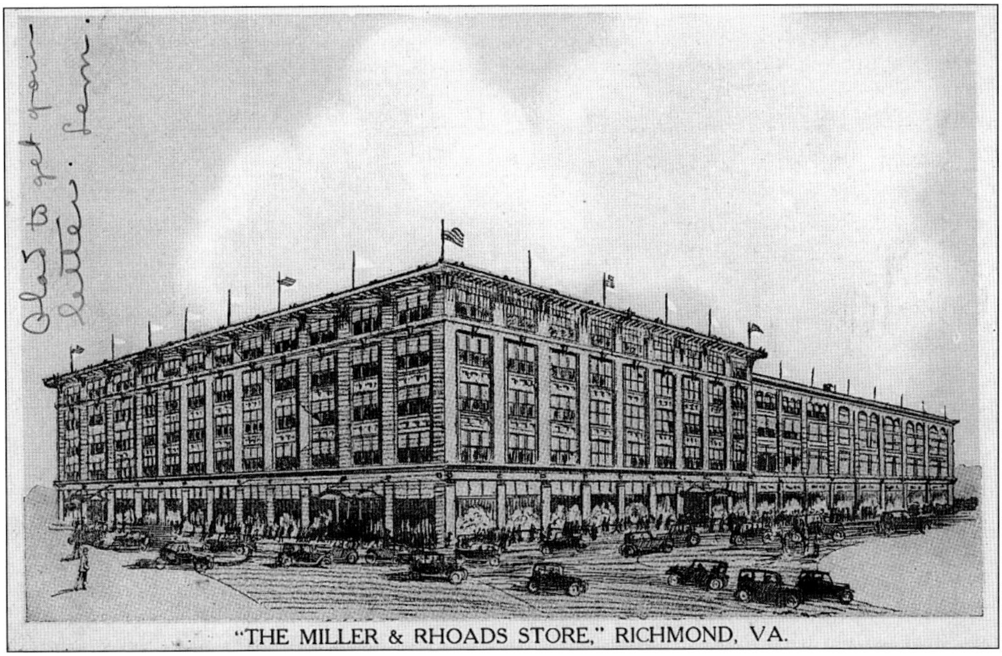

Miller & Rhoads opened on October 17, 1885, and moved to the 500 block of East Broad in 1886. The company continued to expand in the 500 block until 1924 when the store occupied the building shown.

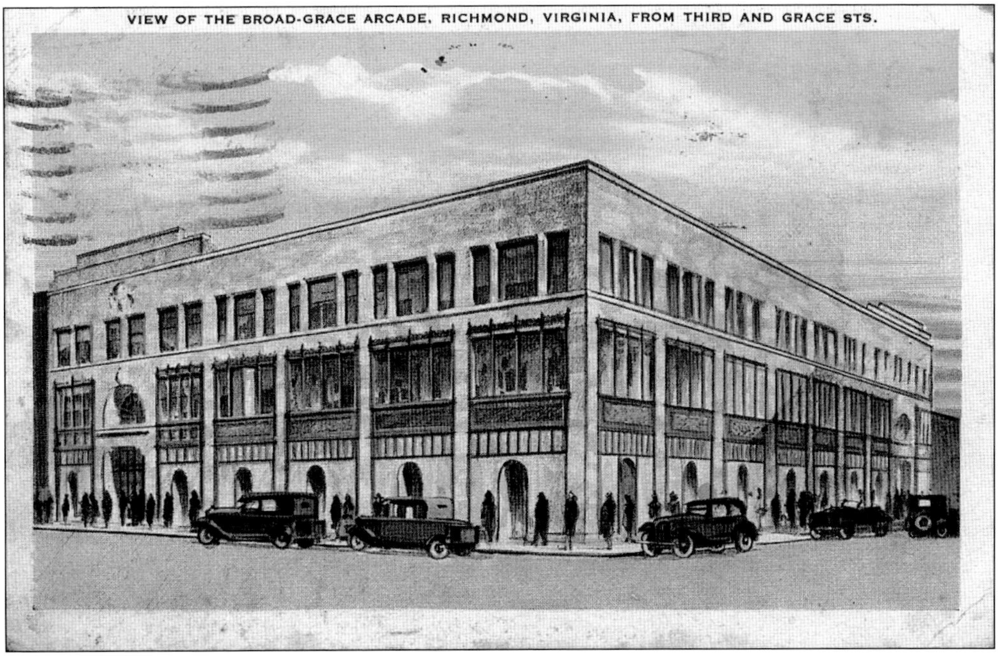

The idea of clustering businesses in an arcade was new to Richmond in 1925. The Broad-Grace Arcade on Third and Grace Streets was the first such venture. The upper floors were used for offices.

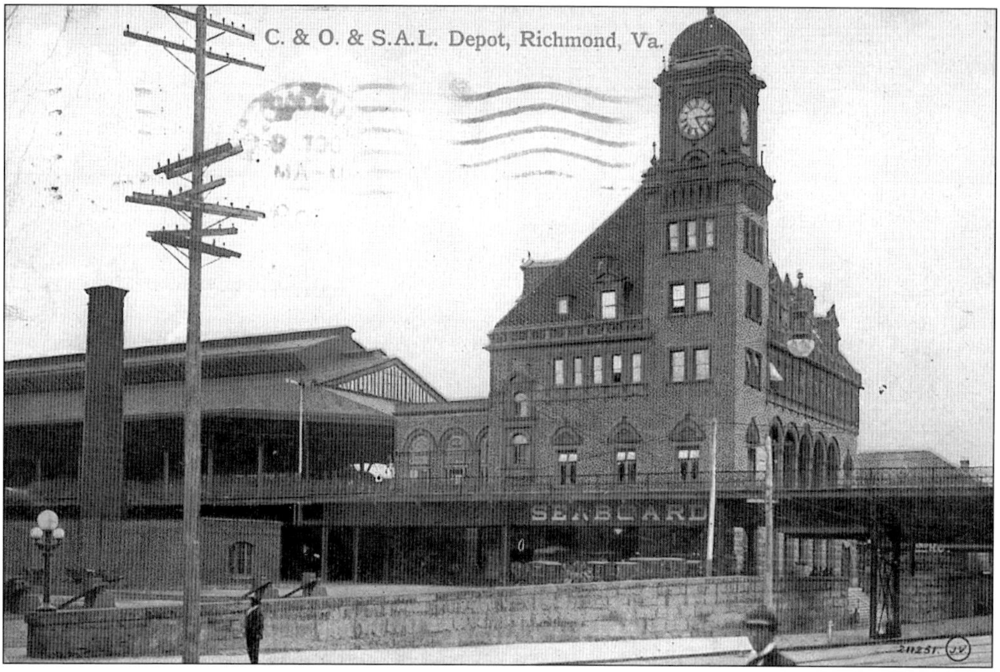

Main Street Station at Main and Fifteenth Streets was built between 1900 and 1901, at a cost of $165,000, to jointly serve the Chesapeake & Ohio, Seaboard Air Lines, and Southern Railroads. It is Richmond's premier example of French Renaissance architecture and was officially opened on November 2, 1901. The extensive viaduct system used to merge the various tracks and the train shed cost approximately $2 million.

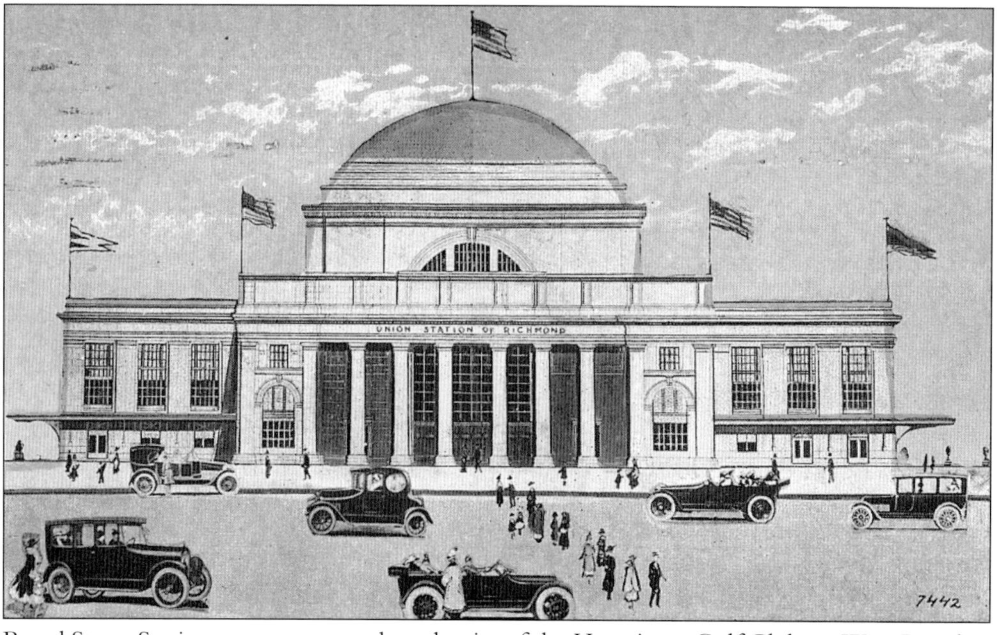

Broad Street Station was constructed on the site of the Hermitage Golf Club on West Broad to jointly serve the Atlantic Coast Line; Norfolk & Western; and Richmond, Fredericksburg & Potomac Railroads. It opened on January 6, 1919.

Five

Hotels and Private Clubs

Richmond's first hostelries generally provided eatables and potables for weary travelers and their horses. Sleeping quarters were usually in an upstairs loft with little privacy. Most notable were the Indian Queen or Washington Tavern at Ninth and Grace Streets and Swan Tavern on Broad Street between Eighth and Ninth Streets. Just north of the downtown area on Brook Turnpike was Goddin's Tavern. As the city grew, the taverns gave way to hotels that provided private rooms in addition to grander dining facilities and spacious bars. These facilities multiplied along Broad Street when the Richmond, Fredericksburg & Potomac Railroad tracks were laid down the street to the train station at Eighth and Broad. Hotels were also built around Capitol Square to provide accommodations for travelers and members of the General Assembly and on Main Street for business travelers. Most notable of these was the Spottswood Hotel on the southeast corner of Main and Eighth Streets. Built in 1860, it was intimately associated with the history of the 1861–1865 period. It burned on December 25, 1870, with the loss of eight lives. When the Jefferson Hotel opened in 1895 with a spectacular lobby, it was the most impressive and attractively ornate hotel in the South.

When the city was young, residents found pleasure in sporting clubs, private military organizations, and social events. The influx of new immigrants injected new and different cultural strains into the city's life. The appearance of musical societies representing the various ethnic groups gave evidence of the city's cultural diversity.

Following the Civil War, the old line political and social elite became allied with the new wealthy industrial powerbrokers and organized private clubs to perpetuate and enhance their beliefs, interests, and lifestyles. Principal among these clubs were the Richmond Club, the Westmoreland Club, and the Commonwealth Club for gentlemen. For women, there was the Woman's Club of Richmond. These clubs maintained their own facilities at which members could enjoy meals and drinks, social gatherings, and overnight lodging when necessary. Servants catered to members and their guests. As with the sporting clubs, military organizations, and musical societies, these private clubs helped to foster pride in the community as well as satisfy individual personal interests.

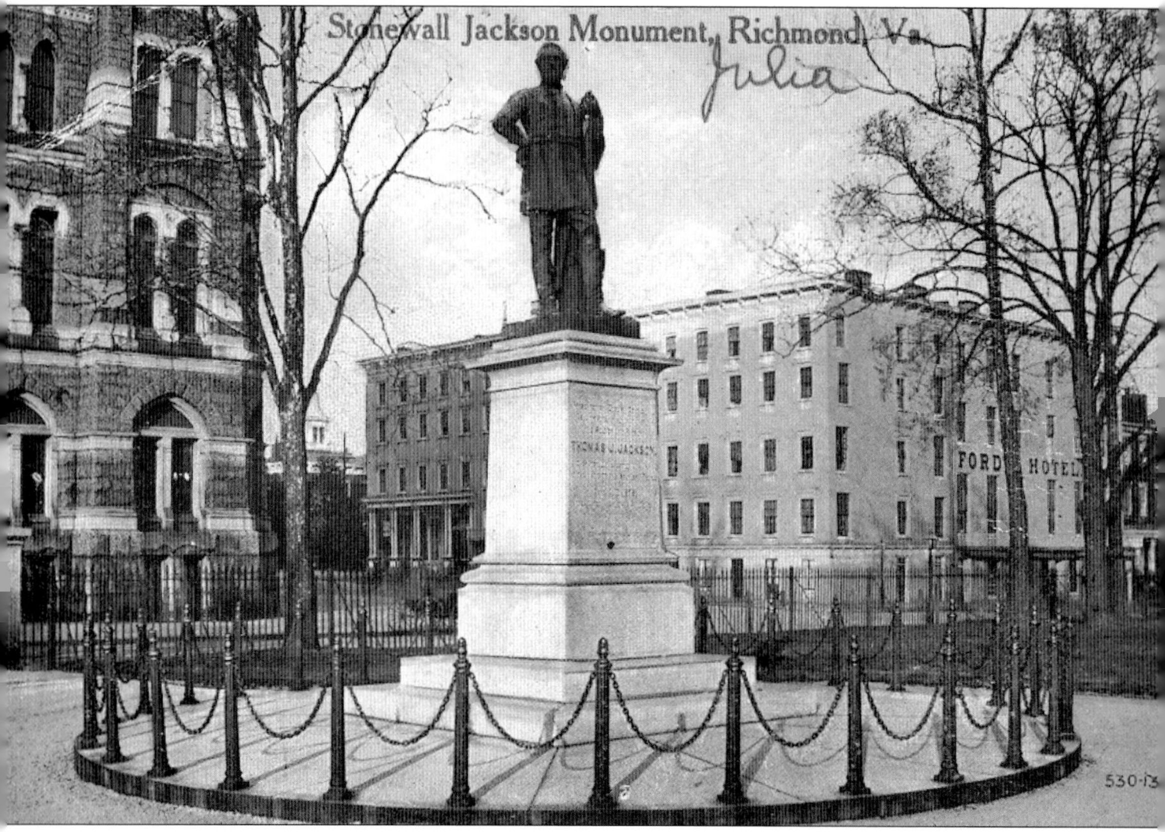

The old Ford Hotel, at right behind the statue of Stonewall Jackson, was on Capitol and Broad Streets between Eleventh and Twelfth Streets and was originally known as the Powhatan House. In 1831 James McKildoe renovated and enlarged a boardinghouse on the southeast corner of Broad and Eleventh Streets and opened the Powhatan House. The body of Mrs. John Tyler, the first wife of a sitting president to die in the White House, was brought to the Powhatan House on September 13, 1842, before being transported to New Kent County the next day. President Millard Fillmore was a guest at the hotel in 1851. By 1870 the old Powhatan Hotel had been renamed for its proprietor, A.J. Ford, and became Ford's Hotel. Even after his death in 1888 it remained Ford's Hotel until 1911 when the property was purchased by the city for a proposed courts building. The next year, Ford's Hotel was torn down.

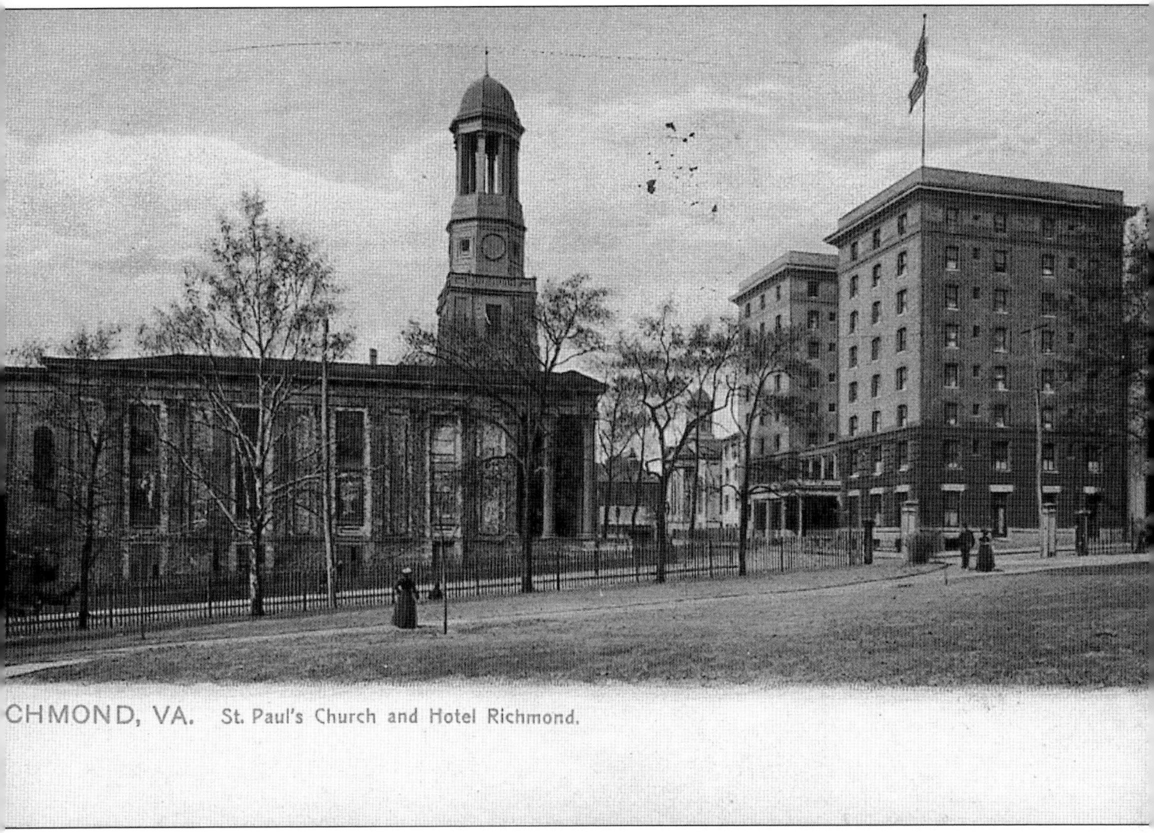

Shortly after the Revolutionary War, Maj. Andrew Dunscombe built a residence on what became the corner of Grace and Ninth Streets, across from the northwest corner of Capitol Square. A portion of his residence became a tavern, thought by some to have been originally called the Indian Queen. In 1797 Parke Goodall used the building as a tavern and it was called Goodall's, or the Indian Queen. By 1810 it was called Washington Tavern. After the 1840s the tavern became known as the Monumental Hotel, and in the 1850s, James Lyons erected a four-story addition on the north side of the original building. During the Civil War it was called the Central (Monumental) Hotel and the second auditor of the Confederate States had his office in the hotel. Around 1870 the name was changed to the St. Claire Hotel, a name that was in use for a little over three decades before the building was torn down in 1903 to make way for a new hotel. The Hotel Richmond, also referred to as The Richmond and the Richmond Hotel, was completed in 1904, thus perpetuating the presence of a hostelry on the same plot of ground from around 1785. This view from Capitol Square shows the Hotel Richmond facing St. Paul's Episcopal Church.

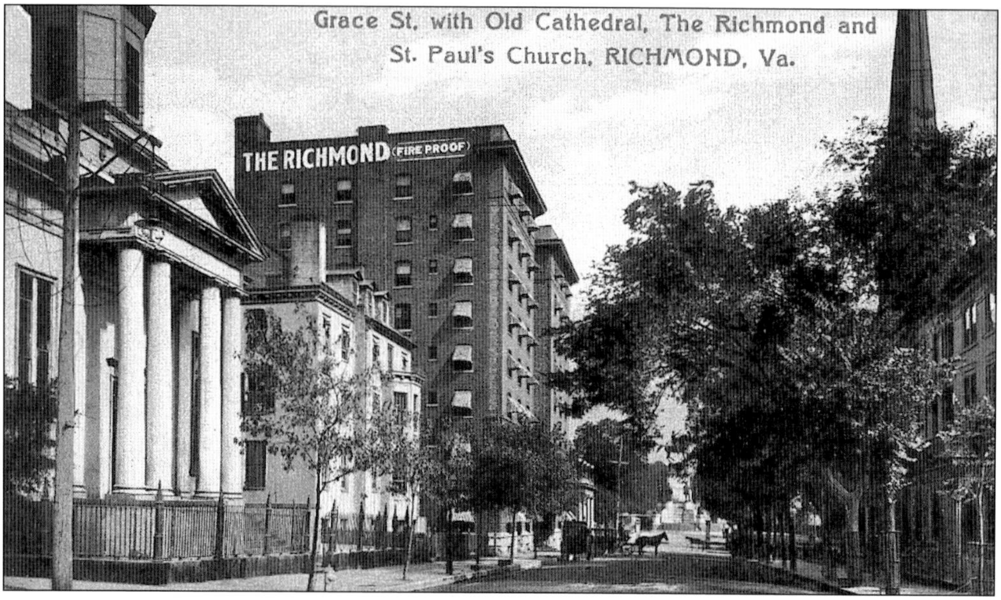

This view from Eighth and Grace Streets looking east shows The Richmond around 1909. The church to the left is St. Peter's Roman Catholic, built in 1841, which served as the cathedral of the Richmond diocese until 1906. On the south side of Grace across the street from The Richmond can be seen the steeple of St. Paul's Episcopal Church, built in 1845. Straight down Grace Street appears the Washington Monument on Capitol Square.

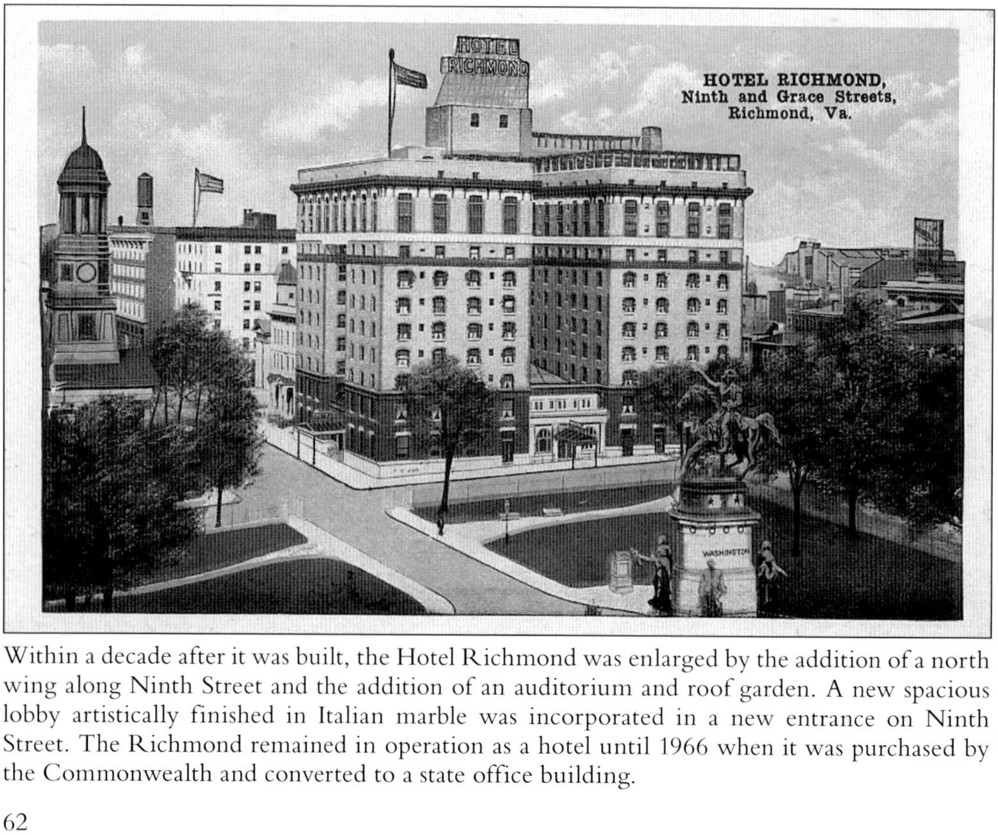

Within a decade after it was built, the Hotel Richmond was enlarged by the addition of a north wing along Ninth Street and the addition of an auditorium and roof garden. A new spacious lobby artistically finished in Italian marble was incorporated in a new entrance on Ninth Street. The Richmond remained in operation as a hotel until 1966 when it was purchased by the Commonwealth and converted to a state office building.

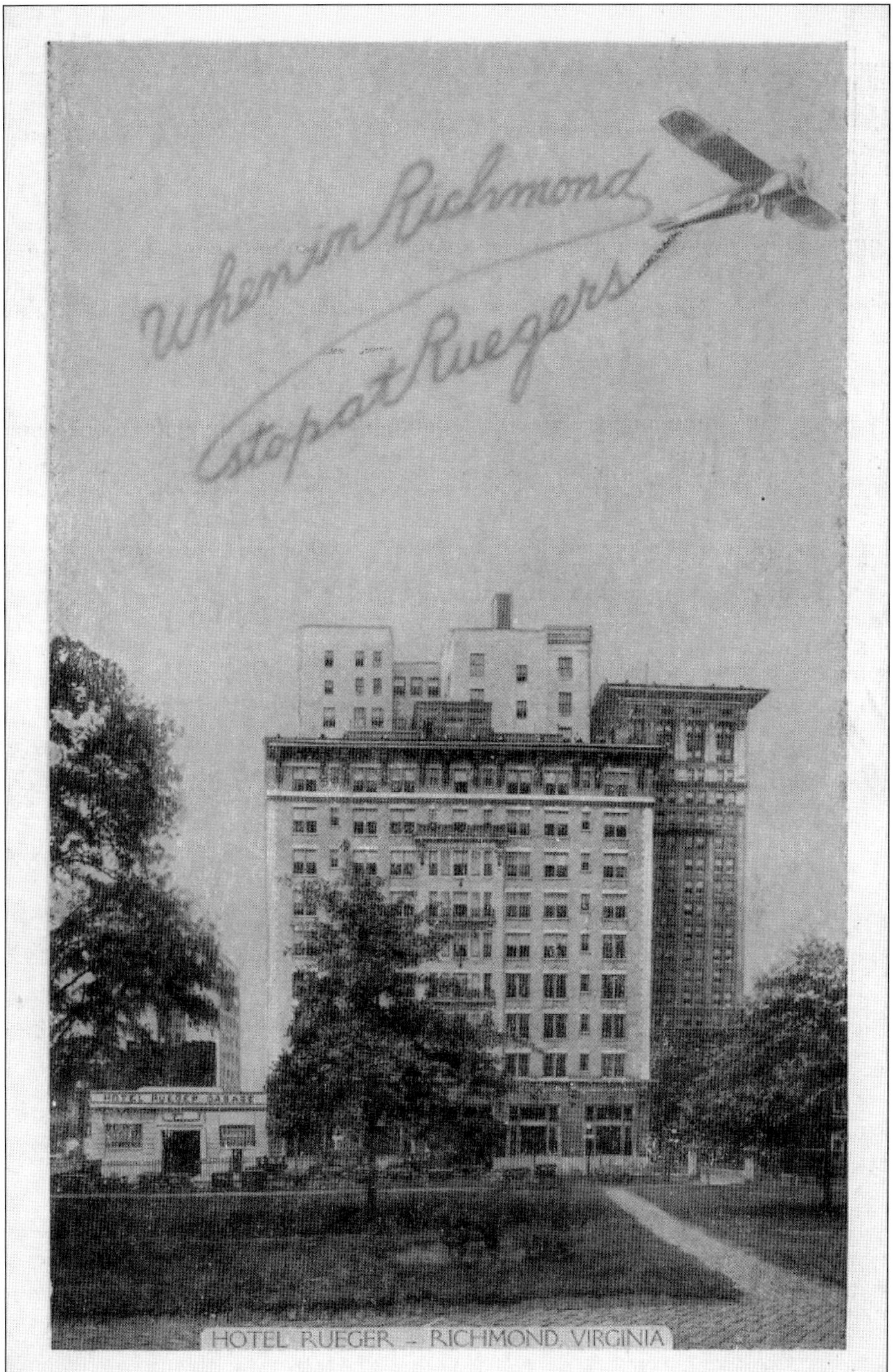

The Hotel Rueger opened in 1912 at the site that was once Rueger's Restaurant, established in 1846 at Ninth and Canal Streets. It became the Hotel Raleigh in 1952 and the Commonwealth Park Hotel in 1982. The building to the right rear is the First National Bank on the southwest corner of Ninth and Main Streets.

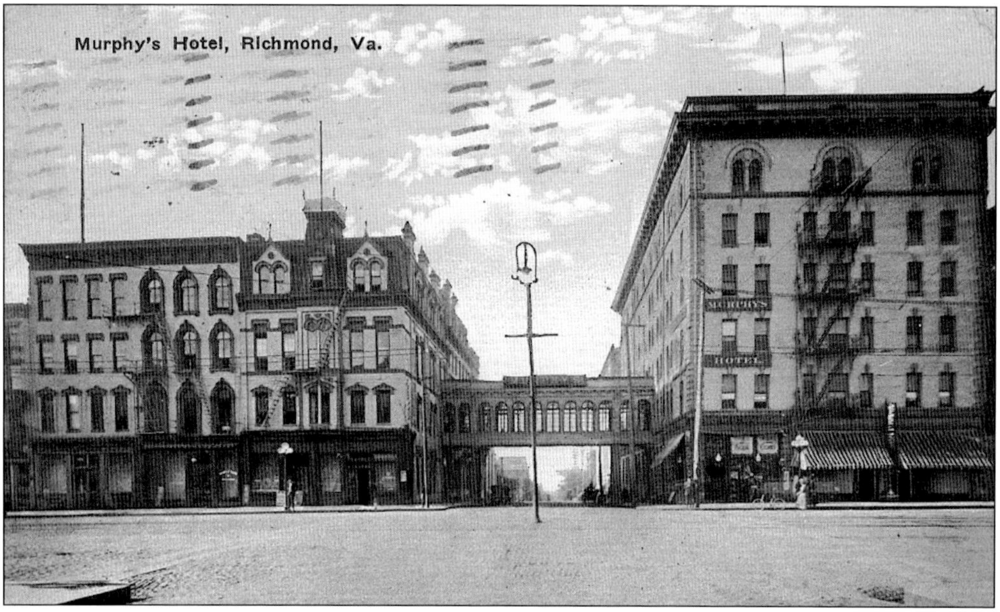

In 1872 Col. John Murphy opened Murphy's Oyster Bar on the southeast corner of Eighth and Broad Streets. In 1886 Colonel Murphy replaced the original building with the structure seen in this postcard. He expanded the hotel by building an annex across Eighth Street on the southwest corner and a bridge was built over Eighth Street to connect the two buildings. The 1886 structure was torn down in 1913 and a New Murphy's Hotel was built. In 1939 the annex was sold and the bridge was removed. Ten years later the New Murphy's Hotel was renamed the King Carter Hotel. The King Carter was purchased by the Commonwealth in 1969 and is now the Eighth Street Office Building.

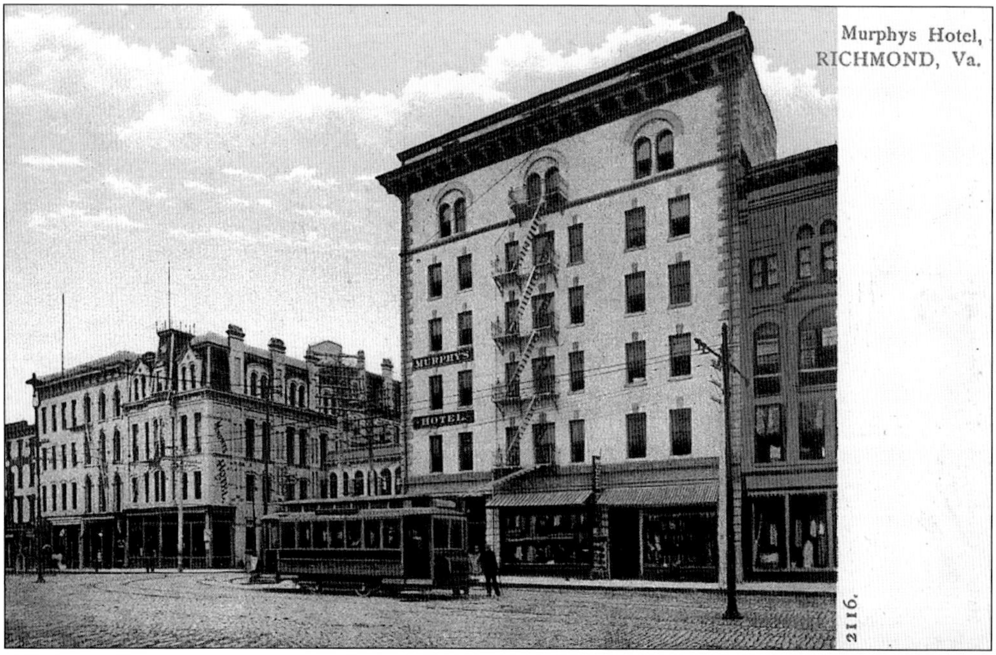

Here is another view of the original Murphy's Hotel and the Murphy's Hotel Annex, *c.* 1907.

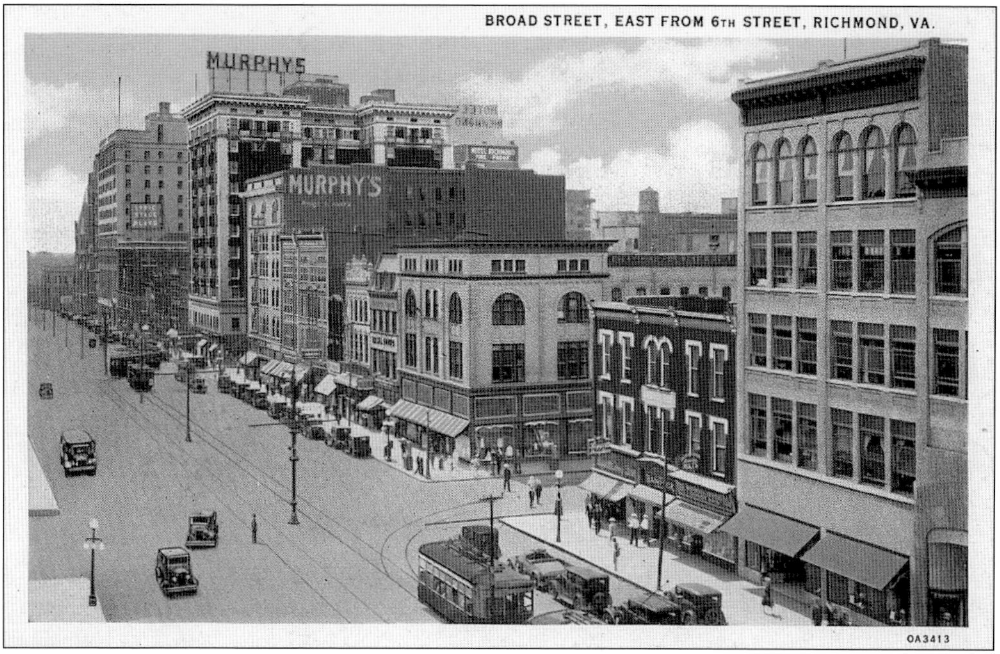

The New Murphy's Hotel, built in 1913, can be been in this bird's-eye view of the south side of Broad Street taken from Sixth Street.

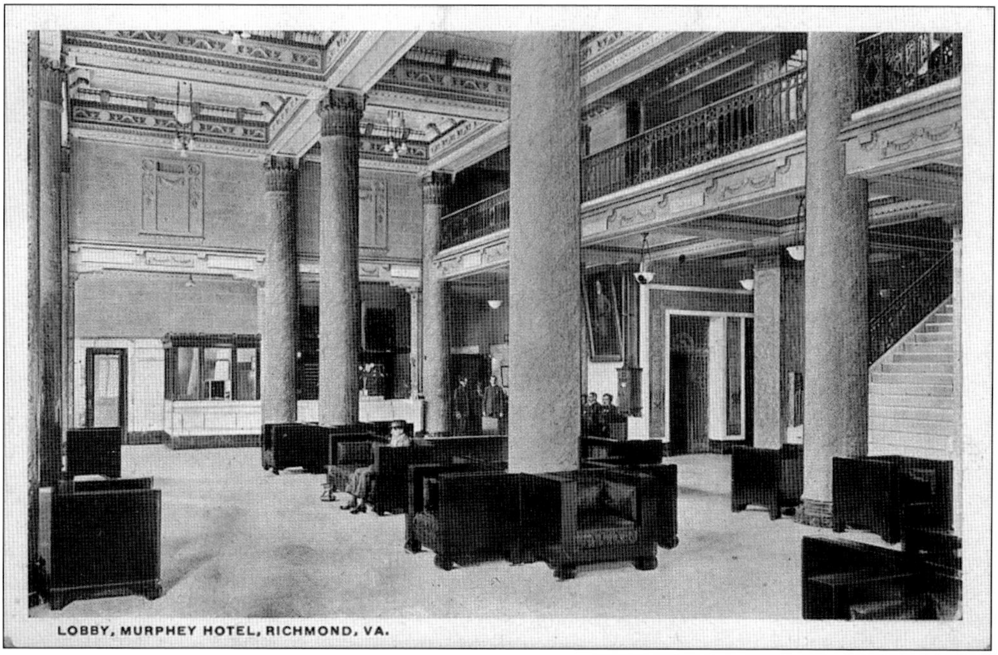

The main lobby of the New Murphy's Hotel was frequented by legislators and lobbyists alike, and many political deals were brokered here between 1913 and 1949.

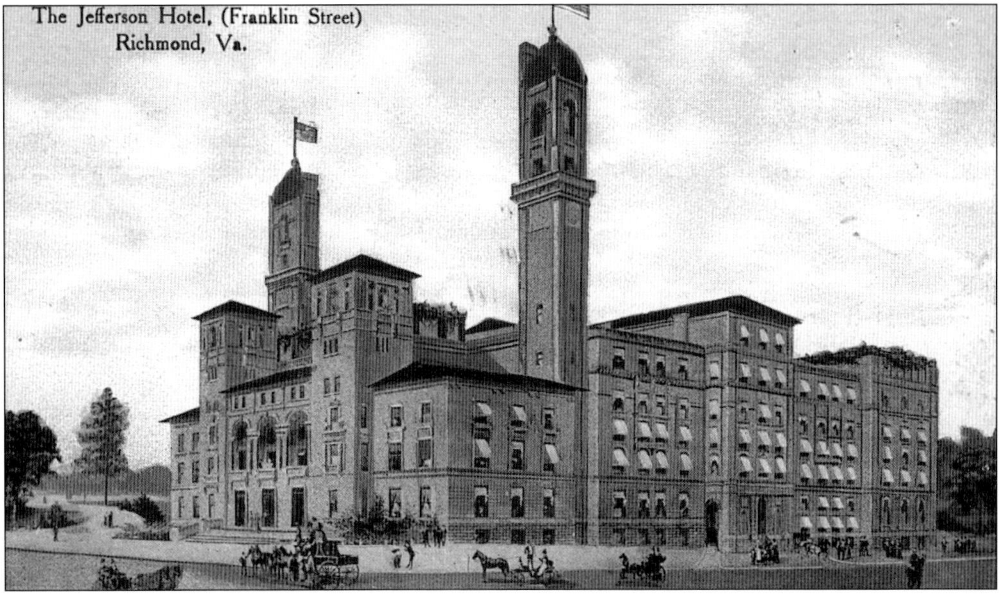

Responding to the need for a hotel in the city's then west end, tobacco magnet Maj. Lewis Ginter, in association with John Pope and George Arents, acquired the 100 block between West Franklin and Main Streets. The architectural firm of Carrere and Hastings designed the Jefferson Hotel to be based on the Villa Medici in Rome. Construction started in 1893, and on October 31, 1895, the hotel officially opened.

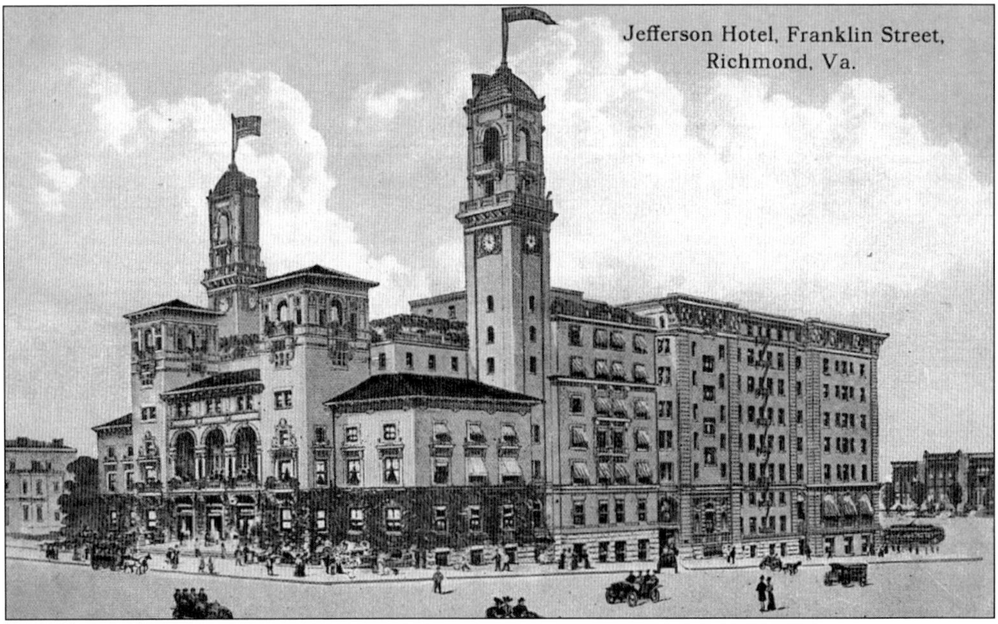

The Jefferson Hotel was enjoying great success when a fire broke out in a fourth-floor blanket room on March 19, 1901. As fire crews fought the flames, all of the hotel's guests managed to flee to safety. The fire destroyed all but the Franklin Street side. No sooner were the flames extinguished than the Jefferson Realty Corporation, with Joseph Bryan as president, began plans to rebuild. The new Jefferson was opened on May 5, 1907 and continues to serve the traveling public.

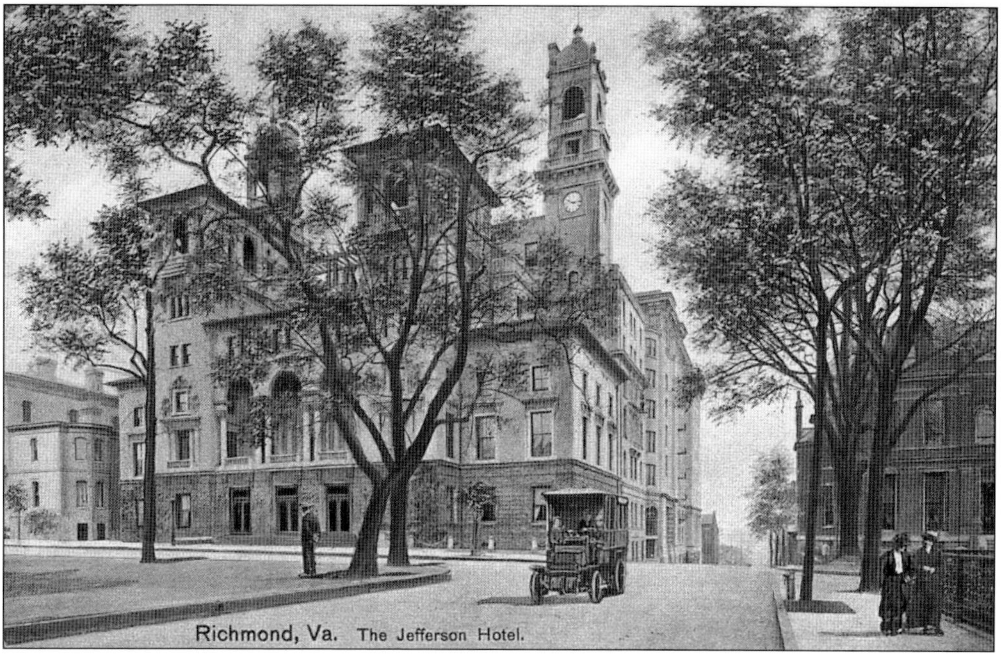

The Franklin Street side of the reconstructed Jefferson Hotel appears in this view taken from Jefferson Street around 1910.

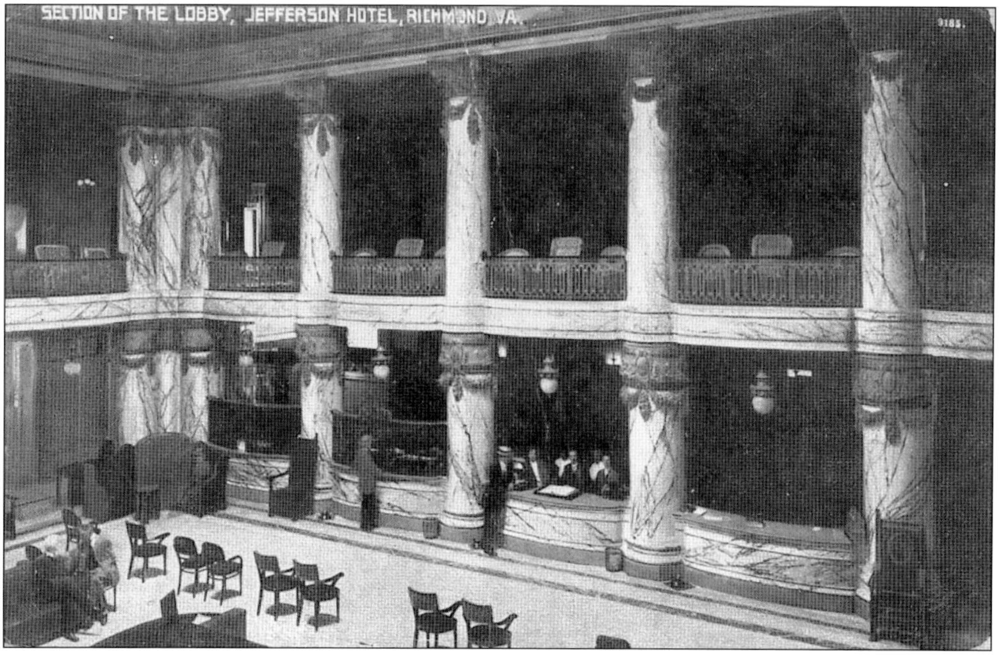

The registration desk located along the west side of the lower, or main lobby is pictured above shortly after the hotel reopened. The lower lobby served guests who entered from Main Street.

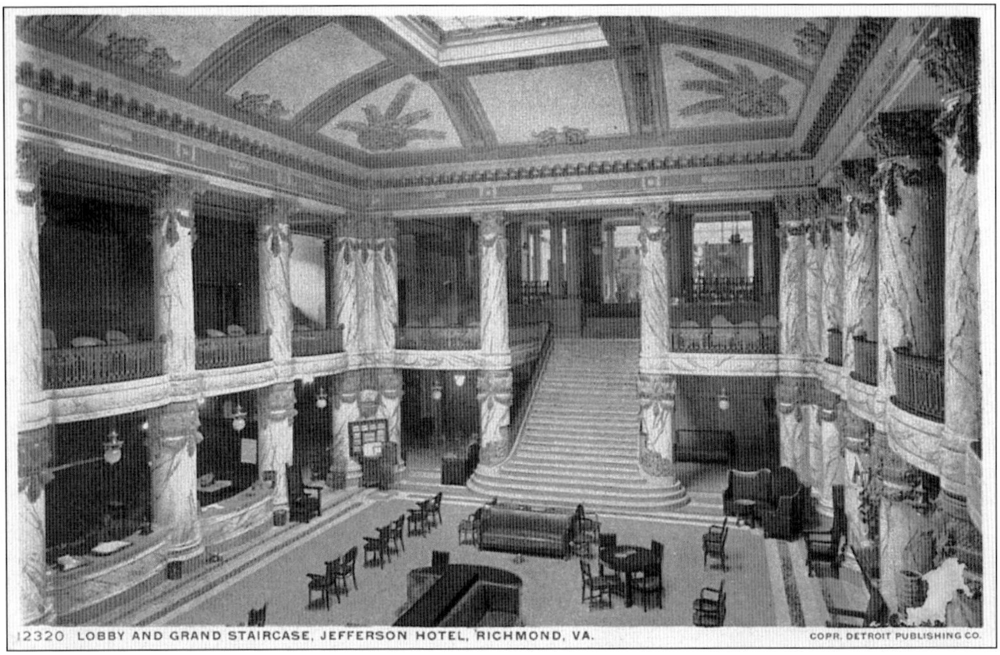

The main lobby of the Jefferson was spacious and ornately grand. These two views of the main lobby were taken after the hotel was rebuilt. The marble staircase leads up to the gallery that surrounds the lobby and to an upper lobby that served guests who entered from Franklin Street.

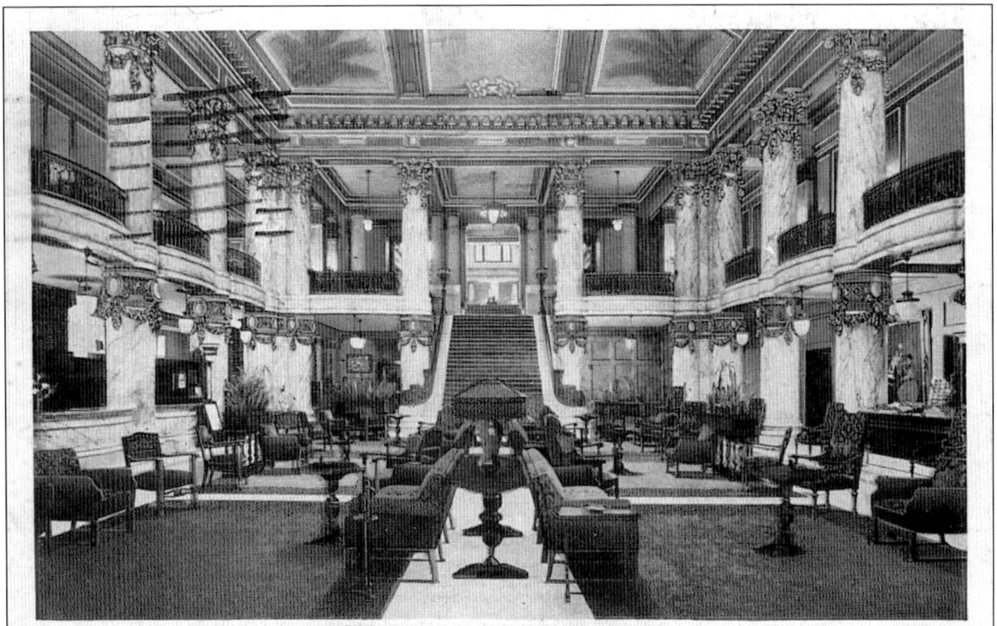

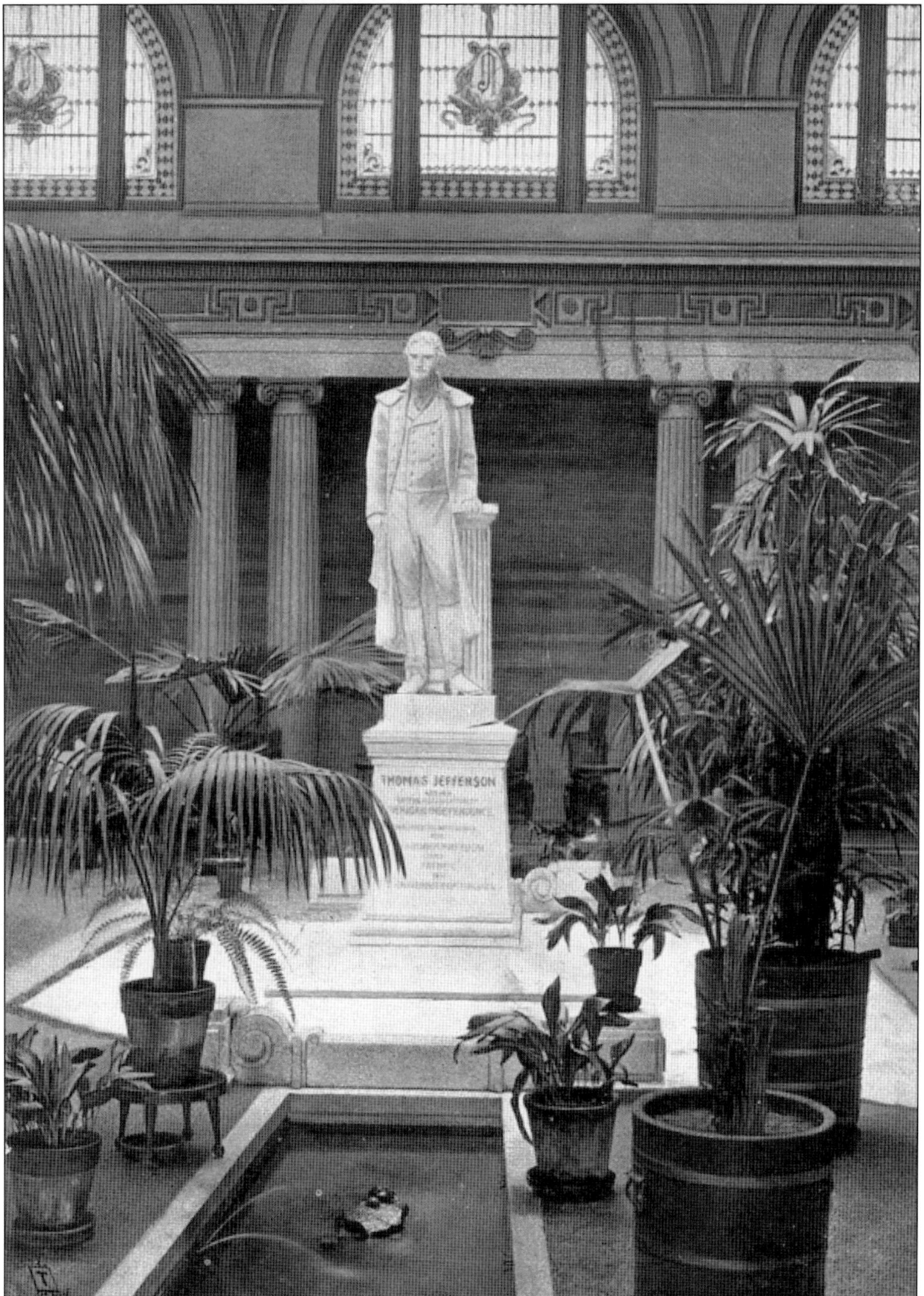

The statue of Thomas Jefferson sculpted by Edward V. Valentine stood in the upper lobby, and during the 1901 fire, several volunteers rushed in to save it. They were successful in rescuing the statue, but the head was broken off in the process. Once the statue was repaired it was replaced in the restored upper lobby, which resembled a Pompeian court.

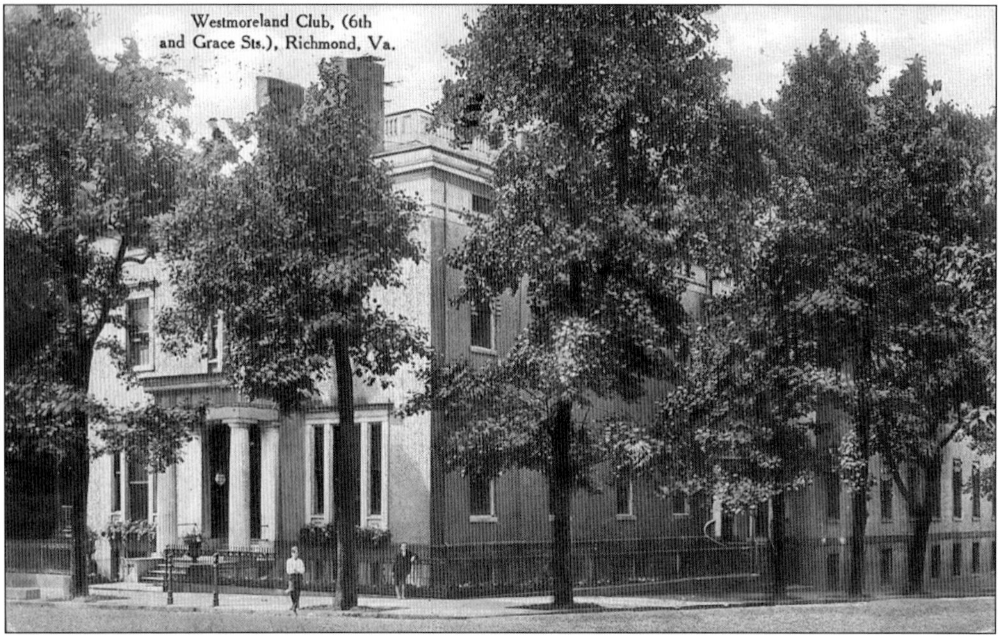

The structure that became the home of the Westmoreland Club at 601 East Grace Street was begun in 1836 by James Gray. In 1879 the Westmoreland Club, a men's social club organized in 1877, acquired the house. Membership in the club was limited to 450 resident and 250 non-resident members. During the early 1930s, the Westmoreland Club fell on hard times and merged with the Commonwealth Club in 1937. The historic clubhouse was torn down to make way for a commercial establishment.

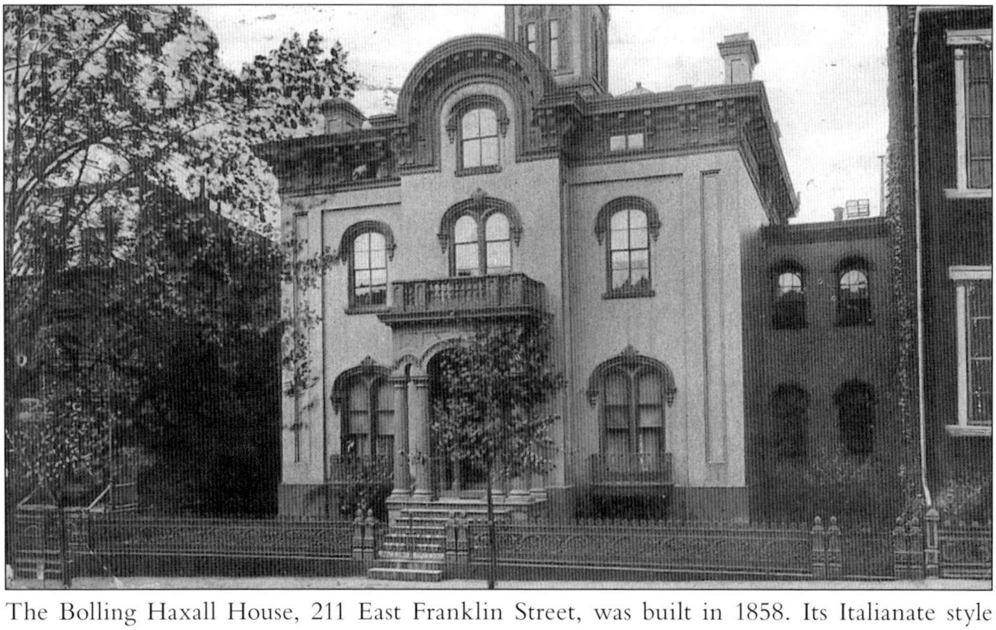

The Bolling Haxall House, 211 East Franklin Street, was built in 1858. Its Italianate style sets it apart from other homes built prior to the Civil War. In 1900 the house became the headquarters of the Woman's Club of Richmond, which had been founded in 1894 by women who were prominent in social, literary, and artistic circles.

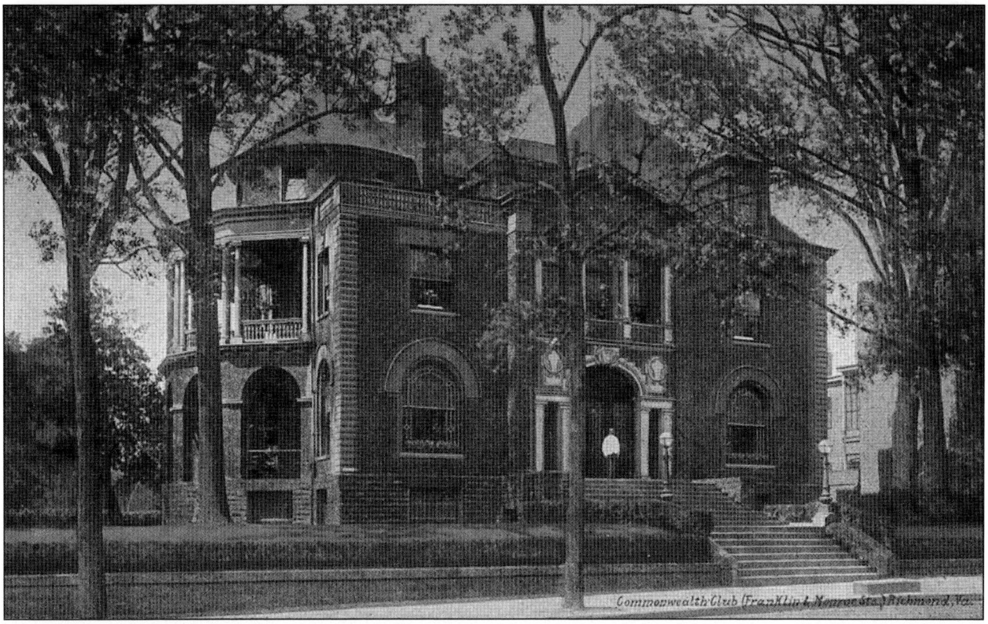

Founded in 1890, the Commonwealth Club acquired property on the southwest corner of Franklin and Monroe Streets. Construction of the handsome brick and brownstone building was completed on October 15, 1891. The men's club has since extended membership to women and continues to flourish as a vital part of the city's social and professional community.

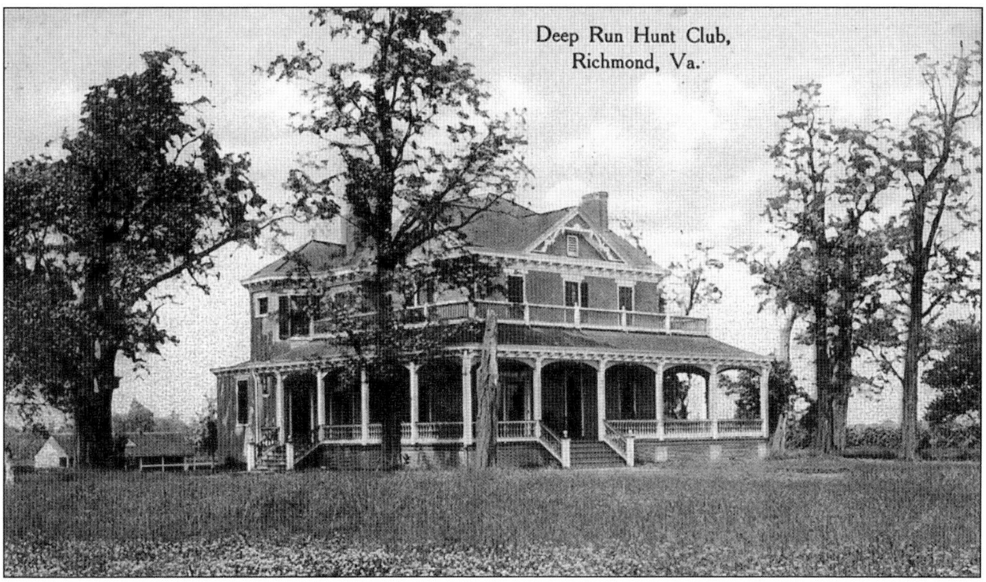

A group of avid hunters who hunted in the western part of Henrico County formed the Deep Run Hunt Club in 1887. In 1896, the membership accepted Maj. Lewis Ginter's offer of 127 acres on Hermitage Road across from the A.P. Hill Monument. There they built their clubhouse, Rosedale Lodge; a stable for 40 horses; a half-mile racetrack; a nine-hole golf course; a steeplechase course; and pens for the hounds. The club remained at Rosedale Lodge until 1910 when it joined with the Country Club of Virginia. The land was subdivided into residential communities and the parcel containing the lodge became a 13-acre park.

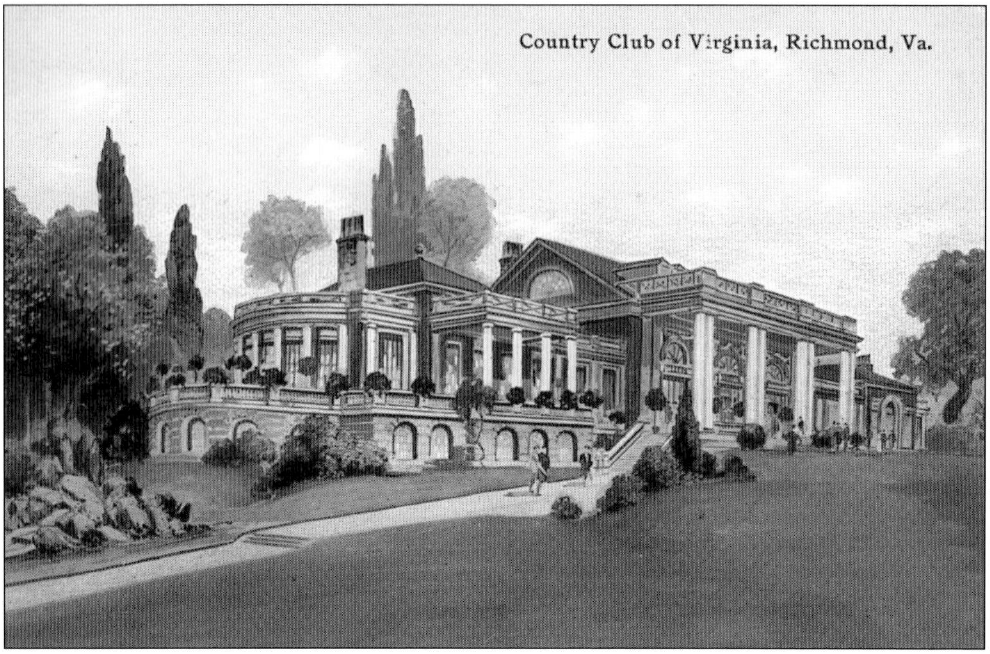

The Country Club of Virginia opened on June 18, 1910, in spacious quarters about three miles from the city limits on Cary Street Road in Rio Vista, Henrico County. It became part of the city through annexation in 1942.

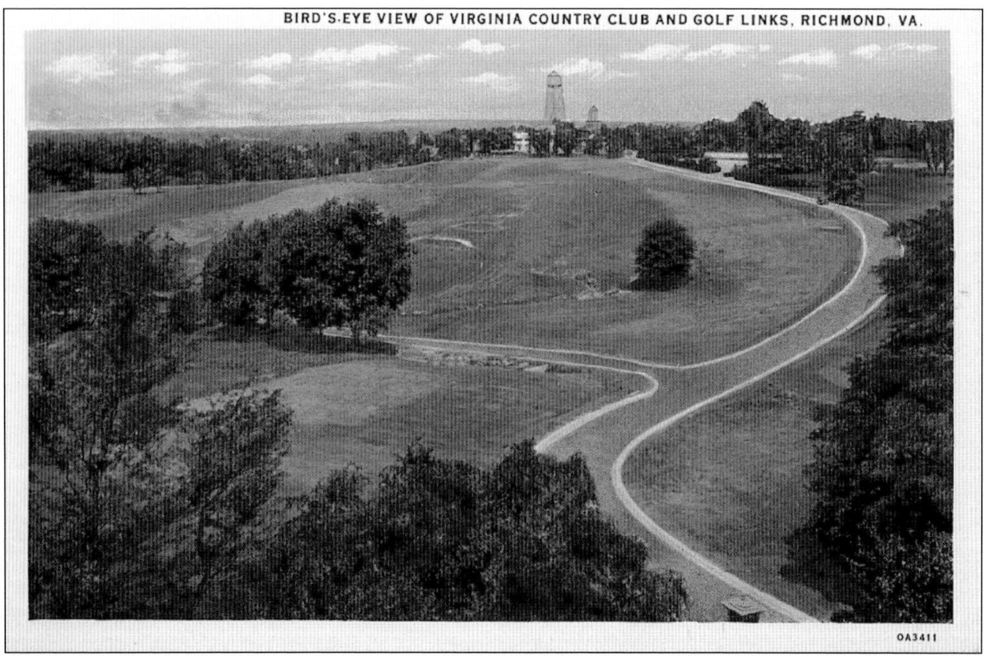

This postcard shows a bird's-eye view of Virginia Country Club and Golf Links as they appeared shortly after the club opened in 1910.

Six

Education

Although Richmond's parent county of Henrico spawned the nation's first university, The University of Henricus, 1619–1622, the city's first educational institution was the Lancaster Private School, which opened in 1759. It was not until Alexandre Marie Quesnay de Beaurepaire, a young French officer who had served on Lafayette's staff, espoused the idea of opening an Academy of Arts and Sciences of the United States in Richmond that the city experienced its first venture into the realm of higher education. Winning local support and financial sponsors, the proposed school was to be built on a site that had been secured on what became Academy Hill. On June 24, 1786, the cornerstone of the Academy of Quesnay was laid. Quesnay's Academy Hall would serve as the meeting place for Virginia's Ratification of the U.S. Constitution Convention in 1788, but it would never serve as a seat of learning. By 1800 Academy Hall was purchased by a theatrical company and served as a theater until it burned in 1803. The square on which it was located was called Academy Square and the hill became Academy Hill. In 1845 the Medical College of Virginia moved to a site on old Academy Square and today engulfs Academy Hill.

The first institution of higher learning to call Richmond home was Richmond College in 1833. The Medical College of Virginia dates from 1838 when Hampden-Sydney established it in Richmond. The Baptists chartered the Richmond Female Institute in 1853 to provide higher education for women. It opened its doors in 1854. That same year the Virginia Mechanics Institute was founded for the purpose of providing educational opportunities in the mechanical and useful arts. The Richmond Theological Seminary, established in 1865, was the first school established to provide African-American men with advanced training for Christian work. In 1898 it merged with other colleges to form Virginia Union University. That same year, Union Theological Seminary in Virginia moved from Hampden-Sydney to Richmond.

It was not until the 20th century that Richmond witnessed the growth of its own university. In 1917, when a group of citizens saw the need for a place for young women to obtain training for social and public health work, they raised funds and chartered the Richmond School of Social Work and Public Health. In 1925, after affiliating with the College of William and Mary, the school purchased a large building at the corner of Franklin and Shafer Streets. Since then it has grown into Virginia Commonwealth University.

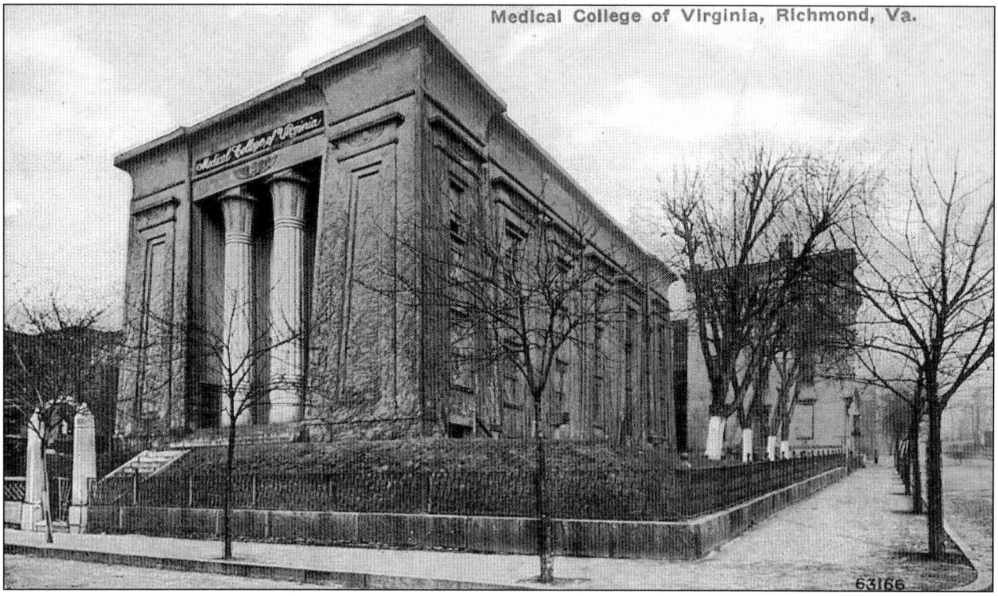

When the medical department of Hampden-Sydney moved to Richmond in 1838, the Union Hotel at Nineteenth and Main Streets was leased for dormitory, classroom, and hospital use. Thomas S. Stewart of Philadelphia was hired to design a permanent home for the department. He did so in the Egyptian Revival style. Built on the corner of College and Marshall Streets, the Egyptian Building was opened in 1845. In 1854, the department became the Medical College of Virginia. During the Civil War it was the only Southern medical college to remain open. It merged with Richmond Professional Institute to form Virginia Commonwealth University in 1968.

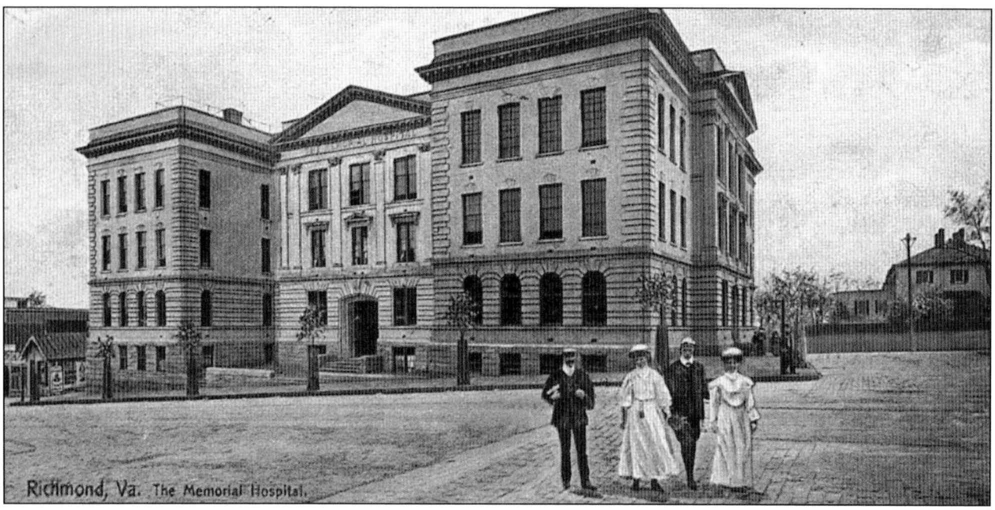

Memorial Hospital was built as a memorial to Miss Charlotte Randolph Williams who drowned at Old Point on July 7, 1884. Her father gave $160,000 to establish a hospital and Memorial Hospital was incorporated October 12, 1899. The site on the southeast corner of Broad and Twelfth Streets was secured and construction began in 1902. Memorial Hospital opened for patients on July 27, 1903. In January 1913 it was conveyed to the Medical College of Virginia. It was eventually transferred to the Virginia Department of Transportation and is presently under that agency's jurisdiction. The Governor's Mansion appears to the right.

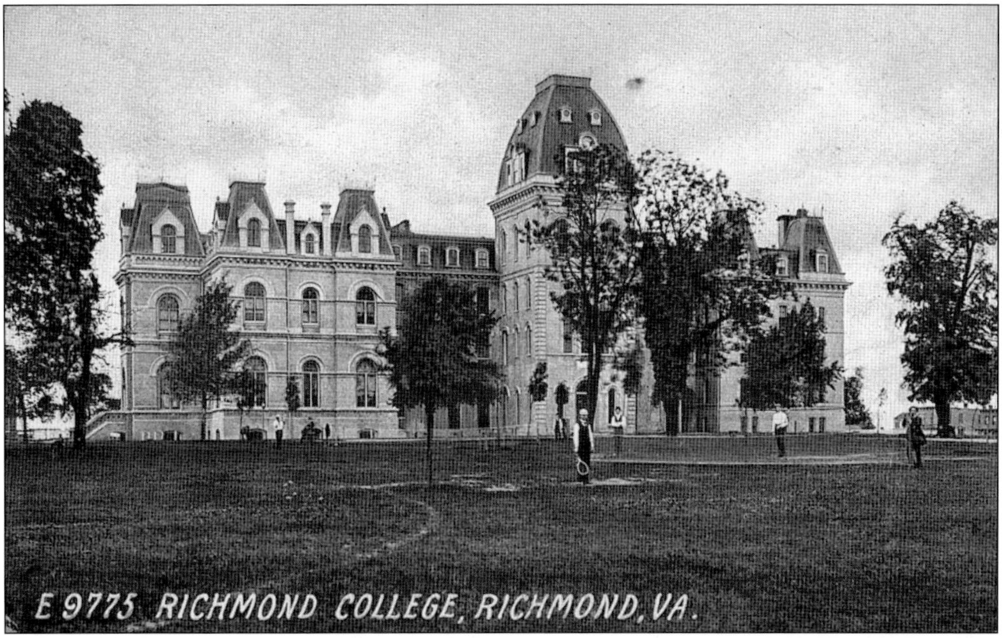

Richmond College's Ryland Hall was built on the west side of Lombardy Street at the end of Grace Street. The college was founded in 1830 and occupied a site at what was then the terminus of Grace Street, between Broad and Franklin Streets. Named for the college's first president, Dr. Robert Ryland, the school began construction in 1872 and was completed by the next year. The north wing of the building burned on the night of December 24–25, 1910, and four years later the college moved to Westhampton. In 1920 it became the University of Richmond. Ryland Hall was torn down after the college moved and Grace Street was extended west through the former campus.

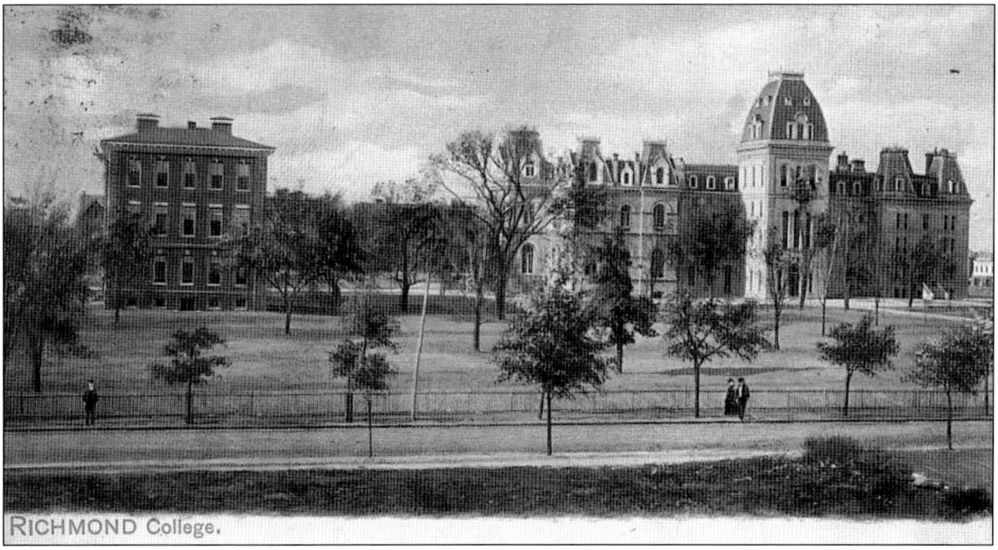

The red brick building on the left in this 1908 view of the campus of Richmond College is Science Hall. Thomas Hall is in the middle, slightly behind Ryland Hall on the right. Thomas Hall housed the college's library and a museum containing a rare collection of paintings, statuary, and curios.

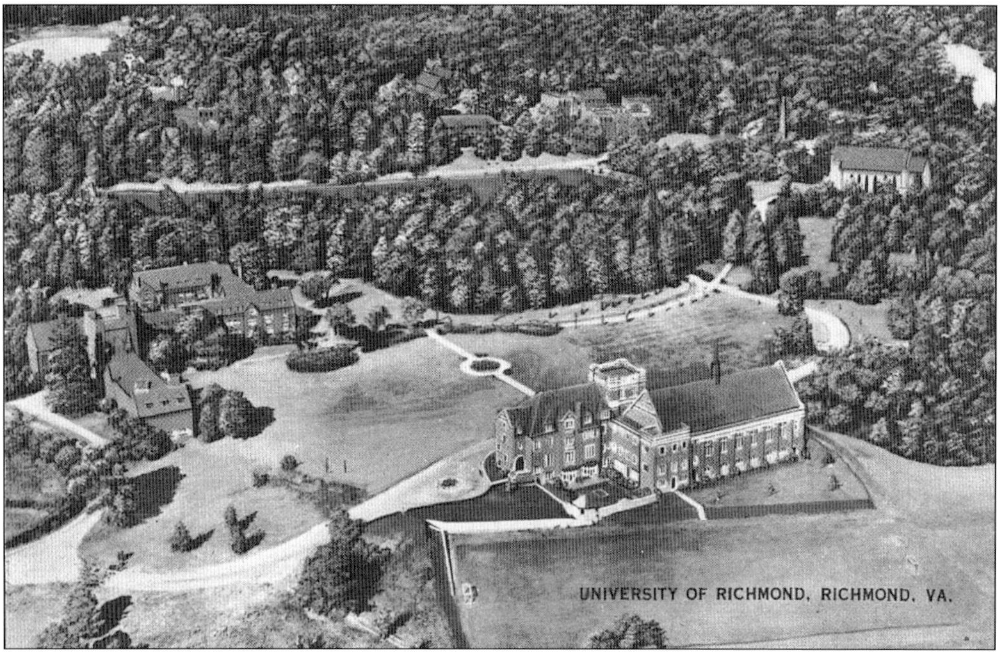

In 1914 Richmond College and Westhampton College (formerly Richmond Female Institute and Richmond Woman's College) moved to Westhampton Park where an old millpond served to divide the two schools. The upper view was taken from the south side of Westhampton Lake showing Westhampton College. Across the lake is Richmond College. The lower view was taken from east of the lake around 1928.

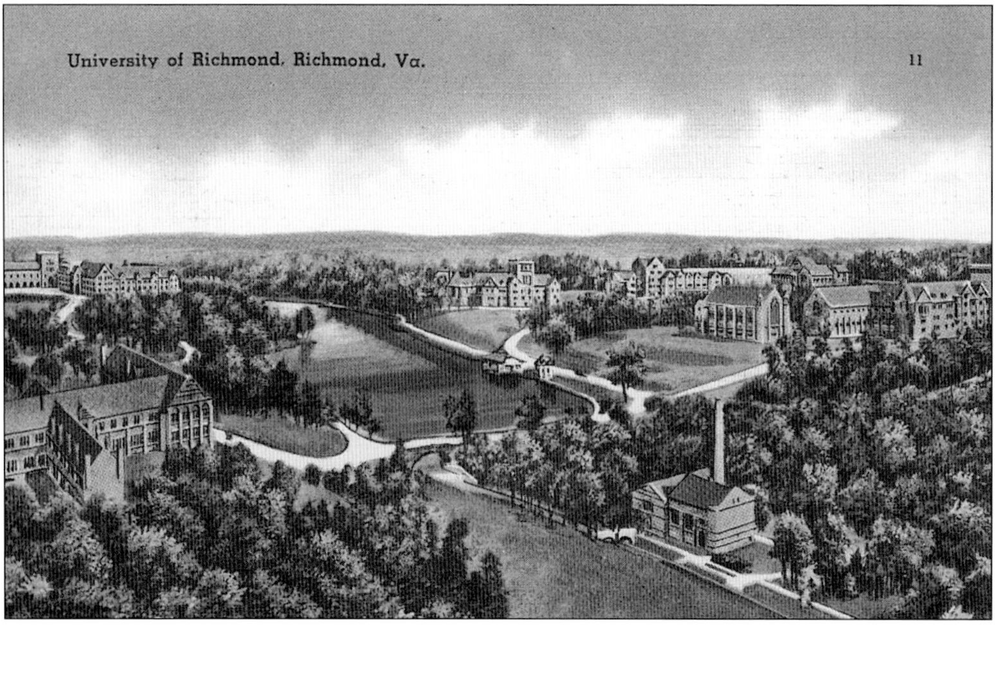

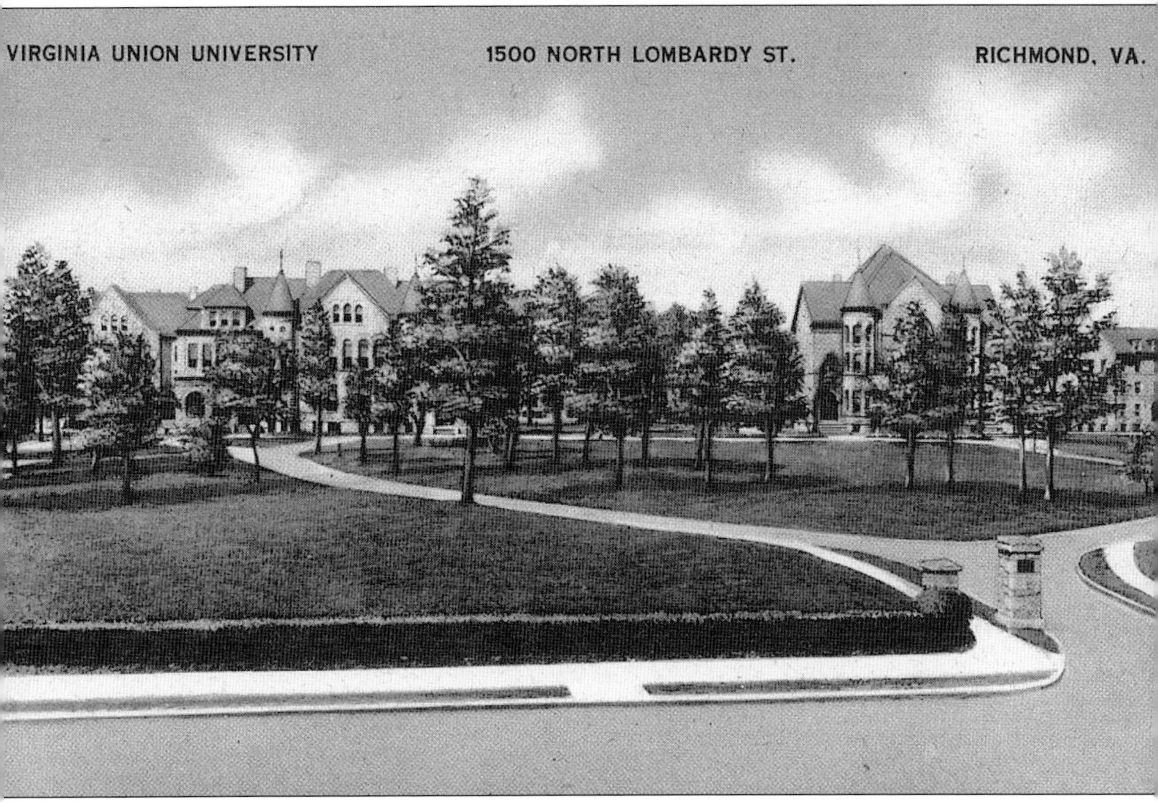

Virginia Union University can trace its origin to the Richmond Theological School for Freedmen founded in 1865 and incorporated as the Richmond Theological Institute in 1867. Its first home was in a former slave jail on Fifteenth Street between Broad and Franklin. The Institute moved to the old Union Hotel at Nineteenth and Main in 1870 and remained there until ground was broken on a 55-acre site on Lombardy Street and Brook Road in 1898. The next year the Richmond Theological Institute merged with Wayland College and Seminary of Washington, D.C. to form Virginia Union University. In 1932 the Hartshorn Memorial School for the Education of Negro Women, founded in Ebenezer Baptist Church in 1883, merged with the University.

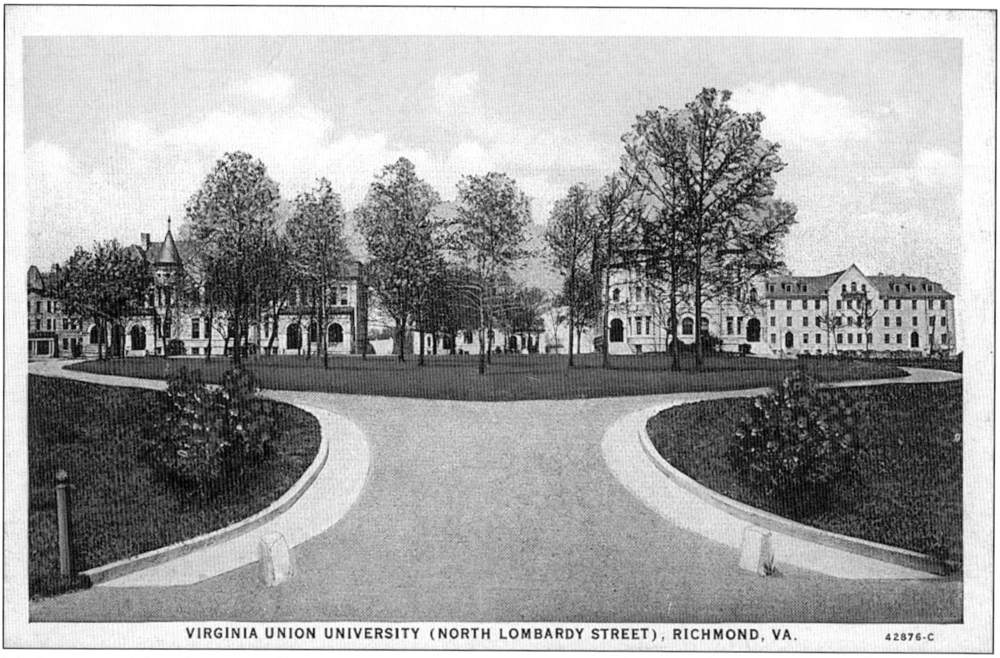

This ground level view of Virginia Union University shows the main entrance from North Lombardy Street.

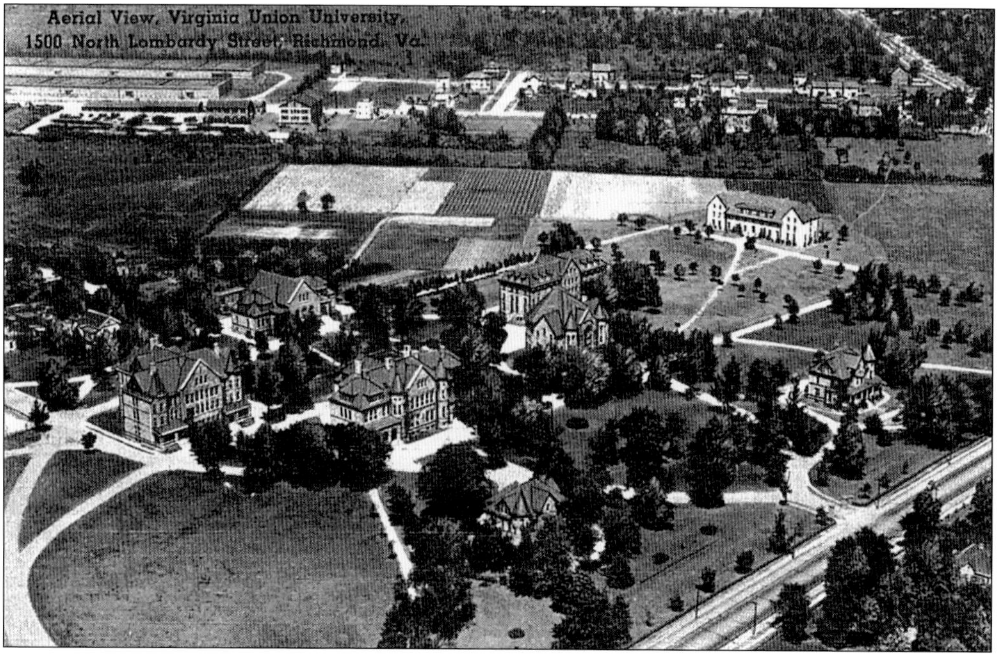

This aerial view of the 55-acre Virginia Union University campus captures all of the academic buildings around 1930. The street on the lower right is North Lombardy, and Brook Road appears in the upper right.

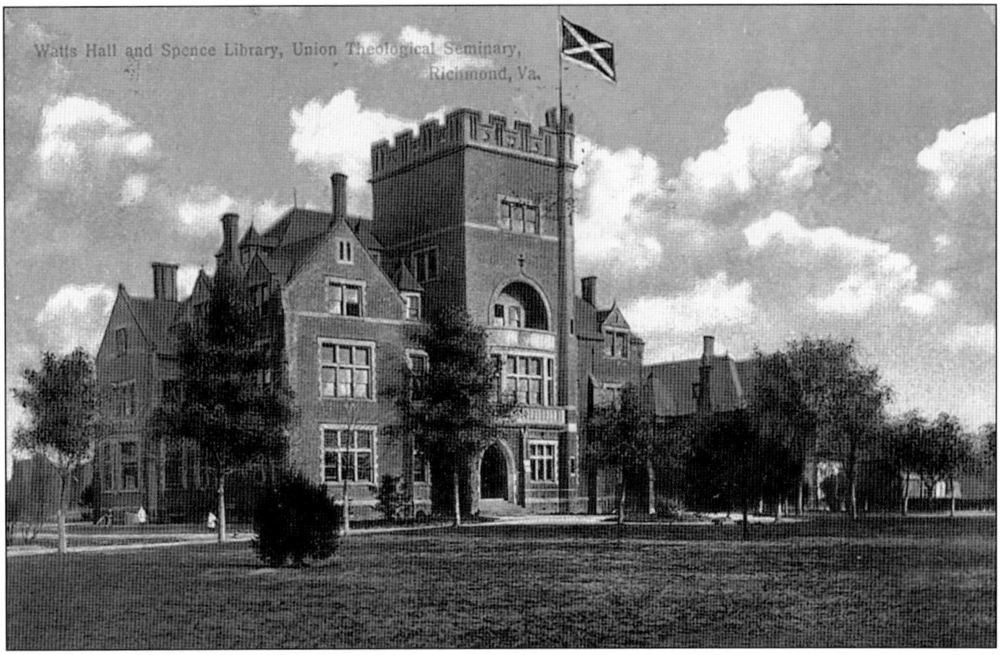

Union Theological Seminary in Virginia, established in 1812, is the oldest theological seminary in the southeastern United States. The seminary was founded as a branch of Hampden-Sydney College and, in 1898, moved to Richmond to occupy an 11-acre site along Brook Road. The land, which extended to Chamberlayne Avenue, was a gift from Maj. Lewis Ginter. The Presbyterian Church U.S.A. accepted the site along with substantial contributions, and the buildings were dedicated on October 5, 1898. Seen here on the left is Watts Hall, the main administration building, and on the right is Spence Library.

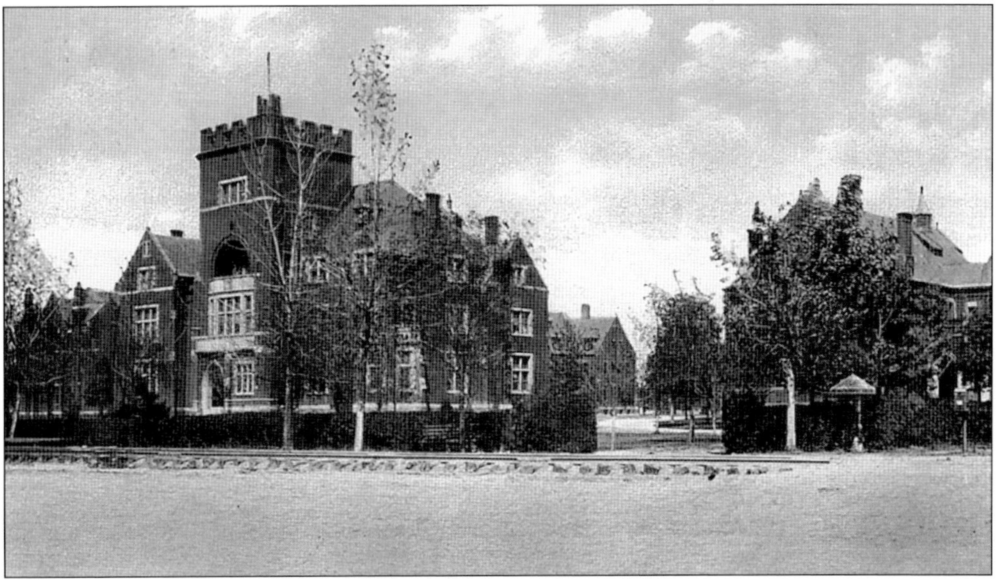

By 1916 the campus of Union Theological Seminary had expanded to 45 acres with some ten buildings. Shown here is Watts Hall. Spence Library is to the right rear. Note the trolley tracks along the side of the street.

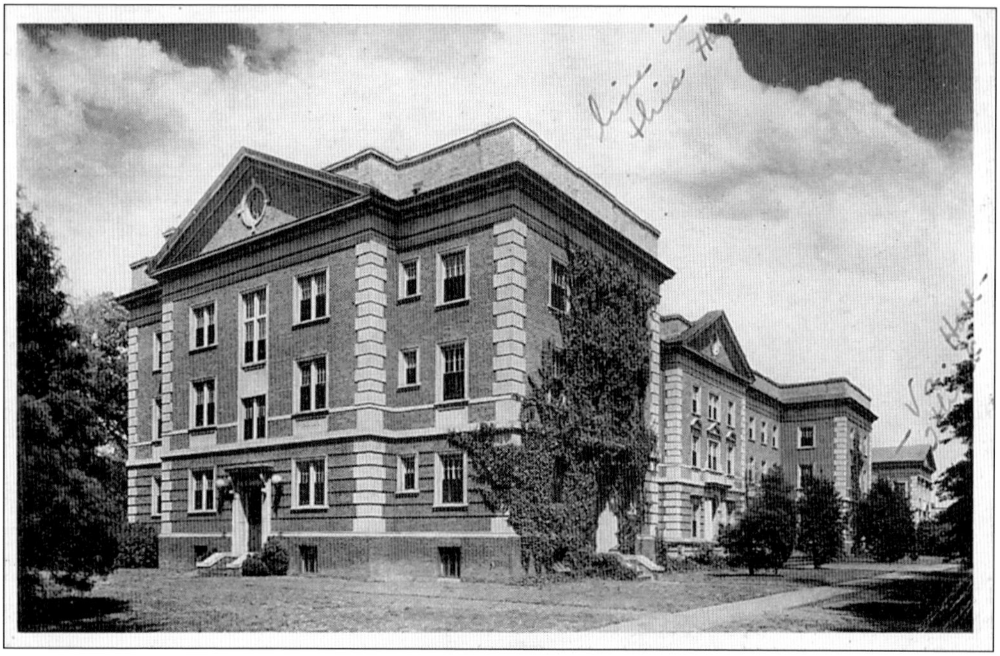

Across Brook Road from Union Theological Seminary, the Presbyterian School of Christian Education was established in 1914. Pictured above is George W. Watts Memorial Hall and below is Virginia Hall.

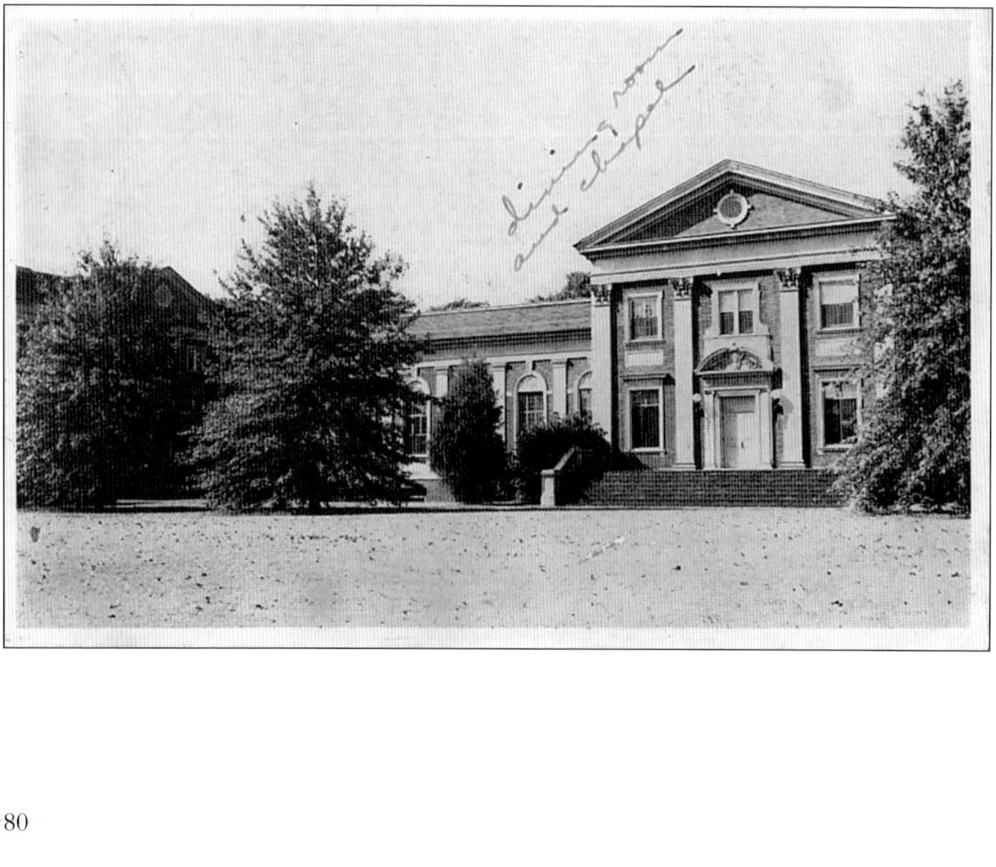

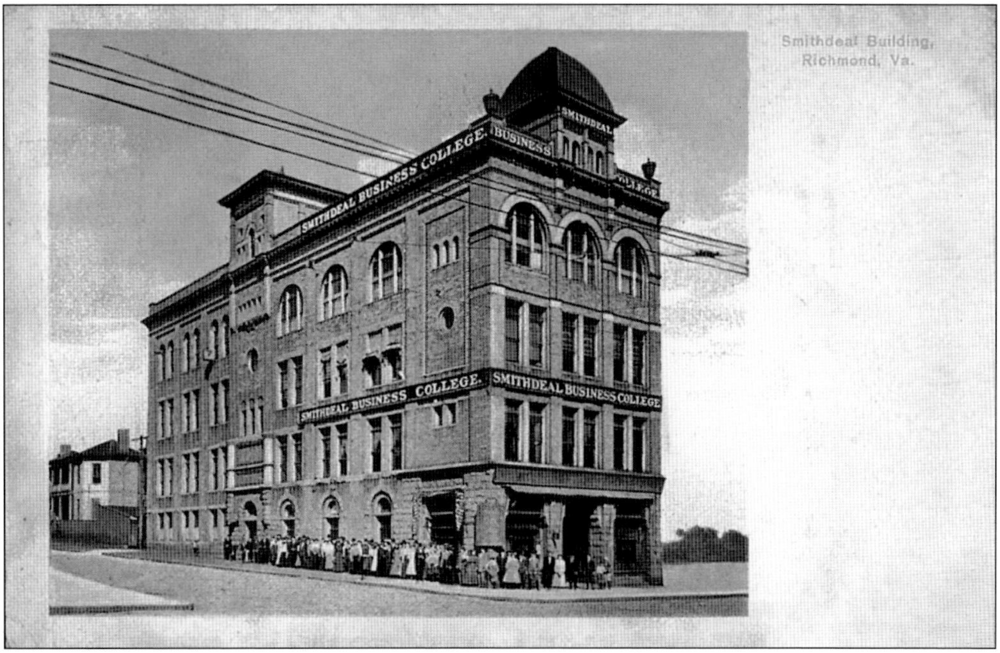

Smithdeal Business College, 900–902 East Broad Street, provided instruction in bookkeeping and secretarial skills. Faculty and students assembled around the college's new building for this picture around 1905.

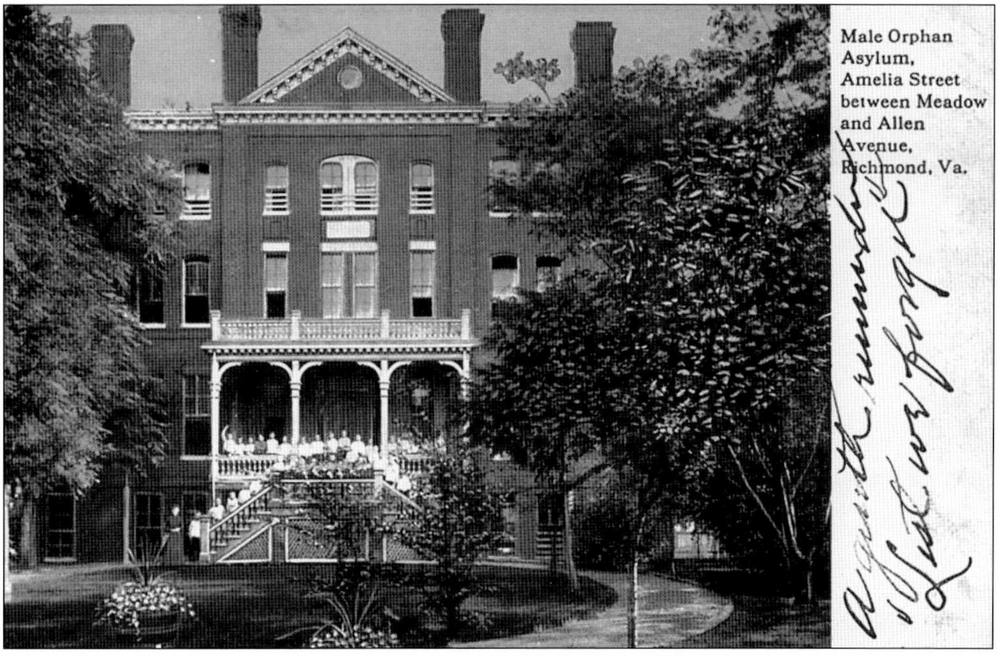

The Male Orphan Asylum started in a small house on Church Hill in 1844 and was incorporated in 1846 as the Richmond Male Orphan Society. It later moved to Amelia Street between Meadow and Allen Avenues. Today it occupies a campus on Broad Street as the Virginia Home and serves both boys and girls.

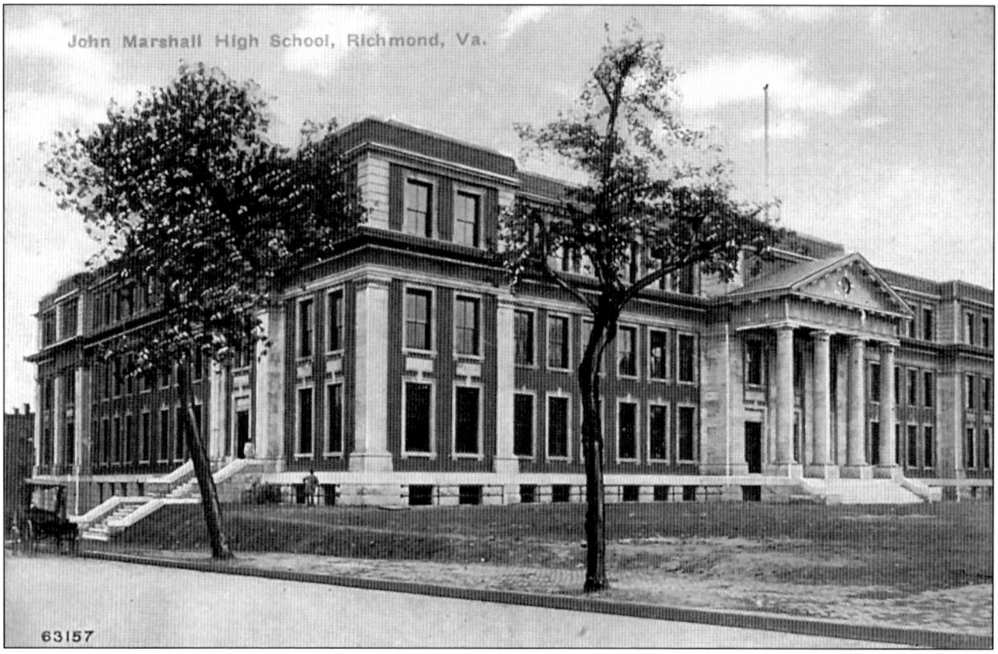

Seen above is John Marshall High School, which was built next to the John Marshall House at Ninth and Marshall Streets. Below is Springfield Elementary School, located at Twenty-sixth and Leigh Streets and built in 1913.

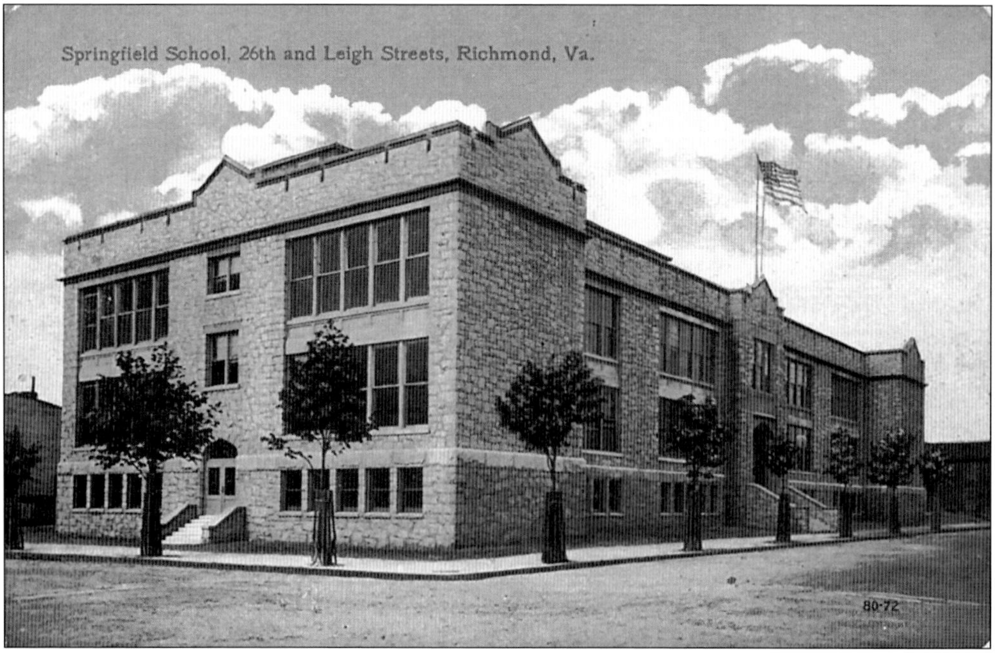

Seven

Houses of Worship

Christopher Newport's planting of the cross on one of the islands below the falls was an act of claiming the land and river for an earthly king. However, as a religious symbol, the cross betokened an attitude of worship to the heavenly King. It implied that the cross would be the guiding force in the lives of those who would come to establish the settlement that would be Richmond.

The Anglican, or Episcopal Church in Virginia was the established church of all the people in the colony for over 125 years. The area around the falls was a part of Varina Parish, and in 1717, the vestry decided to establish a chapel at the falls. Called "The Falls Chapel," it continued in use until the construction of what became St. John's on Church Hill in 1741. For 30 years it was the only church building within the town. The first Baptist services were held in Richmond about 1770. By 1780 a Baptist congregation was meeting and ten years later the Presbyterians organized into a church. The first Catholic services in Richmond were held by Fr. Jean Dubois when he visited the city in 1791. By 1791 there were sufficient members of the Jewish community in the city to organize the first synagogue, Beth Shalom.

After the Capitol was built, the hall of the House of Delegates was used for church services. For more than 20 years Presbyterian and Episcopal services were held there on alternate Sundays. Father Dubois held the first public celebration of the Mass there in 1791, and Rev. Thomas Lyell preached there to a Methodist congregation regularly on Sunday afternoons until the first Methodist church was built in 1799. The Baptists met in a chapel on Cary Street before the completion of First Baptist Church in 1803. The first Presbyterian church was erected in 1812. St. Peter's, the first Catholic church in the city, was erected in 1832. In 1841 the white communicants of First Baptist Church moved into a new building at Twelfth and Broad and gave their old church site to their African-American members. They built their own church on the site—The African Baptist Church. Four years later the Episcopalian congregation, which had met in the hall of the House of Delegates, built St. Paul's at Ninth and Grace Streets opposite the entrance to Capitol Square.

The church was a significant factor in the spiritual life of the community, and adherents who practiced their faith influenced the very life of the city.

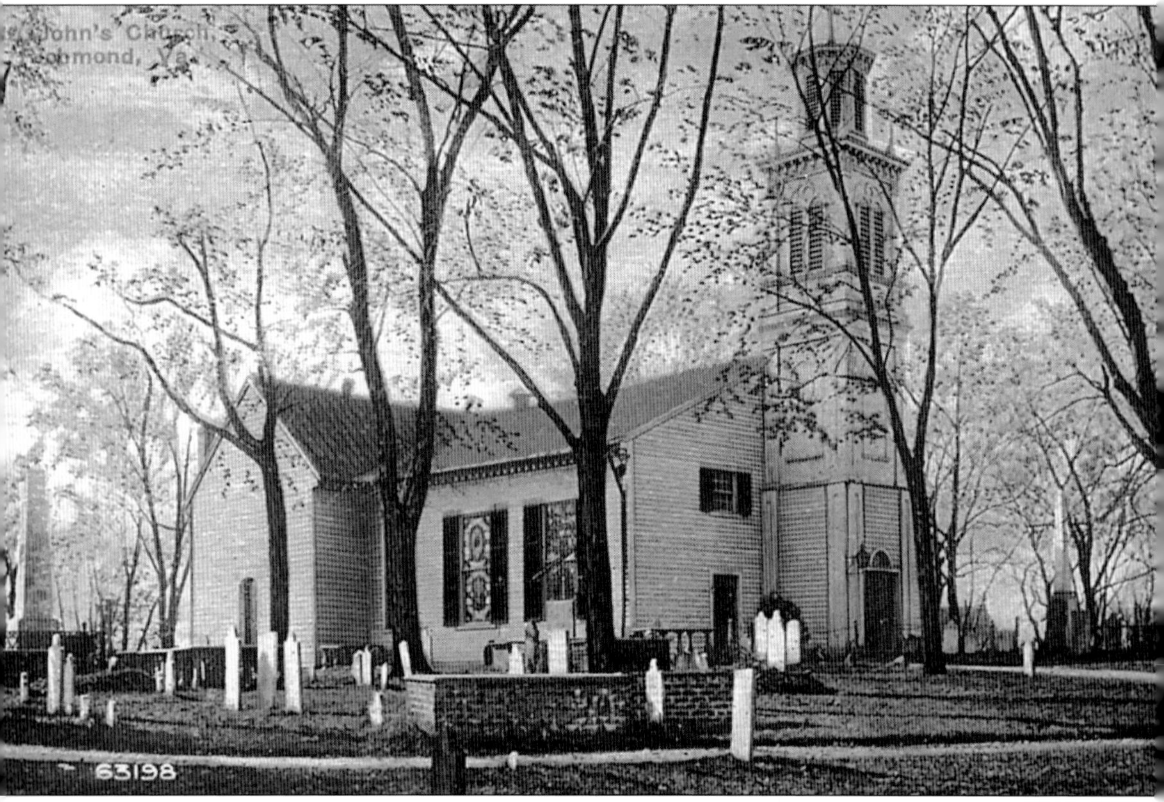

Varina Parish Church was sometimes called the Indian Hill Church, the New Church, the Town Church, the Upper Church, and the Richmond Church before it was named St. John's Church in 1829. Richard Randolph built the original part of the church on two lots given to the parish by William Byrd II. Completed in 1741, its presence soon inspired local citizens to call the hill Church Hill. In 1772 the church was enlarged by the addition of 40 feet on the north side of the original structure. The Second Virginia Convention met in the church on March 20, 1775. It was during this convention that Patrick Henry delivered his famous "Liberty or Death" speech. In 1799 the city acquired the remaining two lots in the square and opened a public burial ground. In 1830 the belfry was erected; it has been replaced twice since then.

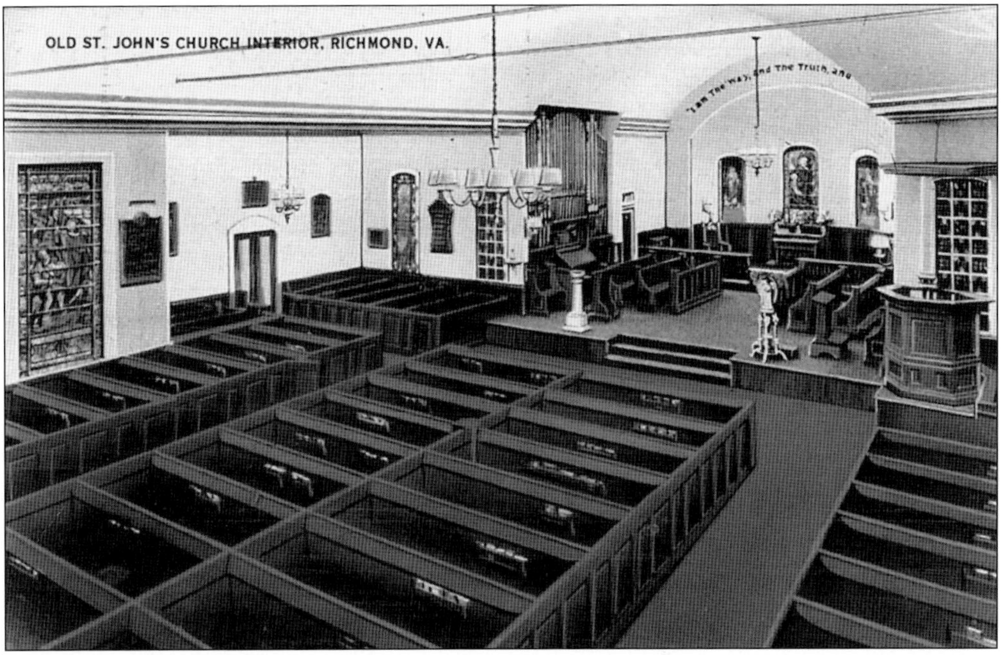

The interior of St. John's Episcopal Church on Church Hill is shown in these two postcard views taken between 1890 and 1920. Patrick Henry was standing in pew 72 when he delivered his "Liberty or Death" speech; a tablet on the wall to the left marks the pew in the upper view.

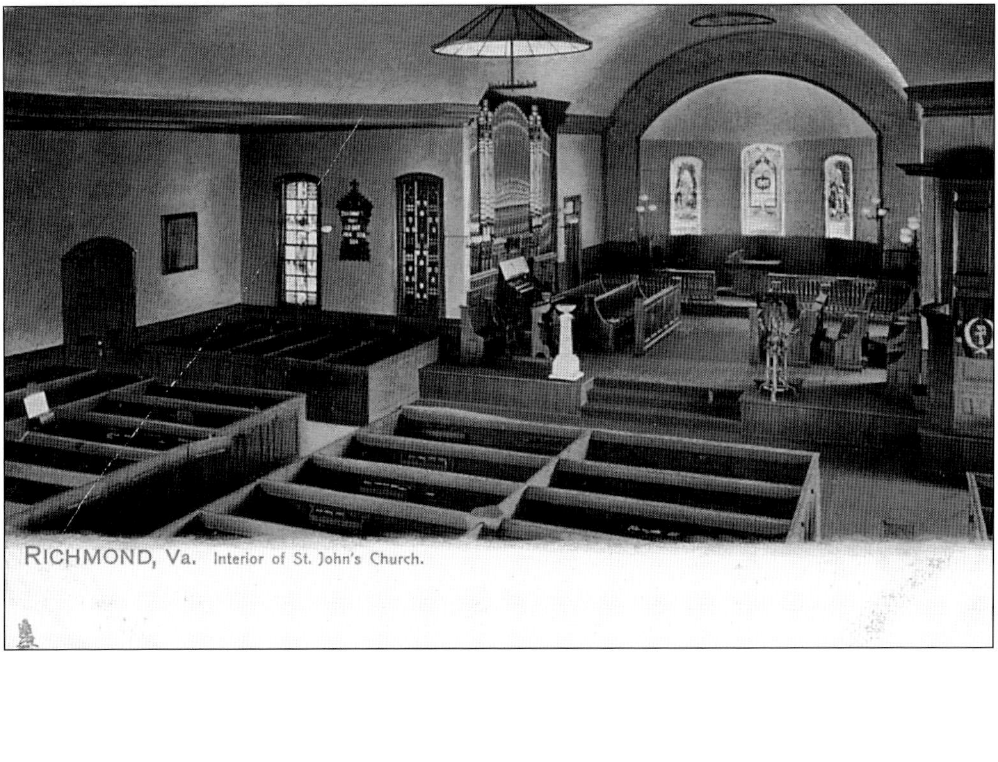

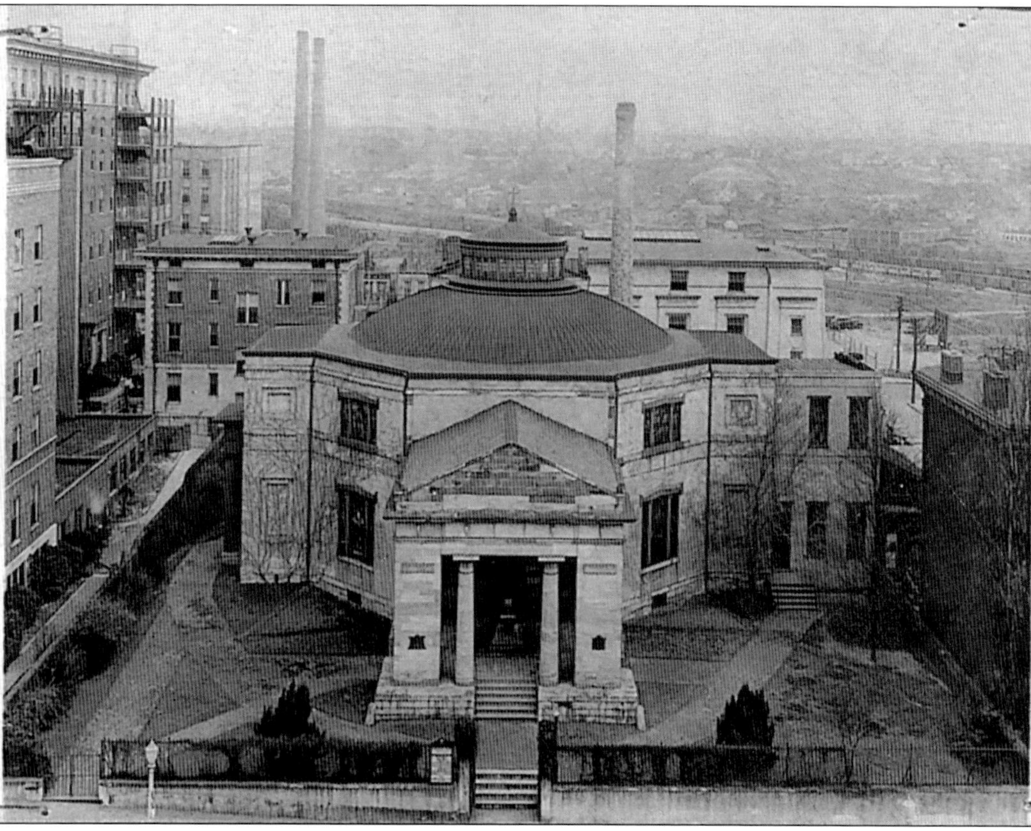

Monumental Church, designed by Robert Mills, was built on the site of the Richmond Theater as a memorial. Mills intended to add a spire, but it was never put in place. The names of the fire victims are inscribed on a monument inside the massive stone portico. Soon after construction was completed in 1814 the Episcopal congregation that had been meeting in the hall of the House of Delegates in the State Capitol moved to the church. It became Monumental Episcopal Church and served as the home of the congregation until it moved to St. Paul's in 1845. Monumental remained an Episcopal church until 1965. Since then it has served as an ecumenical religious center.

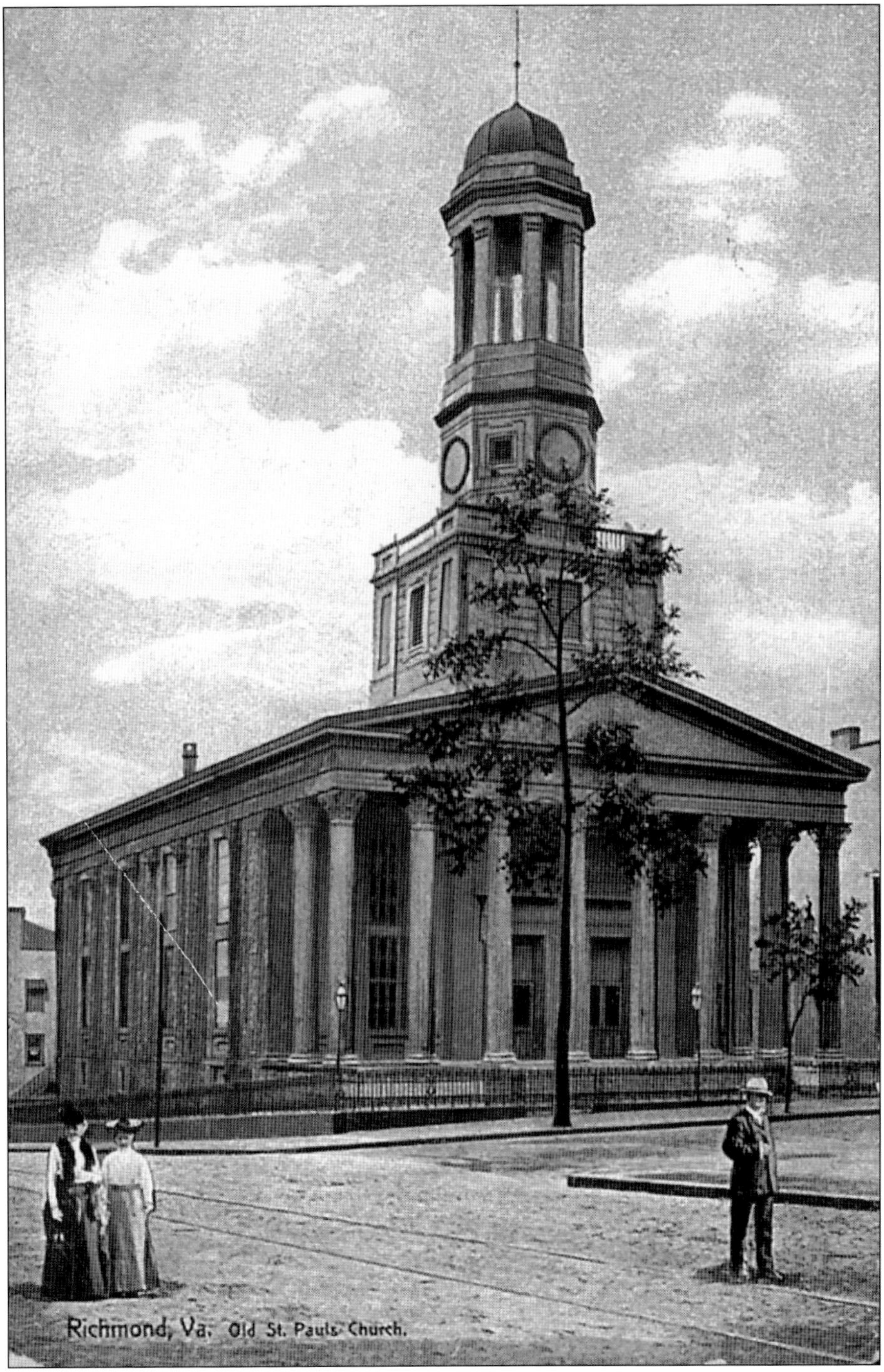

St. Paul's Episcopal Church, at Ninth and Grace Streets, was designed by Thomas S. Stewart of Philadelphia. The cornerstone was laid on October 10, 1843, and the church was consecrated on November 11, 1845. Both Jefferson Davis and Robert E. Lee worshiped at St. Paul's, and it was here that Dr. Charles Minnigerode baptized Davis in May 1862. The church and its congregation continue to serve the community.

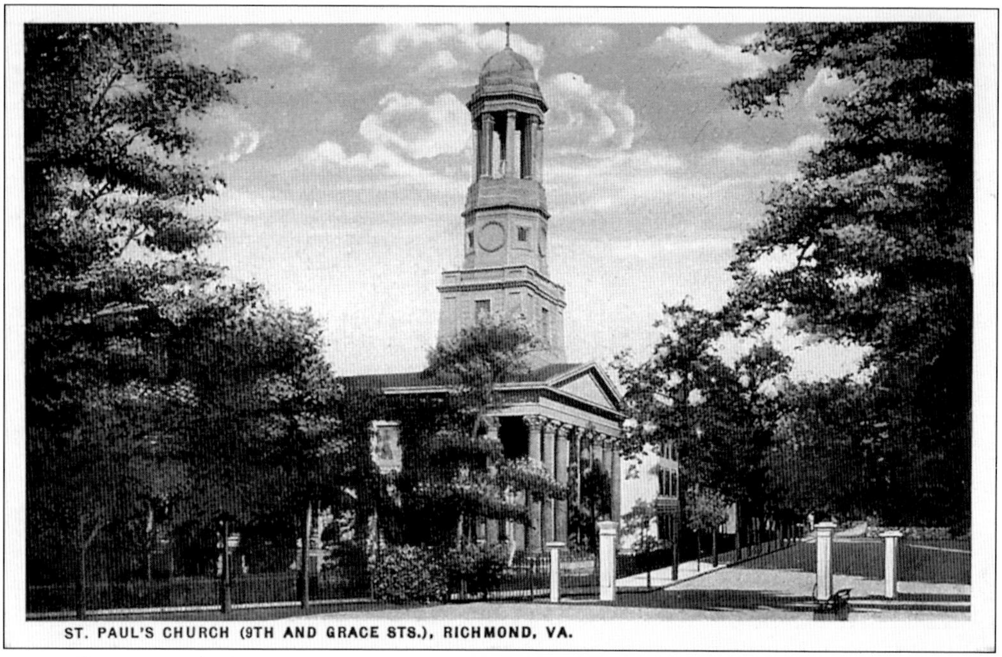

St. Paul's Episcopal church dominates the main entrance to Capitol Square and served as the religious and social center for many Richmonders. This view looks west from Capitol Square up Grace Street.

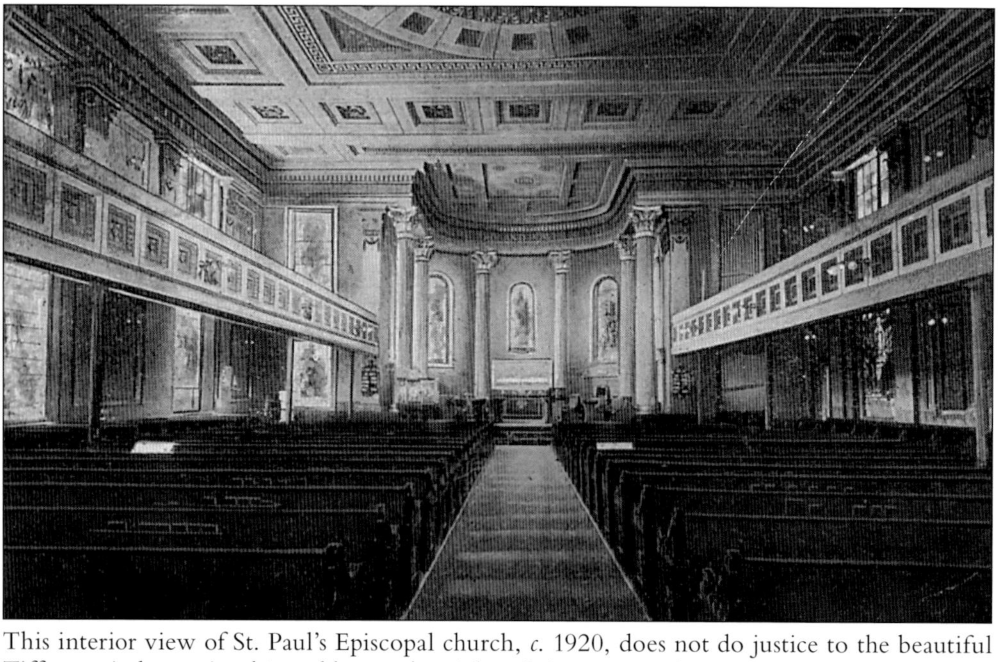

This interior view of St. Paul's Episcopal church, *c.* 1920, does not do justice to the beautiful Tiffany windows. A white tablet to the right of the main aisle identifies President Davis's pew. He was in his pew on April 2, 1865, when he received a telegram from General Lee announcing that Richmond would have to be evacuated. The pew used by General Lee is to the left of the main aisle and it, too, is marked by a white tablet.

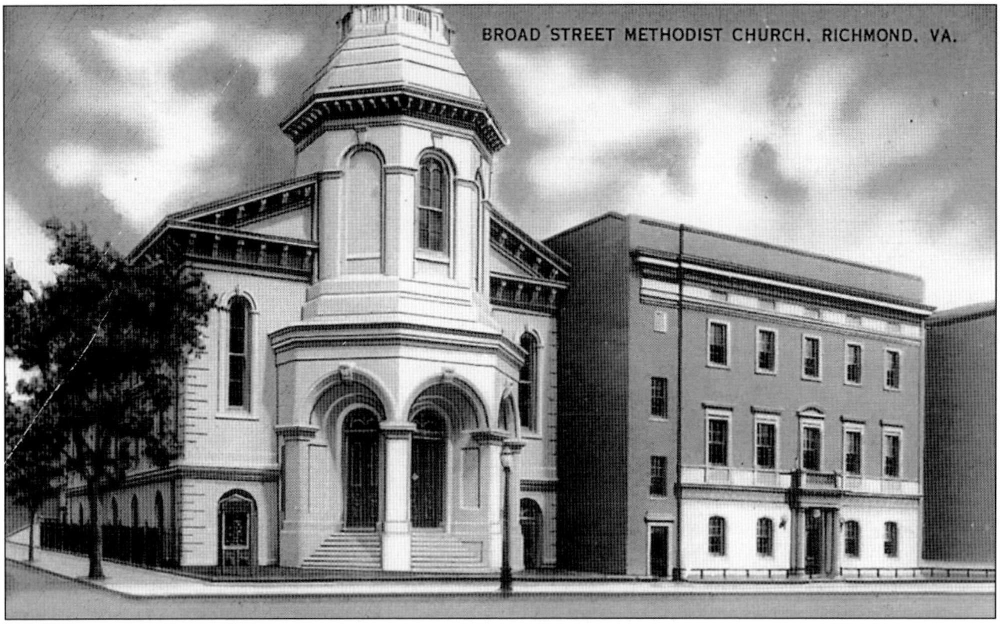

Albert L. West, a local architect, designed Broad Street Methodist church at Tenth and Broad and it was built in 1859. When the congregation moved to a new edifice in the western suburbs the building remained empty until it was acquired by the city. It was used as a visitor's center until it was torn down to make way for a parking lot.

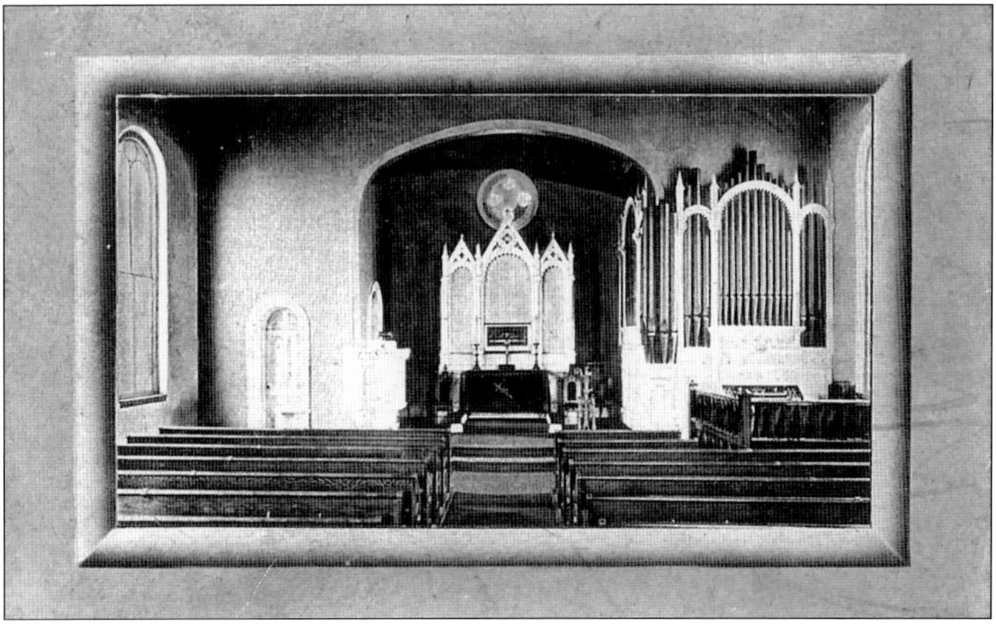

In 1853 a group of German Lutherans built a small meetinghouse at Sixth and Clay and called it Bethlehem Evangelical Lutheran Church. Fifteen years later a church was erected, and it served the congregation until they moved to a new building on Ryland and Grace Streets. The old building was sold to an African-American congregation and became Sixth Street Baptist Church. This view depicts the sanctuary of the original Bethlehem Evangelical Lutheran Church.

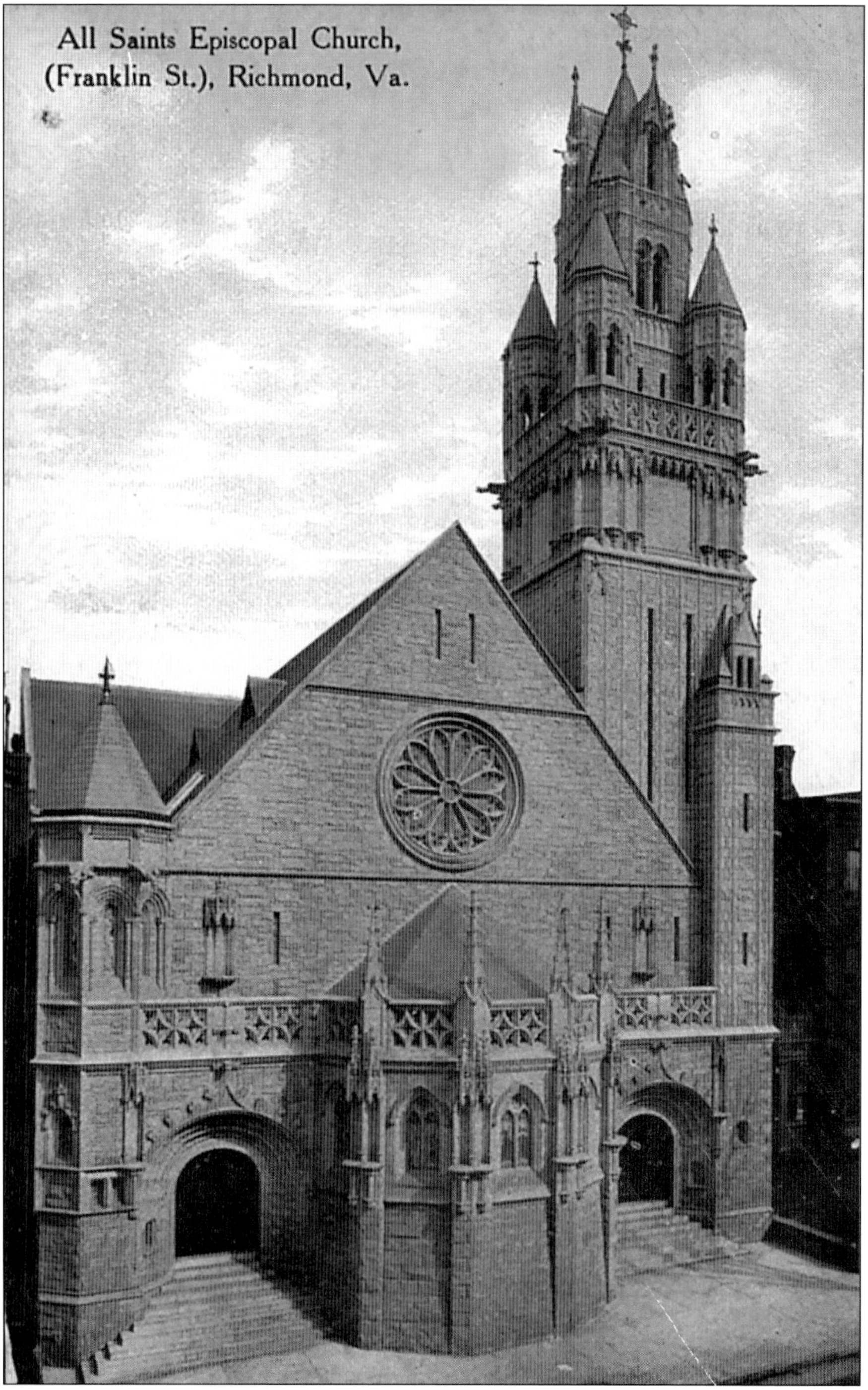

In 1883 several members of Monumental Church established a chapel at Madison and Grace Streets and called the new parish All Saints. The parish was admitted into the diocese of Virginia in 1889. On December 7, 1898, the cornerstone was laid for All Saints Episcopal Church on the north side of Franklin between Madison and Monroe Streets. The church was consecrated on the Feast of the Epiphany, January 6, 1901.

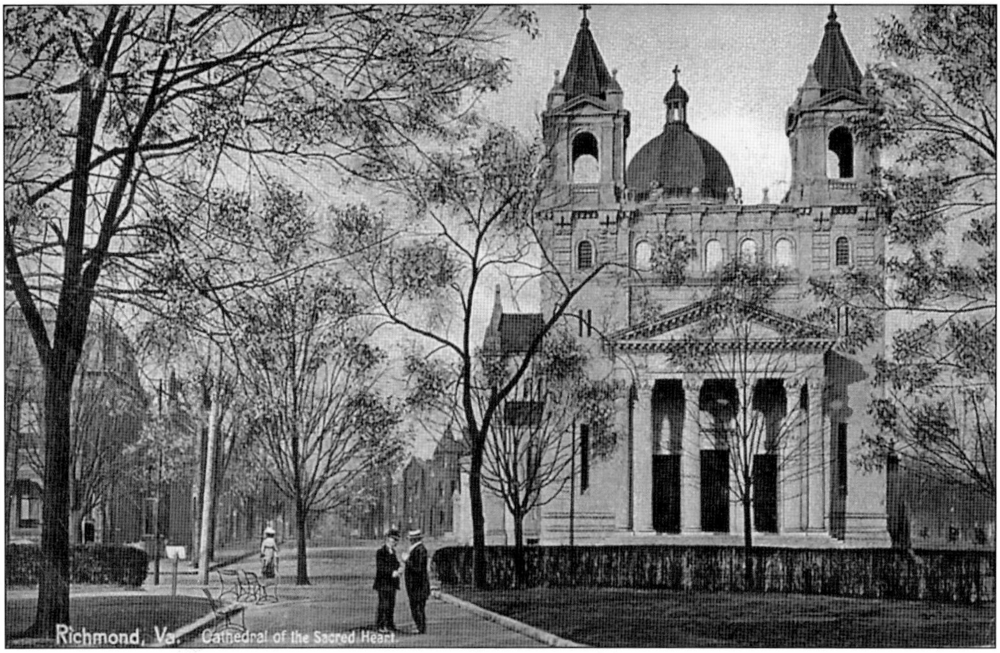

Realizing a need for a new church, Richmond's Catholic community purchased land opposite Monroe Park on Laurel Street at Floyd and Park Avenues in 1883. With a gift of $300,000 from Mr. and Mrs. Thomas F. Ryan the cornerstone of the Cathedral of the Scared Heart was laid on June 4, 1903. The cathedral was consecrated on November 19, 1906, and it continues to serve as the cathedral of the Richmond Diocese.

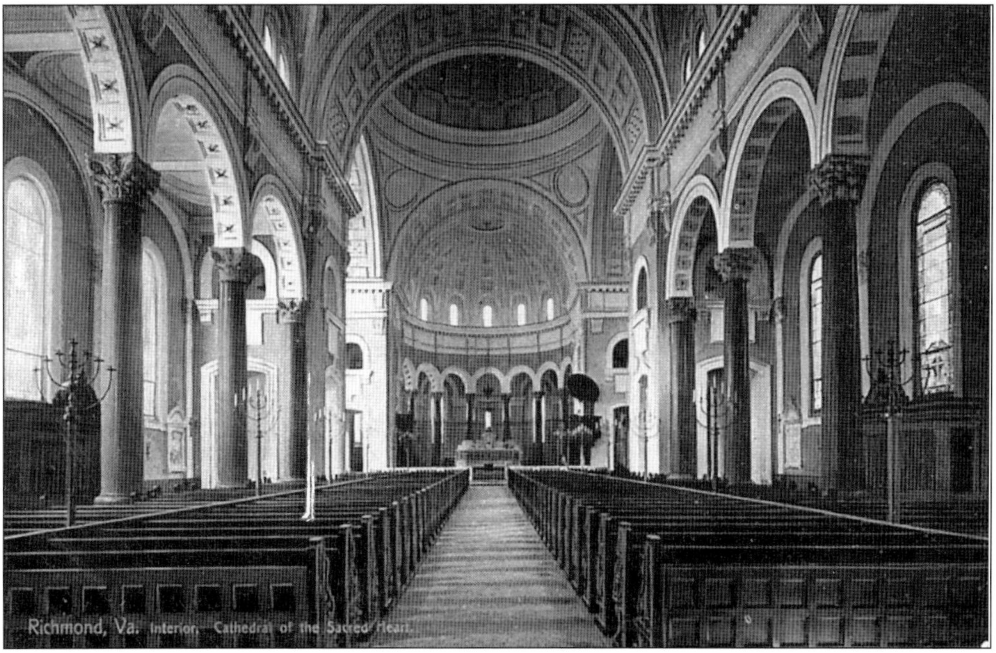

The interior of the Cathedral of the Sacred Heart replicates the Gothic cathedrals of Europe with a magnificent vaulted ceiling and interior colonnade.

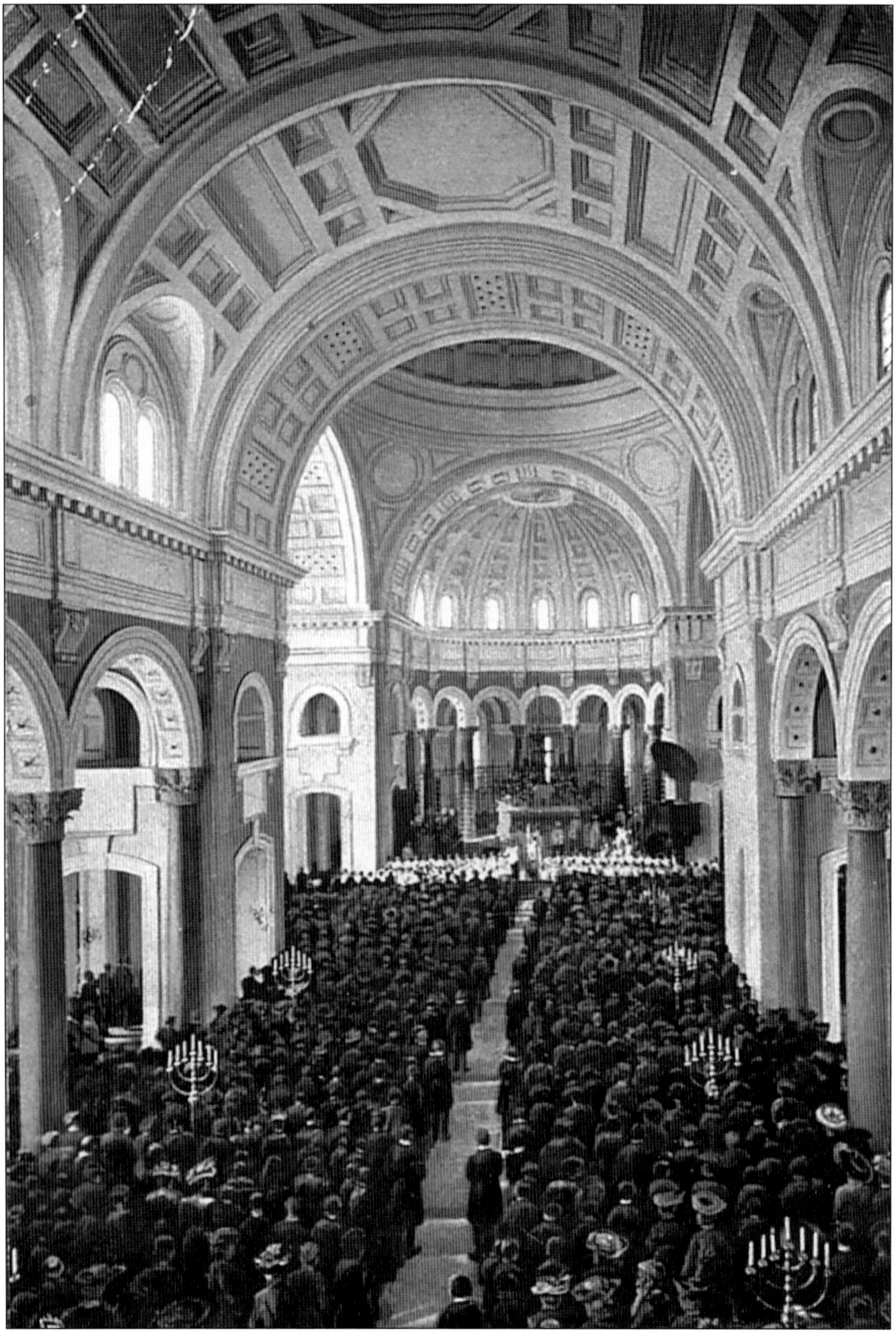

The nave of the Cathedral of the Sacred Heart is more than 200 feet long, and there are five altars and two chapels.

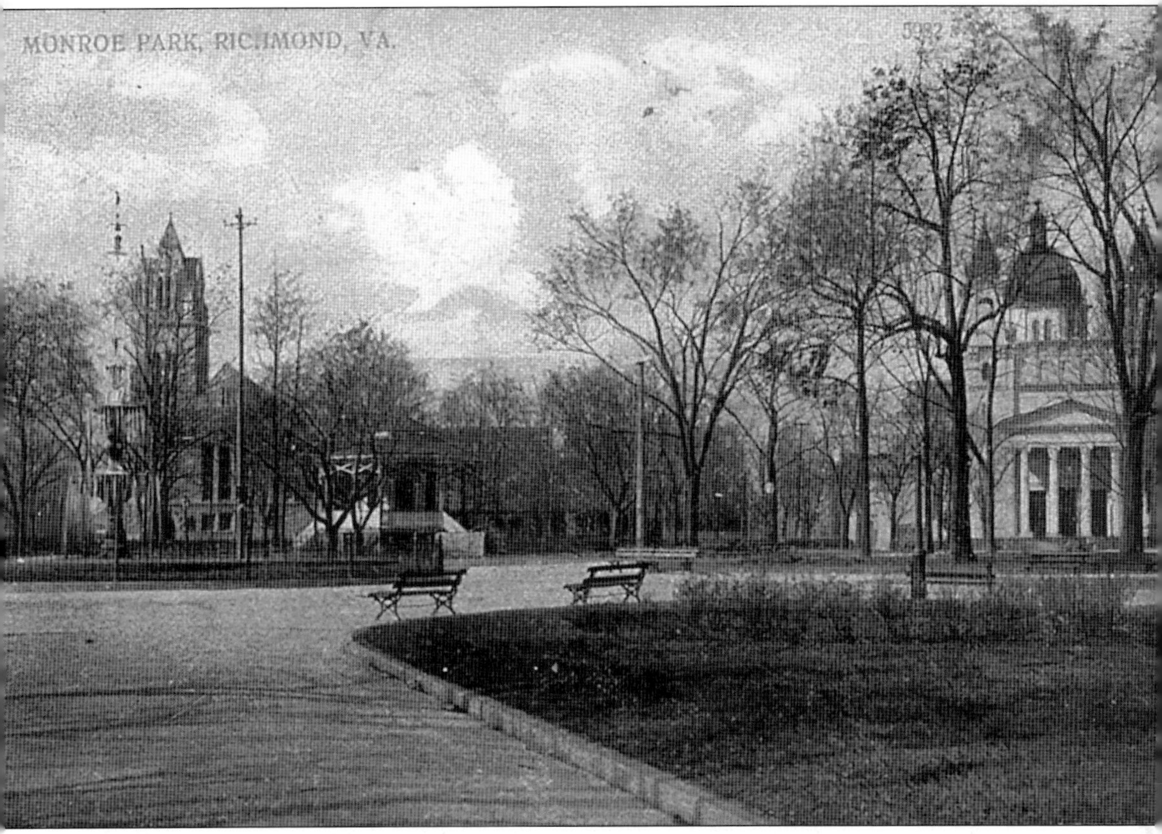

The Cathedral of the Sacred Heart appears on the right of this postcard view taken from Monroe Park. To the left, behind the fountain is Holy Trinity Episcopal Church, completed in 1894. It was consecrated on October 1, 1907, with the Bishop of London, the Right Reverend A.F. Winnington-Ingram present. In 1924 the congregation of Grace Church combined with Holy Trinity and the church became Grace and Holy Trinity.

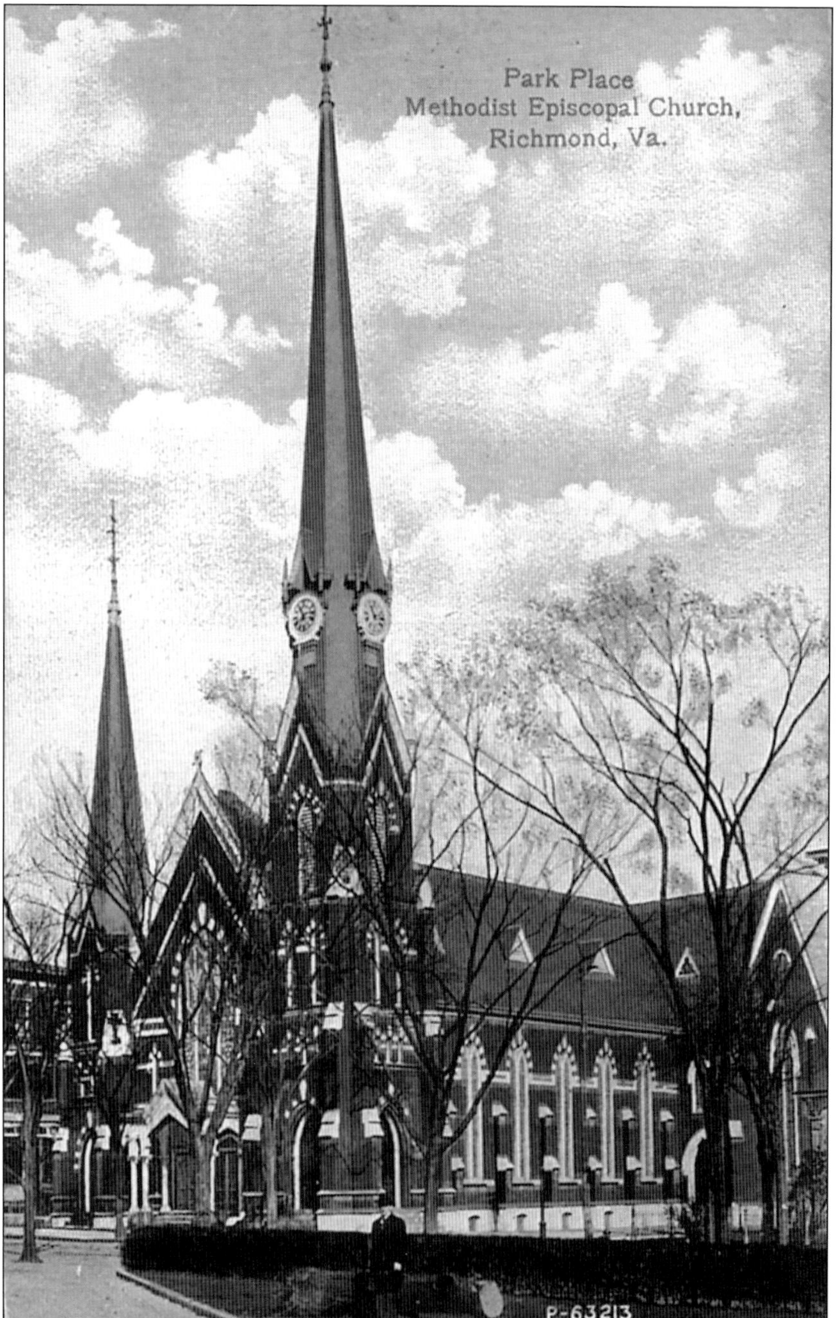

On the corner of Franklin and Pine Streets opposite Monroe Park, the cornerstone for Park Place Methodist Episcopal church was laid June 18, 1877. Albert L. West, a Richmond architect and church member, designed the two-steeple, Gothic-style structure. Richmond businessman James B. Pace, who had donated the land, was also a member. When the church was completed in 1886 it was dedicated to two of Pace's children who had died while it was under construction. After Pace's death in 1920 the church was renamed Pace Memorial Methodist. On December 11, 1966, the building was destroyed by fire.

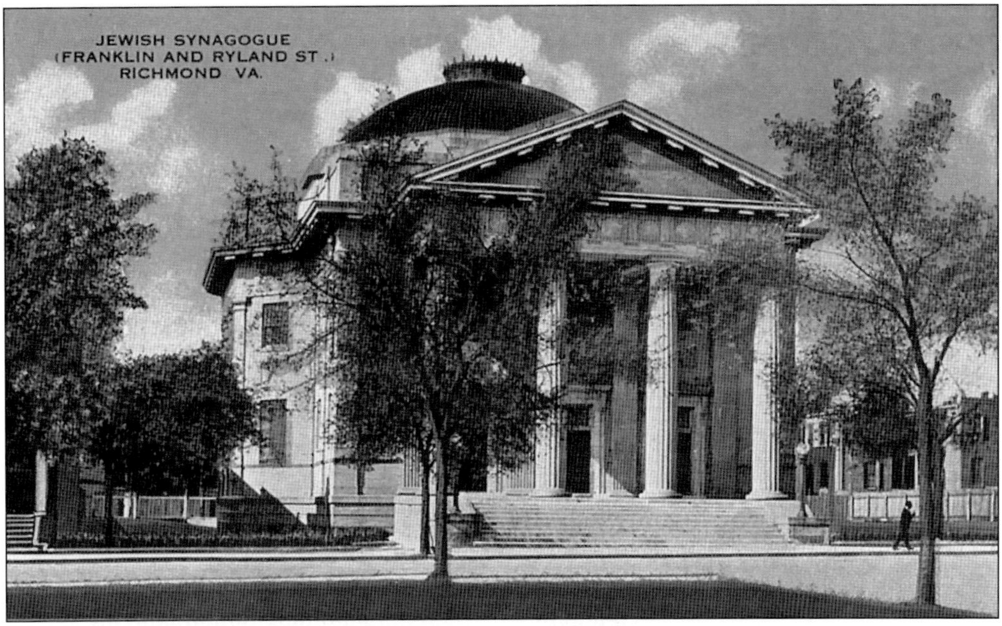

Beth Ahaba "House of Love" Synagogue, located on South Franklin Street facing Ryland Street, was dedicated on December 9, 1904. The cornerstone had been laid on March 4. The congregation moved from its former synagogue on Eleventh Street near Marshall and continues to occupy this building, which has been expanded by the addition of an annex to meet the congregation's needs. The original structure seen here is a perfect octagon with a Doric portico and front columns.

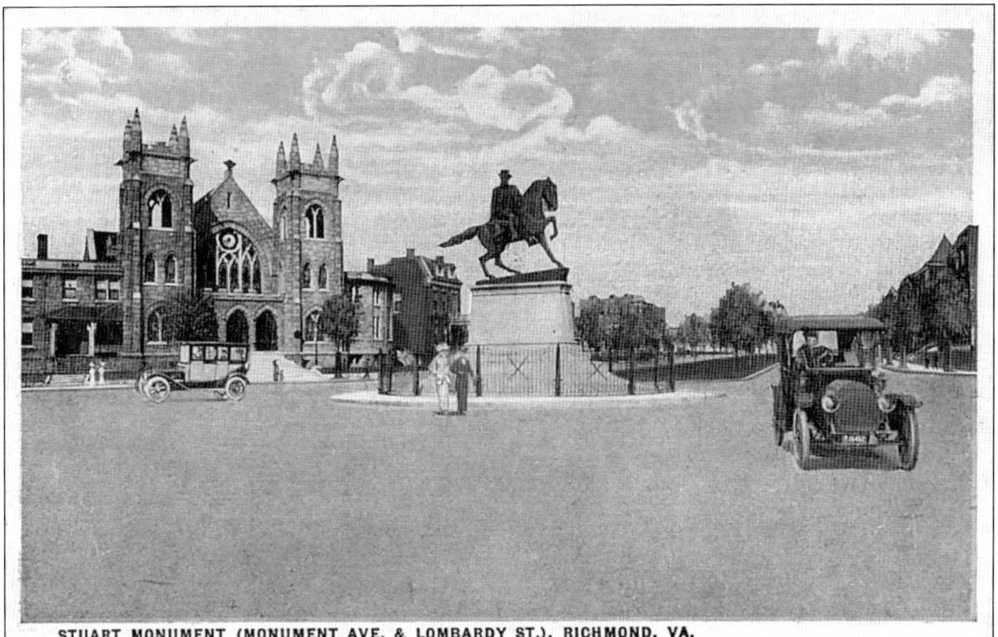

First English Lutheran Chapel was established at Seventh and Grace Streets on April 8, 1877. The congregation moved to their new building on Stuart Circle at Monument and Lombardy Streets in 1910. The church was designed by Charles M. Robinson.

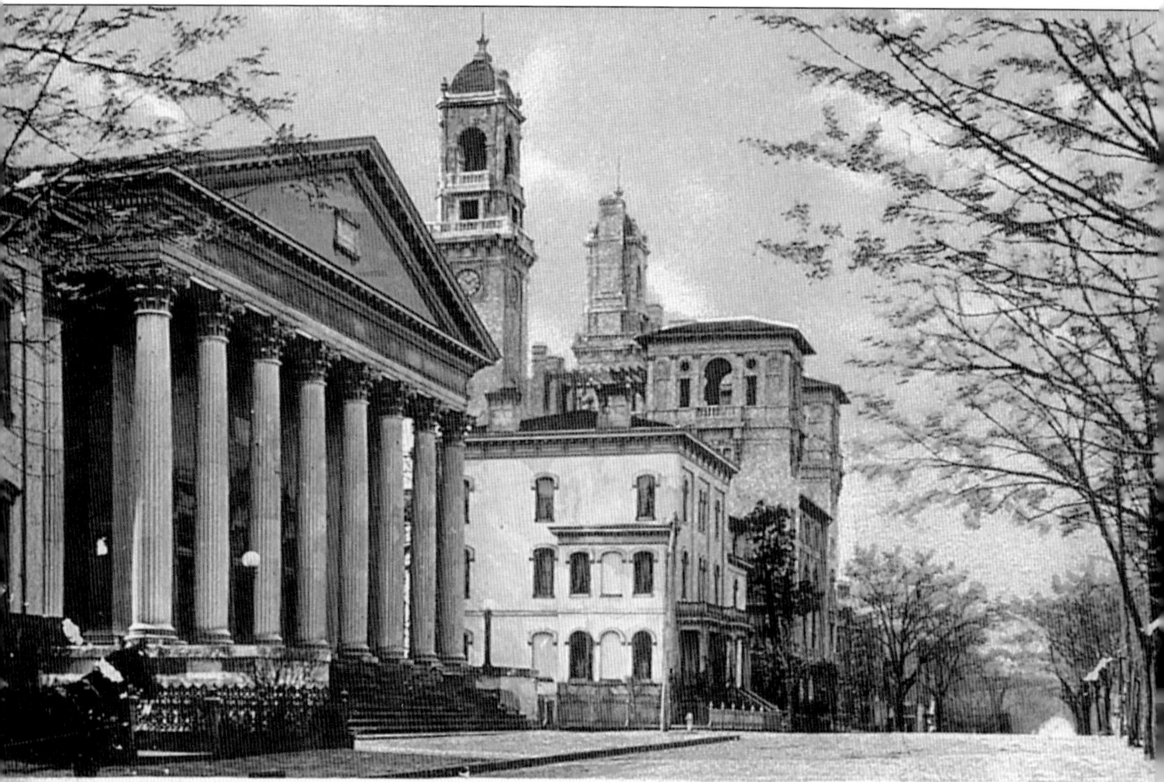

Franklin Street West, Richmond, Va.

Richmond Lodge No. 10, A.F. & A.M laid the cornerstone of the new Second Baptist Church, at the southeast corner of Franklin and Adams Streets, on July 16, 1904. The congregation moved from its former church at Sixth and Main Streets when the church was dedicated February 11, 1906. Dr. W.W. Landrum, a former pastor, preached the sermon on that day. Across Adams Street is the Archer Anderson house, built in 1815. Just beyond the house is the newly reopened Jefferson Hotel.

Eight

NEIGHBORHOODS

The original town of Richmond was laid out east of Shockoe Creek, which ran down the valley between the two principal hills on which the city was founded. On the southern slope of the hill along the east side of the creek was the site of Powhatan's tribal village, so the area was first called Indian Town Hill. After the construction of the parish church, St. John's, the area became known as Church Hill. In time, as residential and commercial communities extended south, east, and north of the area known as Church Hill, they were given their own names even though they were topographically part of the same geographic feature. South of Church Hill the commercial area became Shockoe Creek Bottom and Rockett's Bottom. On the southeastern boundary the new residential area became Libby Hill and to the east it became Chimborazo Hill. Along the northern boundary of Church Hill, north of Broad Street, the residential community became known as Union Hill. As these communities grew and became integral parts of Richmond's life they lost their individual identity and became known simply as Church Hill.

West of Shockoe Creek along the creek bank a residential community was laid out, but it had to give way to the seat of government. The selection of Shockoe Hill as the site for the State Capitol in 1780 hastened expansion to the west of the governmental complex. However, for more than a 100 years the residential area north and northeast of Capitol Square was known as Court End, and east of the square down to Shockoe Creek was called Council Chamber Hill because of the presence of the Council of State Meetinghouse. Both these areas, first Council Chamber Hill, which gave way to commercial enterprises, and later Court End, which experienced the expansion of both state and city government, ceased to be residential areas. New immigrants arriving after 1830s moved into Jackson Ward, north of Broad Street and west of Court End. After the Civil War, African Americans moved into this area as the white residents moved to the city's western and northwestern suburbs.

West of Capitol Square to the pre–Civil War western boundary of the city, present-day Belvidere Street, was the principal residential area of Richmond's upper- and middle-class white residents. Large houses used to line Grace, Franklin, and Main Streets. These gradually gave way to commercial businesses that either adapted the houses or tore them down. As Richmond's economy rebounded in the post–Civil War period, Richmonders began moving west, and Grace and Franklin as well as other city streets began to experience the construction of spacious new suburban homes along the avenues. In time, these western suburbs would be annexed into the city.

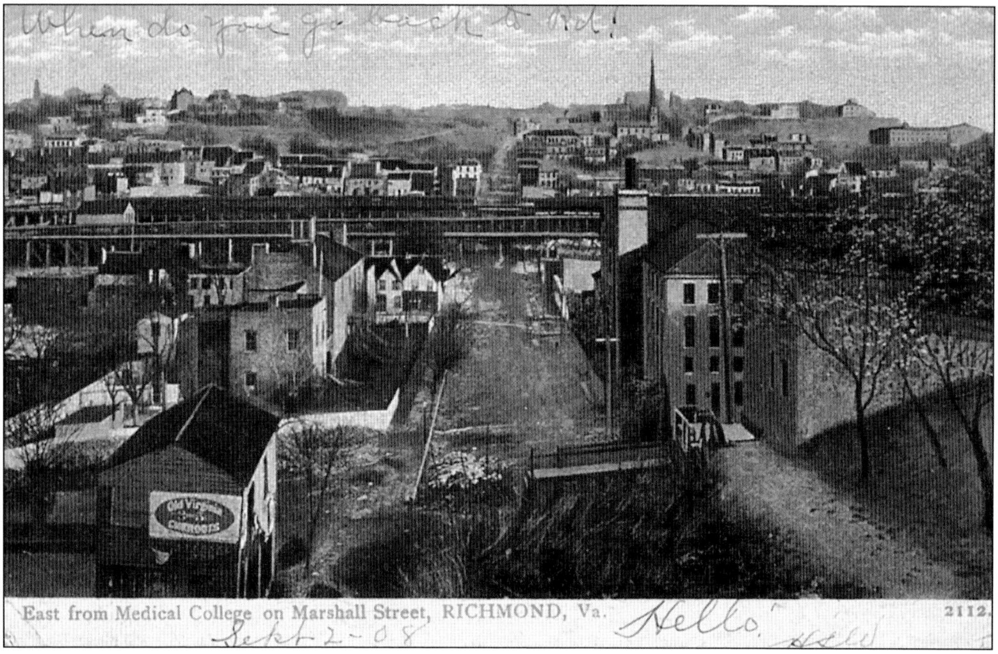

Union and Church Hill, pictured above, are seen across Shockoe Valley from Marshall Street in Court End around 1905. Trinity Methodist Church built in 1860 at Twentieth and Broad Streets is visible just below the ridgeline. The bottom of Shockoe Valley was lined with railroad tracks.

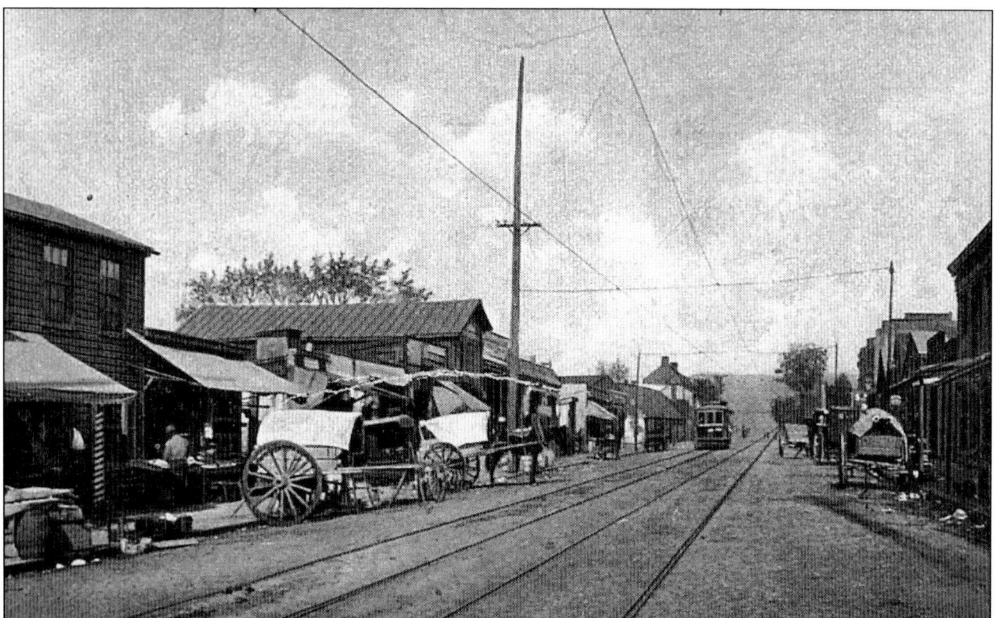

The area along Eighteenth Street on the western base of Church Hill had experienced decline around the turn of the 19th century. Because it was the home of the poorer laboring class, it was considered Richmond's slum area prior to World War I. Expanding commercial, produce, and industrial businesses associated with the railroads gradually encroached on the area.

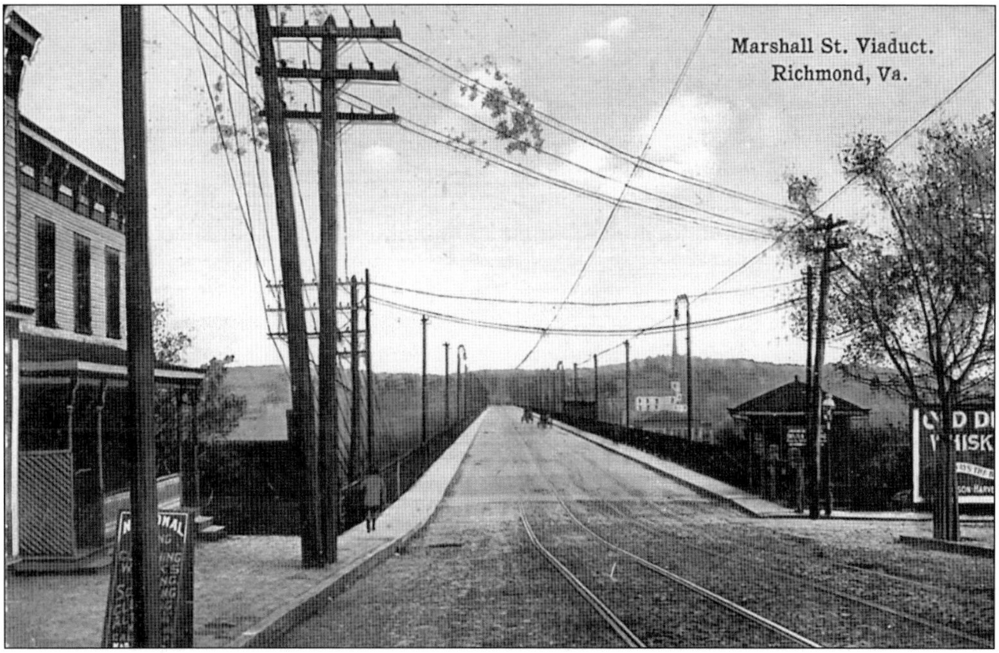

Built by the Richmond & Henrico Railway Company, the Marshall Street viaduct connected Court End with Union Hill when it was completed July 24, 1911.

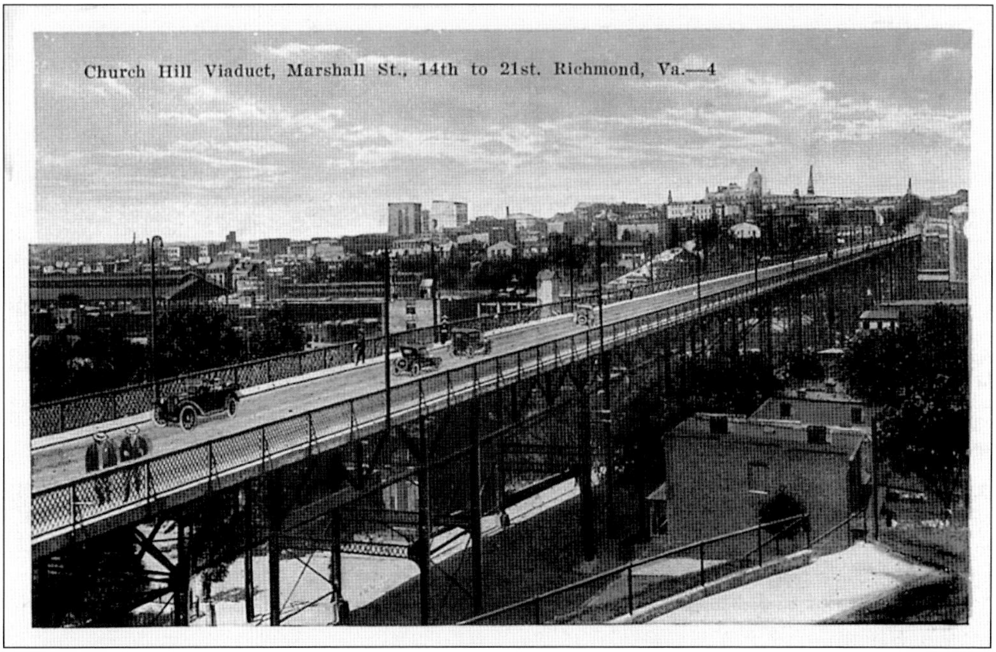

The Marshall Street viaduct was 2,800 feet long and, at its highest point, was 95 feet above the 17 railroad tracks it spanned. From the Union Hill side can be seen Monumental Episcopal Church, City Hall, the State Capitol, and the steeple of Broad Street Methodist Church in Court End.

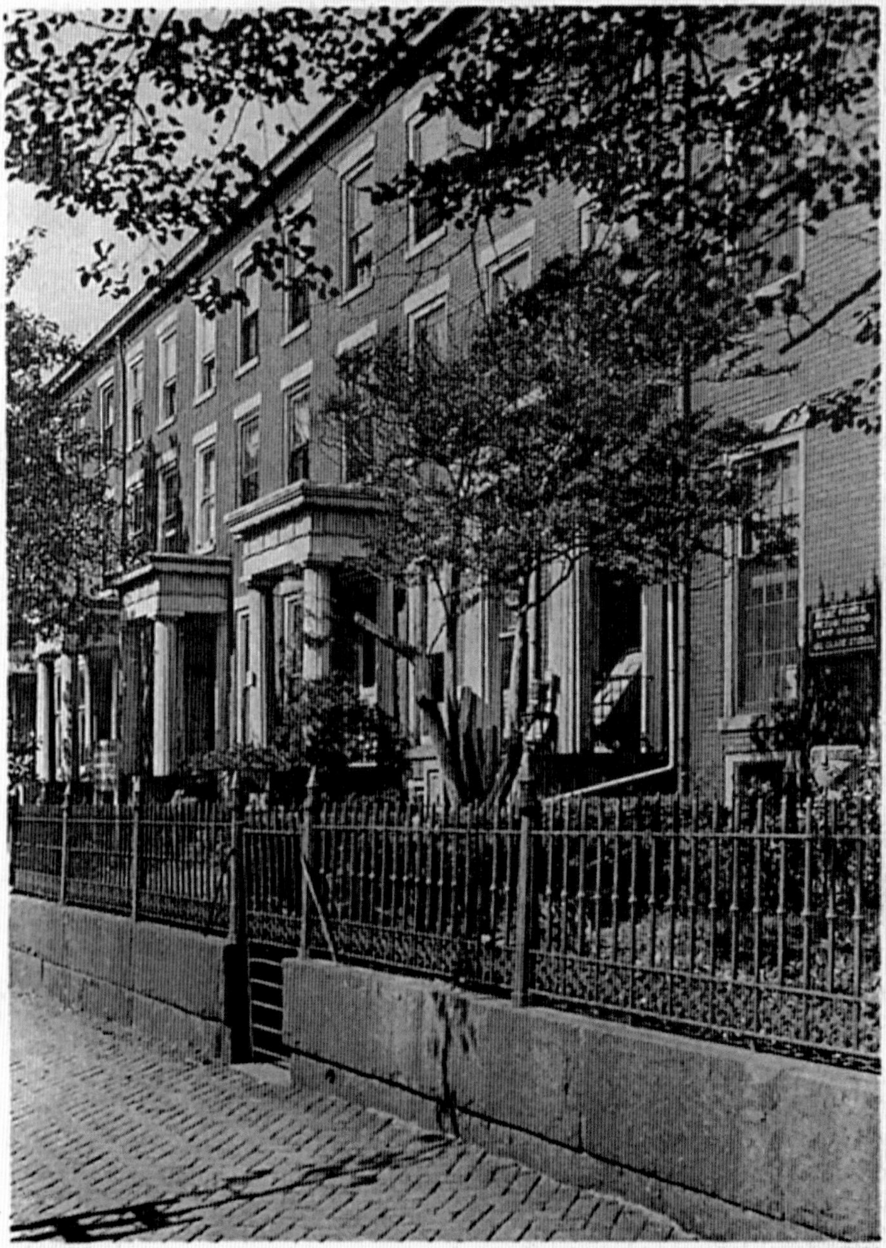

Several rows of houses were built on Franklin Street during the 1840s. Between First and Second Streets, Fleming James built five row houses, and six years later, five more were built, thus making a row of ten houses. Known as Linden Row, eight of the ten houses remain standing.

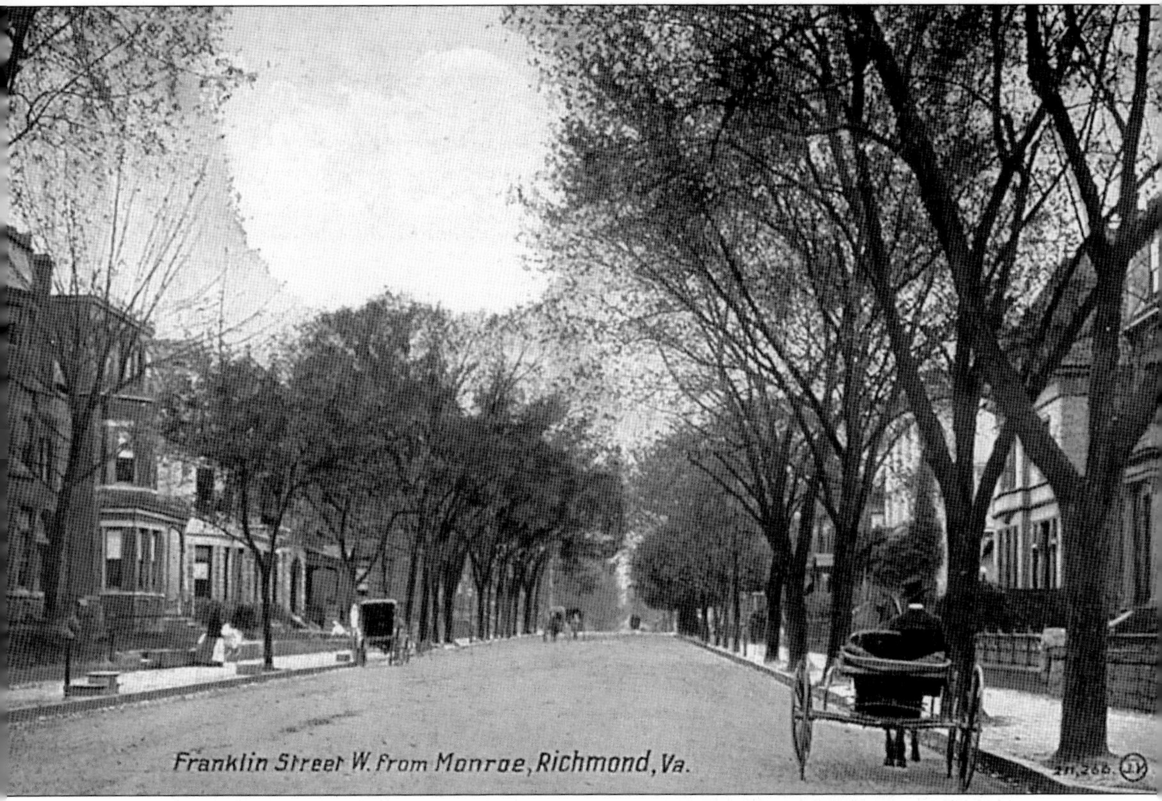

Even though the western boundary of the city was Belvidere Street at the time of the Civil War, residential structures were being built west of the city limits. The area west of Belvidere to Lombardy was annexed by the city in 1867, and plans were implemented to extend city streets and services in the newly annexed area. The extension of city water, sewer, and gas lines facilitated the development of residential neighborhoods along the newly extended streets. These stately homes on Franklin Street, west of Monroe Street, were built just before and after the Civil War.

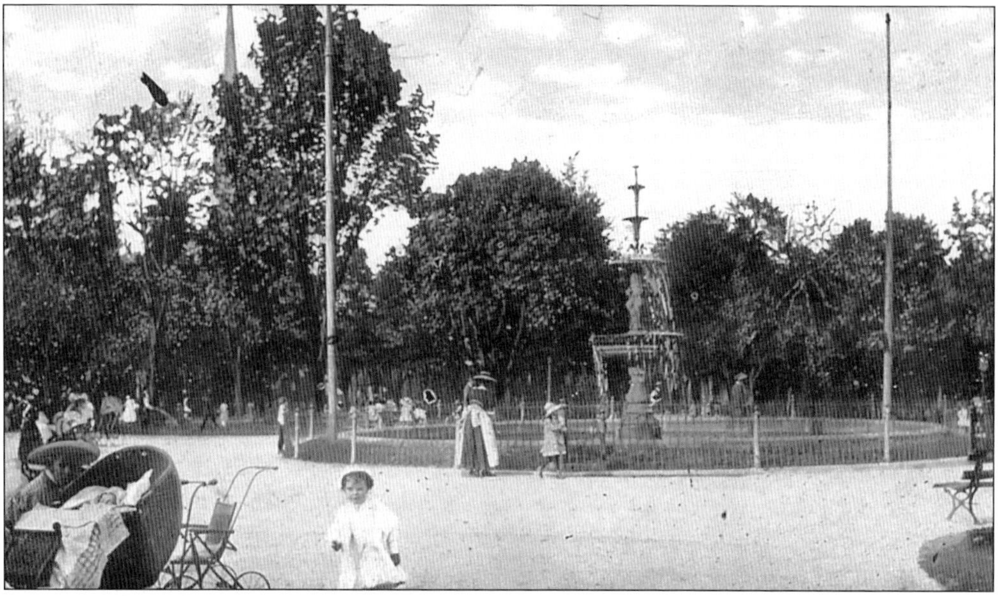

Monroe Park occupies the site of what was originally called Western Square, which was on the western edge of pre–Civil War Richmond. It was here that the early agricultural fairs were held. At the outbreak of the Civil War these fairgrounds served as a camp of instruction for volunteers. After the war, as the city began to develop to the west, the fairgrounds were moved further out Broad Street. Western Square, renamed Monroe Park in honor of President James Monroe, found itself surrounded by residences and churches. The park's shady walks, fountain, and velvety grass provided opportunities for a variety of recreational activities for residents.

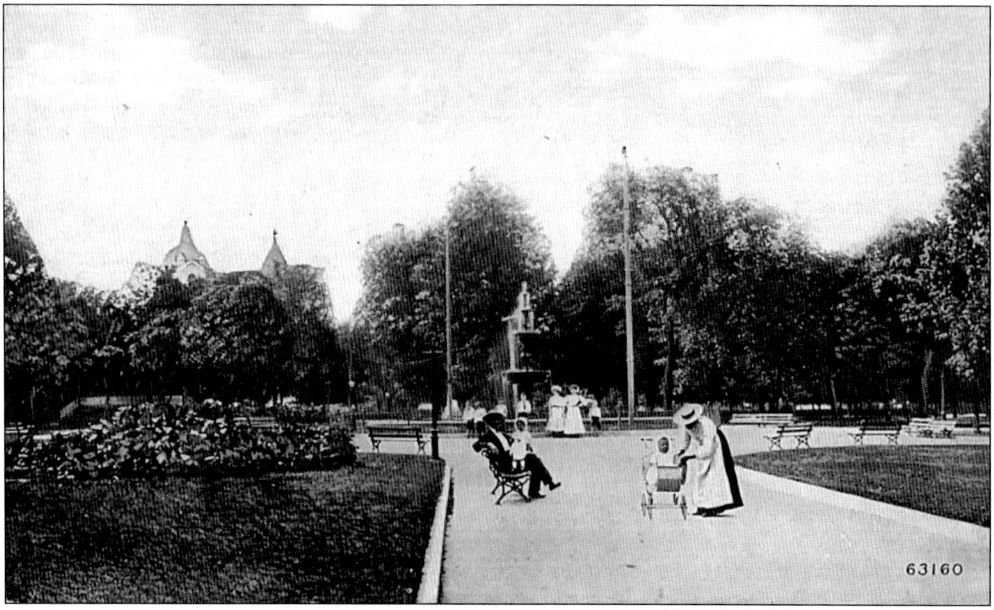

Around the turn of the century, Eugene Walton became the keeper and gardener of Monroe Park. He landscaped the park with flowers, shrubs, and trees. Paving along walkways was installed and a four-tier, cast-iron fountain designed by city engineer Col. William E. Cutshaw was installed around 1908.

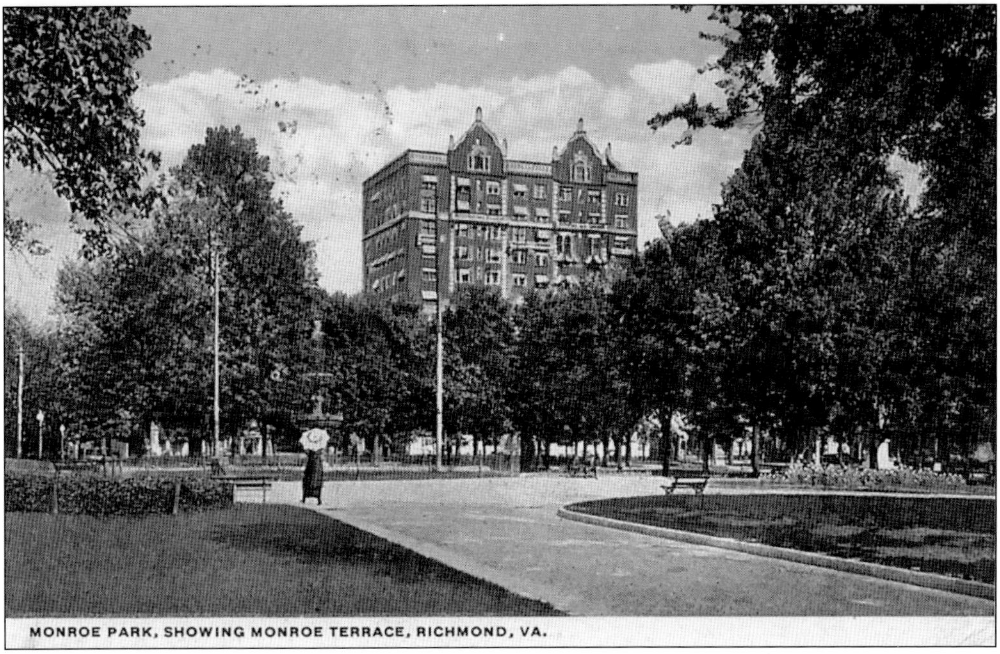

Residences surrounded Monroe Park prior to the end of the 19th century, but these gave way to churches and eventually to apartment buildings. Rising above the park's trees is Monroe Terrace Apartments at the corner of Franklin and Laurel Streets. Built in 1915 this 12-story apartment building is now a dormitory of Virginia Commonwealth University.

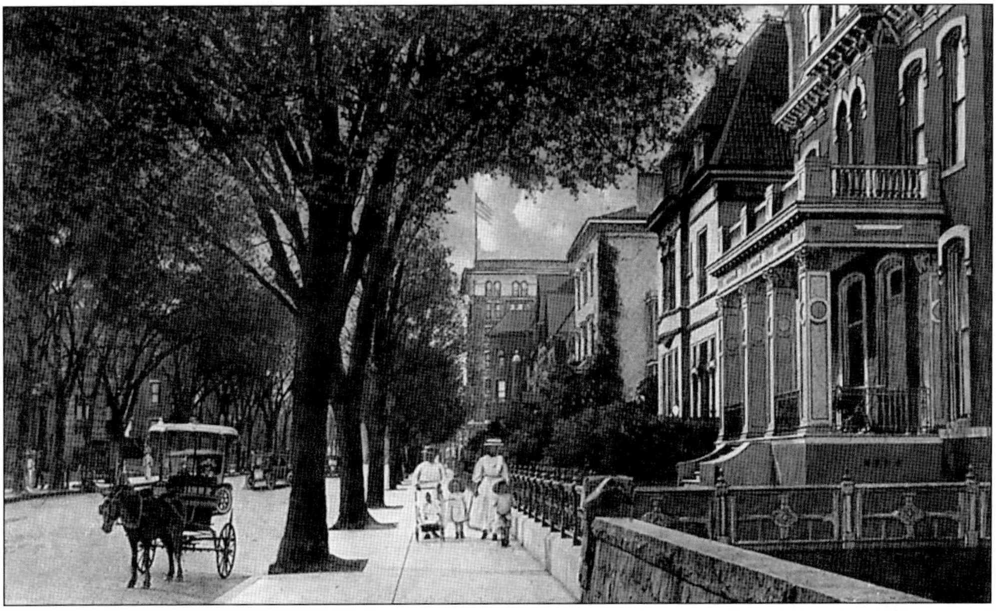

Large stately houses were built along Franklin Street west of Monroe Park between 1890 and 1920. This image shows the north side of Franklin and appears to have been taken from the northwest corner of Monroe Park. The tall building in the background with the flag on its roof is the Chesterfield Apartments at 900 West Franklin Street. Built in 1903, this was one of the first high-rise apartment buildings in the city.

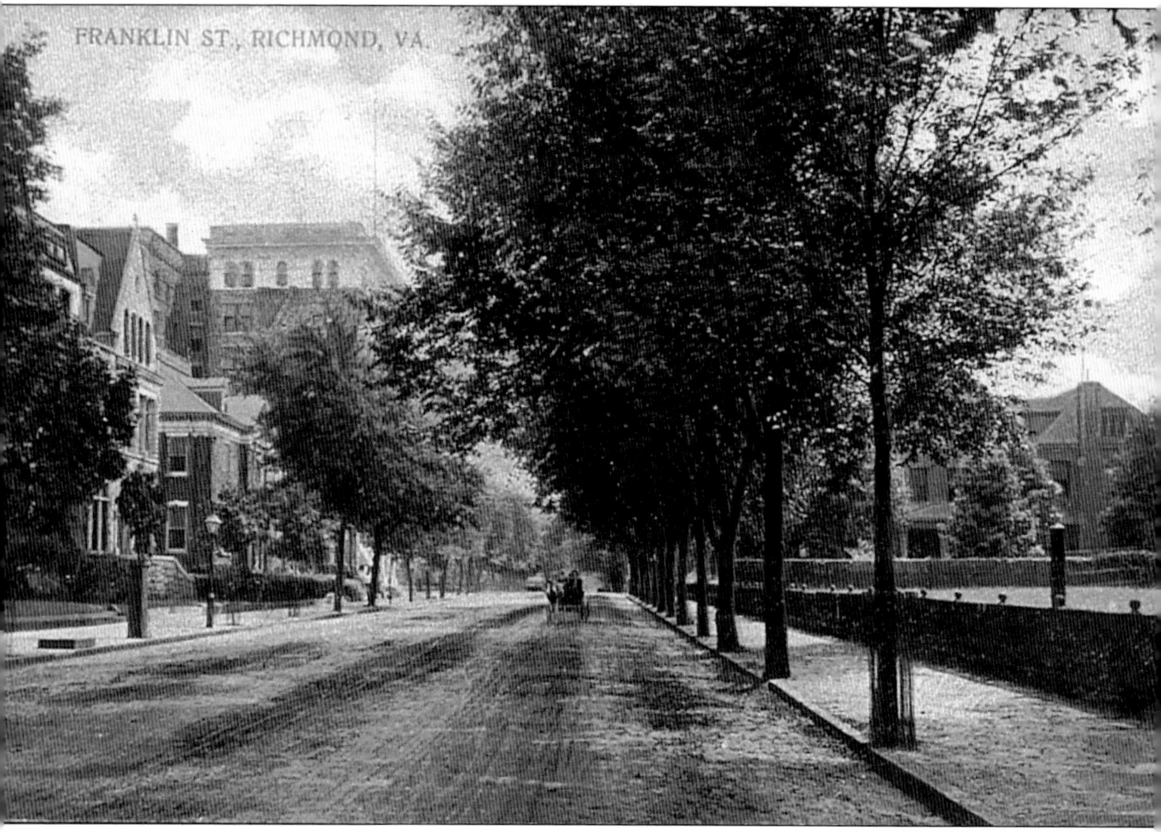

Not all of the lots on West Franklin were occupied with homes. The Chesterfield Apartments at 900 West Franklin appears on the north side of the street. As seen, some of the lots on the south side were vacant.

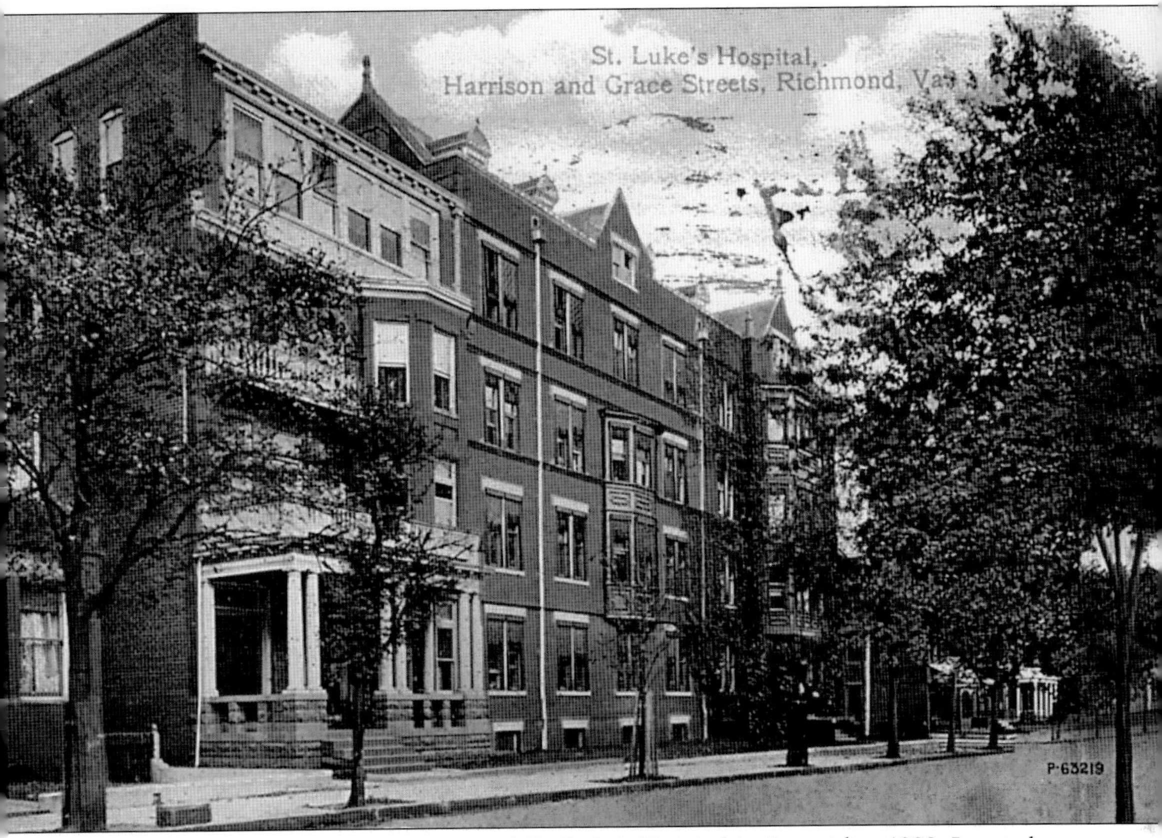

Drs. Hunter and Stuart McGuire opened St. Luke's Hospital in September 1899. Located on the corner of Harrison and Grace Streets, it was in the middle of a growing residential area.

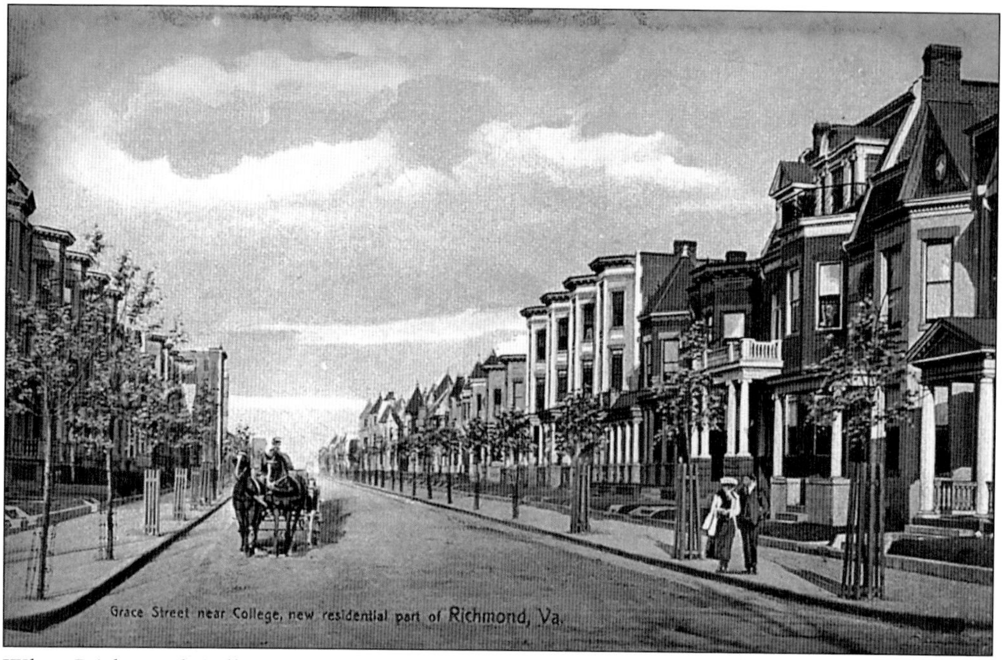

When Richmond College moved to Westhampton in 1914, the old college campus was sold for development and Grace Street was extended west. New residential developments soon appeared along Grace Street as Richmonders eagerly sought to move to the suburbs.

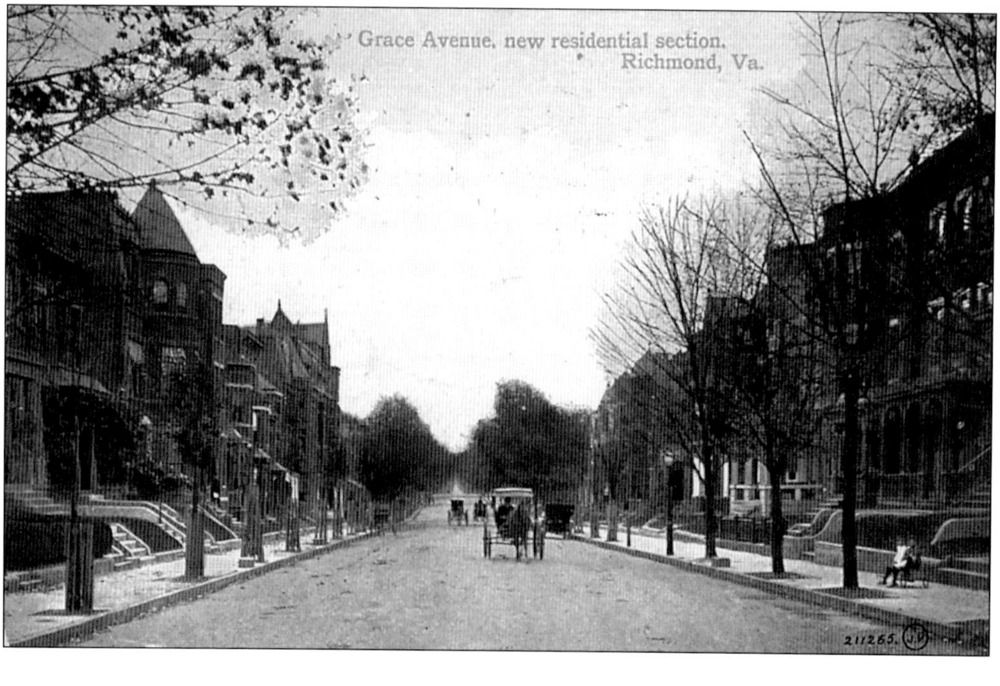

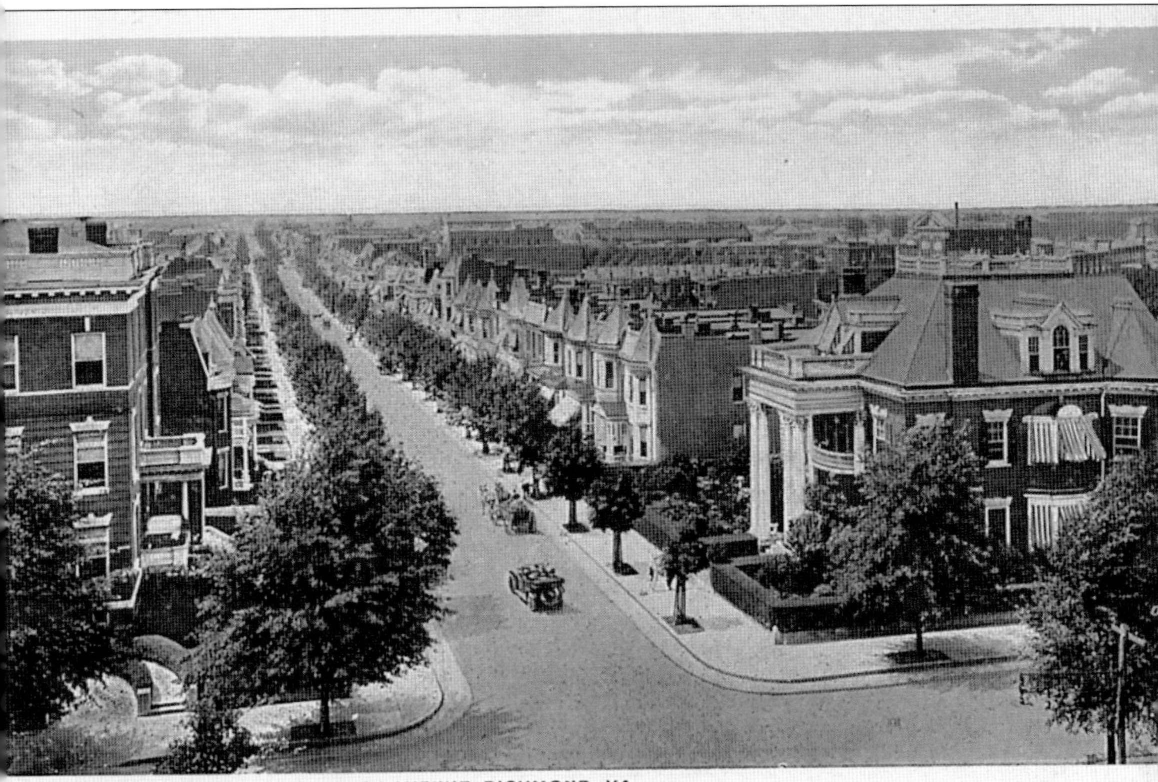

GRACE STREET, WEST FROM ALLEN AVENUE, RICHMOND, VA.

This postcard provides a bird's-eye view of Grace Street from Allen Avenue, just one block north of the Robert E. Lee Monument at Allen and Monument Avenues. The city annexed the land from Lombardy to the Boulevard in 1892, but an economic depression that swept the nation in 1893 delayed development for over ten years. By World War I, developers and land speculators were eagerly building apartments and rowhouses along Grace Street.

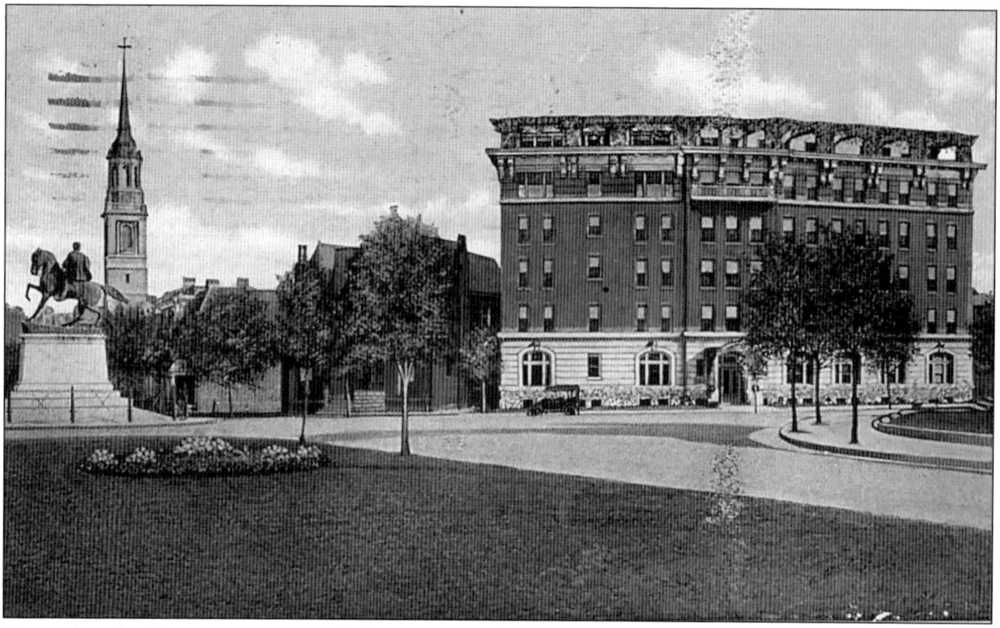

Extensive development occurred west of Lombardy Avenue after the turn of the 19th century. Franklin Street ended in a circle where Lombardy crossed, and west of that circle, Franklin became Monument Avenue. The J.E.B. Stuart Monument, which was erected in 1907, was joined by Stuart Circle Hospital in 1913. The new St. James Episcopal Church, along with Franklin and Birch Streets, can be seen behind the monument.

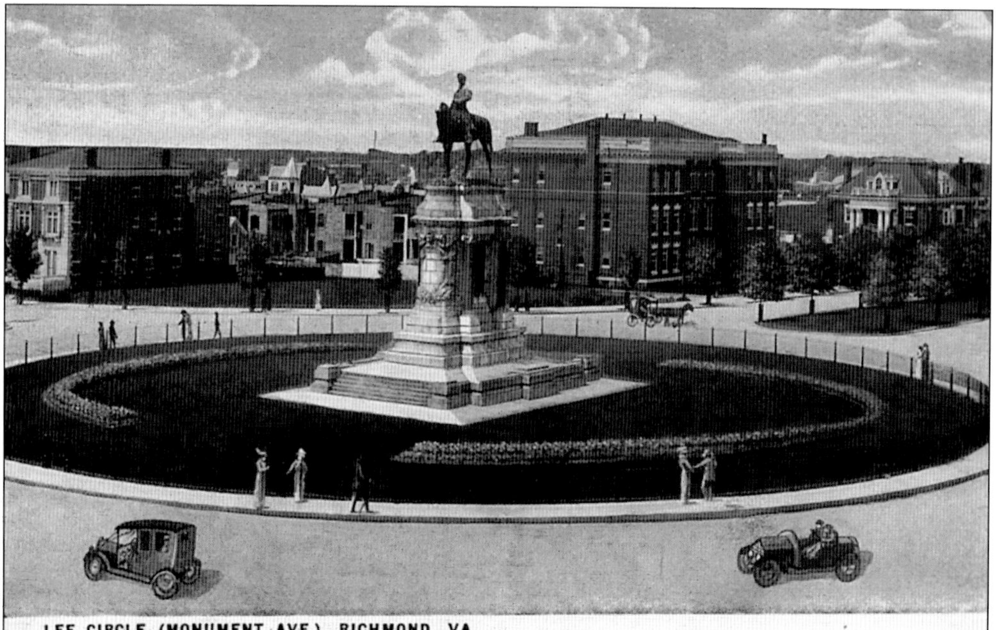

The R.E. Lee Monument, erected in 1890, was originally surrounded by open country but, by 1910, was virtually surrounded by residential structures.

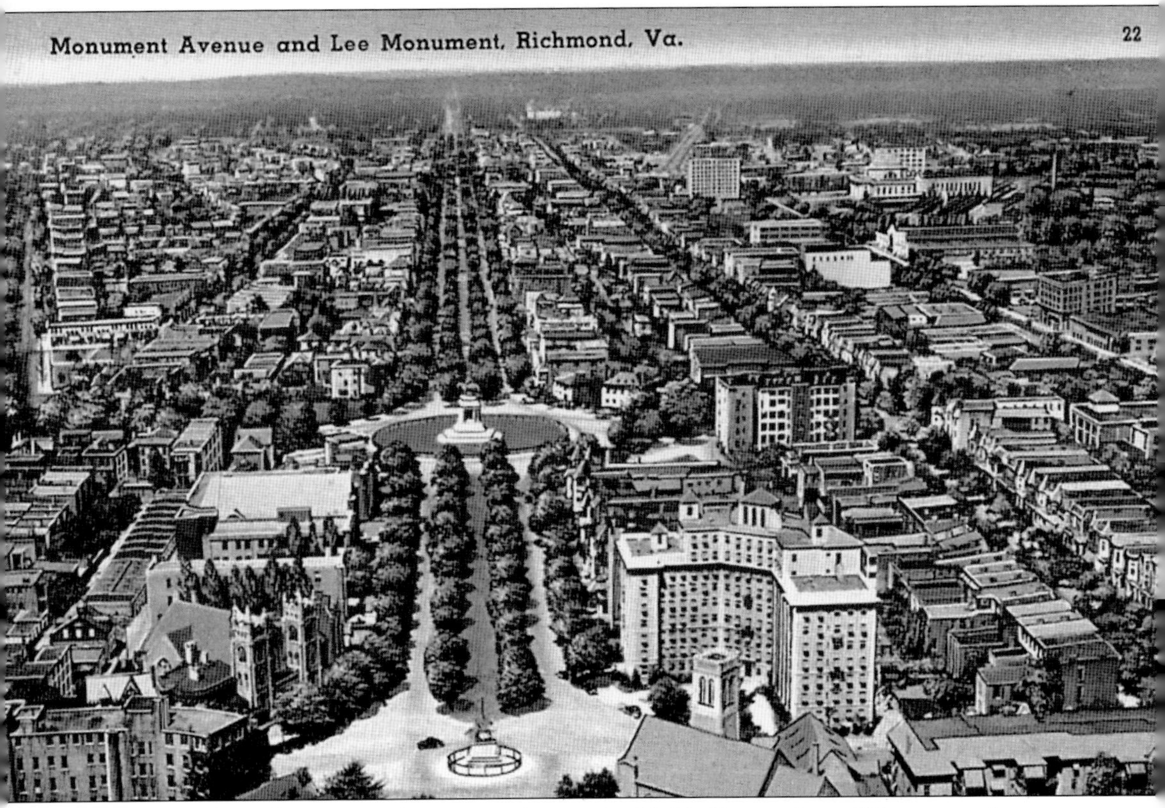

The extent of development to the west can be seen in this bird's-eye view of Monument Avenue, *c.* 1920. Running parallel to Monument to the north, both Grace and Broad Streets show the amount of development.

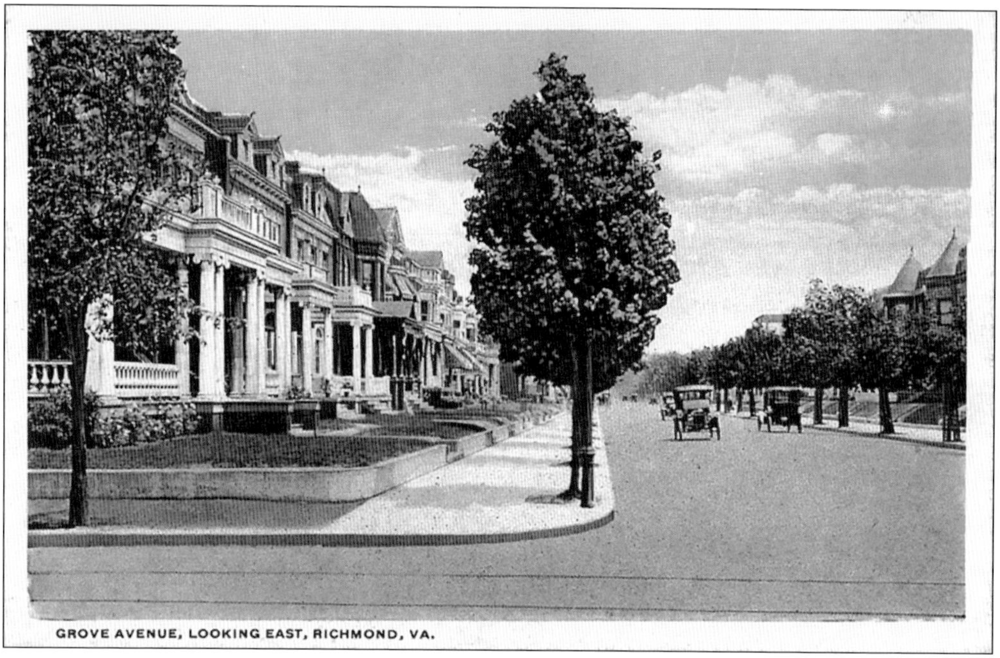

Grove Avenue was another of Richmond's residential thoroughfares. Looking east from Boulevard, one sees the heavy column porches that typified homes of the period.

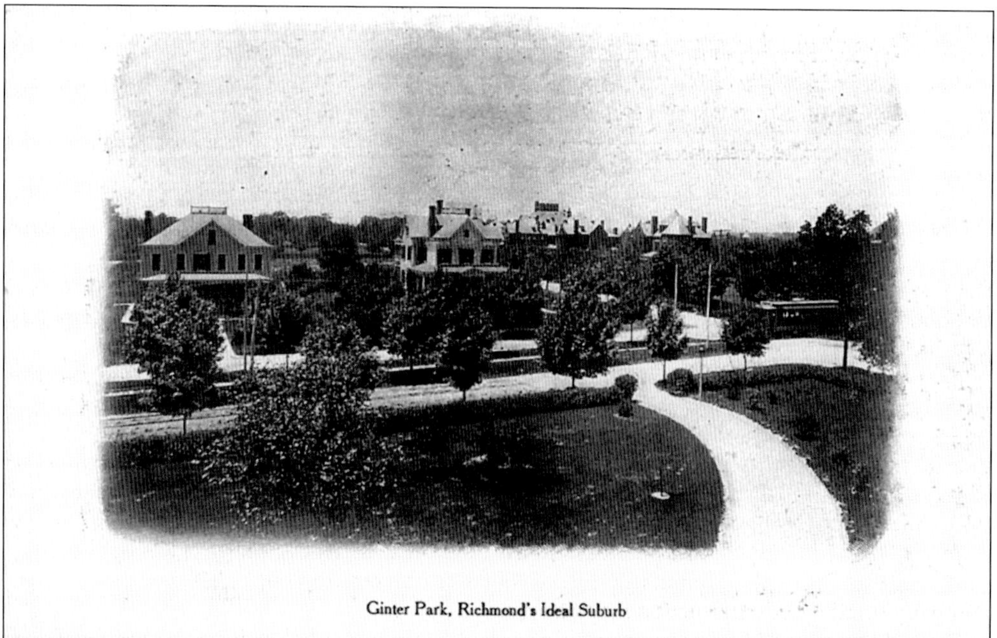

In 1895, Maj. Lewis Ginter began purchasing land along Brook Road just north of Richmond. After his death in 1897, the Ginter Park Land Company developed Ginter Park as a suburban community, and in 1914, Ginter Park was included in an area annexed by the city.

Nine

Burial Grounds

When the town of Richmond was established the common practice was to inter the dead in family burial grounds, in church cemeteries, or in isolated graves. When St. John's Episcopal Church was built in 1741 space was limited for interments, so families such as the Adamses, Carringtons, and Picketts set aside land for family burial grounds. In 1791 the Jewish community acquired a parcel on the western slope of Church Hill and established the Middle Street Burying Ground. In 1799 the city purchased the two lots adjacent to St. John's and opened a public burying ground.

The same year it purchased the two lots adjacent to St. John's, the city purchased land for a burial ground north of Shockoe Hill in what was to become Jackson Ward. On the northwestern edge of this tract the city set aside a cemetery for free blacks, a small one for slaves, and an additional plot for paupers and transients. In 1816 the city council gave Beth Shalome congregation an acre of land on the northern edge of its larger parcel, and it became the New Hebrew Cemetery. In November 1820 the city enclosed four acres of the larger parcel and established Shockoe Hill Cemetery, which became the principal burial ground for most of the city's well-to-do citizens between 1822 and 1850. In 1855 the city purchased 60 acres in the Union Hill section of Church Hill to help relieve the crowding in Shockoe Hill Cemetery. This new city cemetery became Oakwood Cemetery.

Even though the city maintained its burial grounds, a group of local citizens interested in establishing a landscaped rural cemetery organized a private cemetery company. On June 3, 1847, the company purchased 42 acres atop a steep granite bluff overlooking the falls of the James a quarter mile west of the city. Late in December 1847, John Notman, a Scottish architect living in Philadelphia, visited the site and prepared a design for the cemetery. Observing a large number of holly trees on the property, Notman suggested the name Hollywood. The cemetery was laid out in July 1848, and Hollywood Cemetery, the first private cemetery in the city, was dedicated on June 15, 1849. Twice defeated in its efforts to obtain a charter from the legislature, the cemetery company finally met with success in 1856.

West of Hollywood Cemetery overlooking the James, the Catholic diocese acquired land for Mt. Calvary Cemetery in 1885. In March 1887 the city purchased 52 acres between Hollywood and Mt. Calvary and later opened Riverview Cemetery. These three cemeteries were eventually annexed into the city.

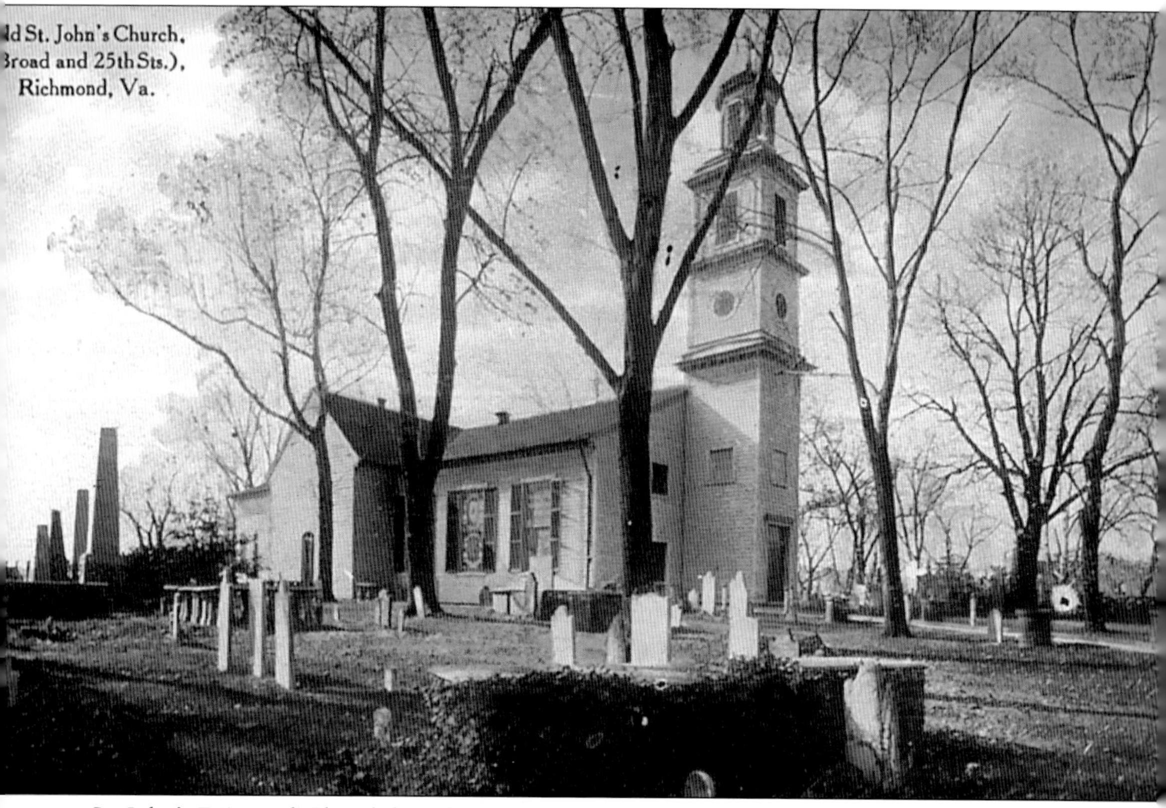

St. John's Episcopal Church burial ground became the city's first public burial ground when the city acquired the two lots adjacent to the church in 1799. Except on approval of council, interments ceased in 1821.

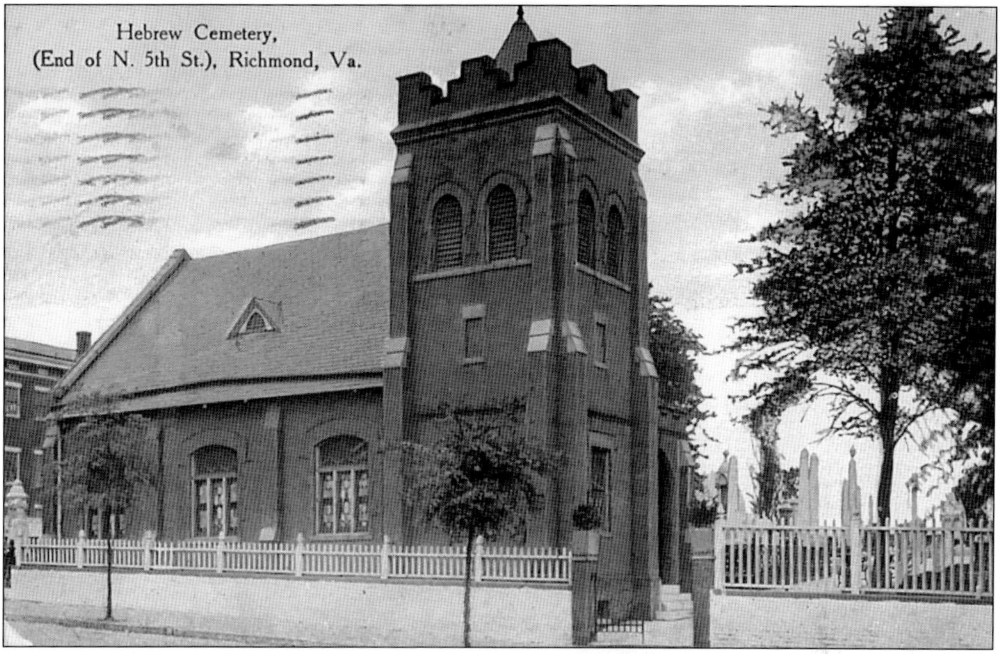

In 1816, Benjamin Woolfe, a member of the city council, obtained the council's approval to set aside one acre of ground to be used for burial purposes by the congregation of Beth Shalome. He was the first to be interred in the New Hebrew Cemetery. Additions were made over the years, and the mortuary chapel seen in this view was added in 1894.

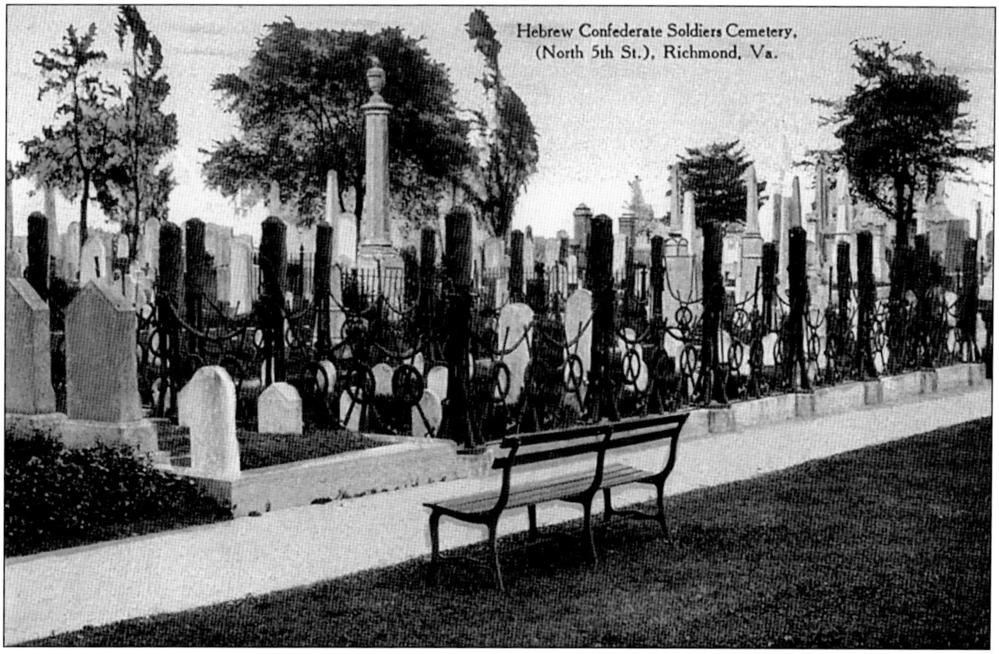

The Hebrew Confederate Soldiers Cemetery occupies a section of the New Hebrew Cemetery; it is under the care of the Hebrew Ladies Memorial Association. A cast-iron fence of stacked rifles and crossed sabers surrounds the Confederate section.

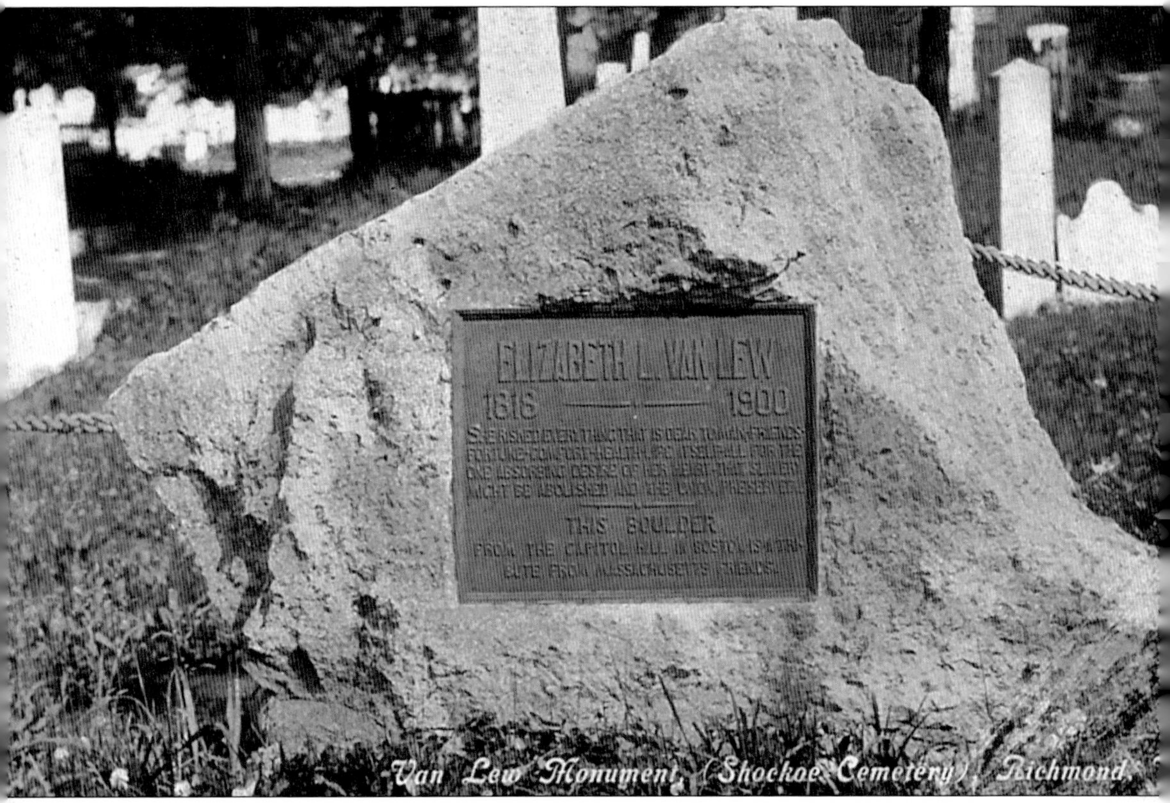

Miss Elizabeth Van Lew was a Union sympathizer who lived on Church Hill during the Civil War. In 1869 President U.S. Grant appointed her postmaster of Richmond. Because of her activities as a Union spy, post-war Richmonders shunned her. She died November 25, 1900, and her remains were interred in Shockoe Hill Cemetery. A monument in the form of a bolder from Boston's capitol hill was placed on her grave as a tribute from her Massachusetts friends.

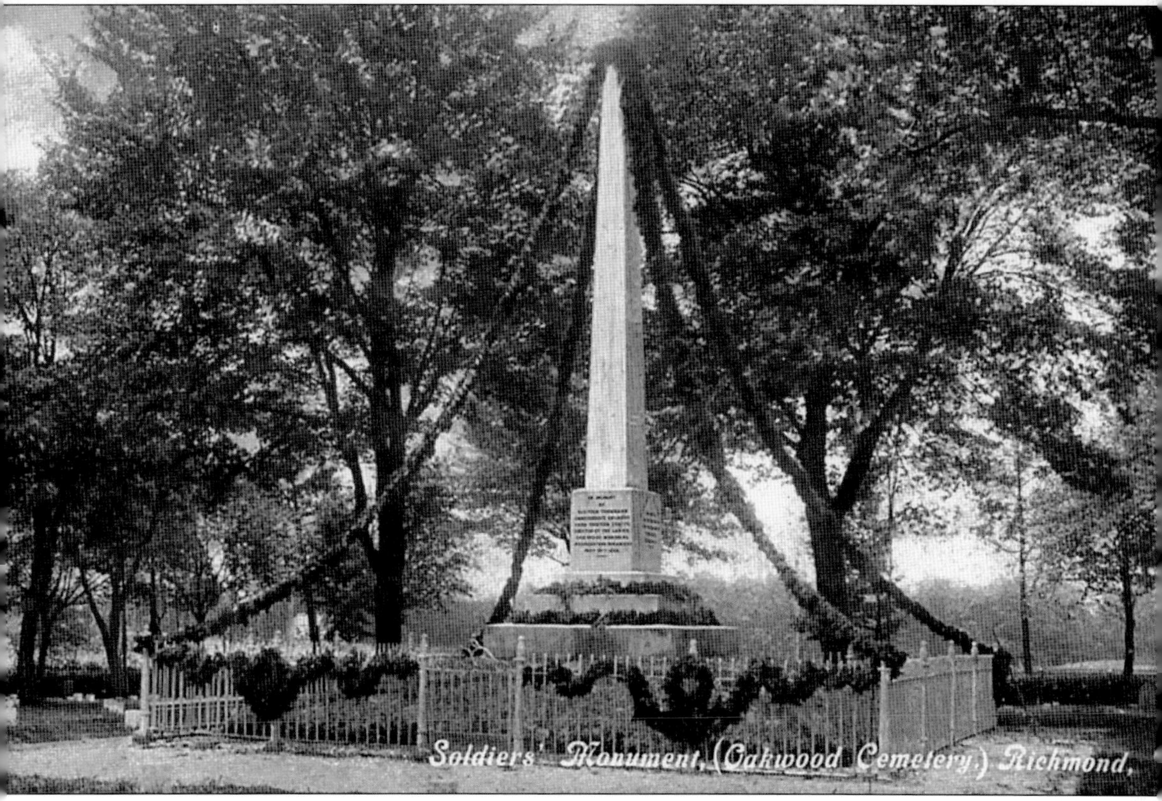

During the Civil War deceased Confederate soldiers were buried in both Oakwood and Hollywood Cemeteries. The granite monument erected by the Oakwood Ladies Memorial Association marks the center of the area in which 17,000 Confederate dead are buried.

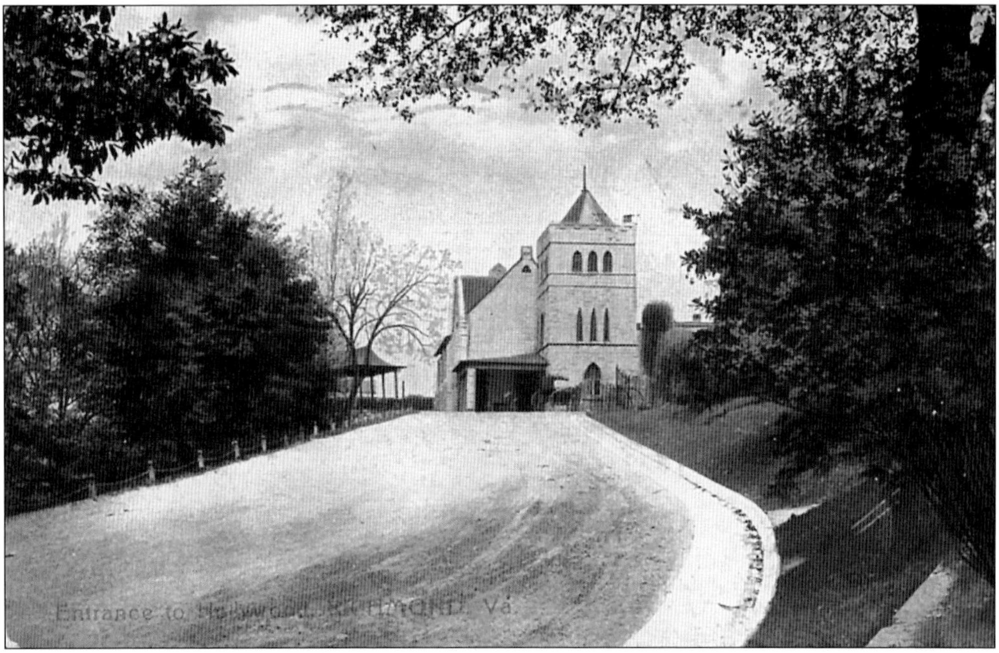

Originally, the entrance to Hollywood Cemetery was guarded by two frame structures that served as the keeper's house and office. Marion J. Dimmock designed a new stone mortuary chapel and office building in 1897–1898 that was constructed at the entrance.

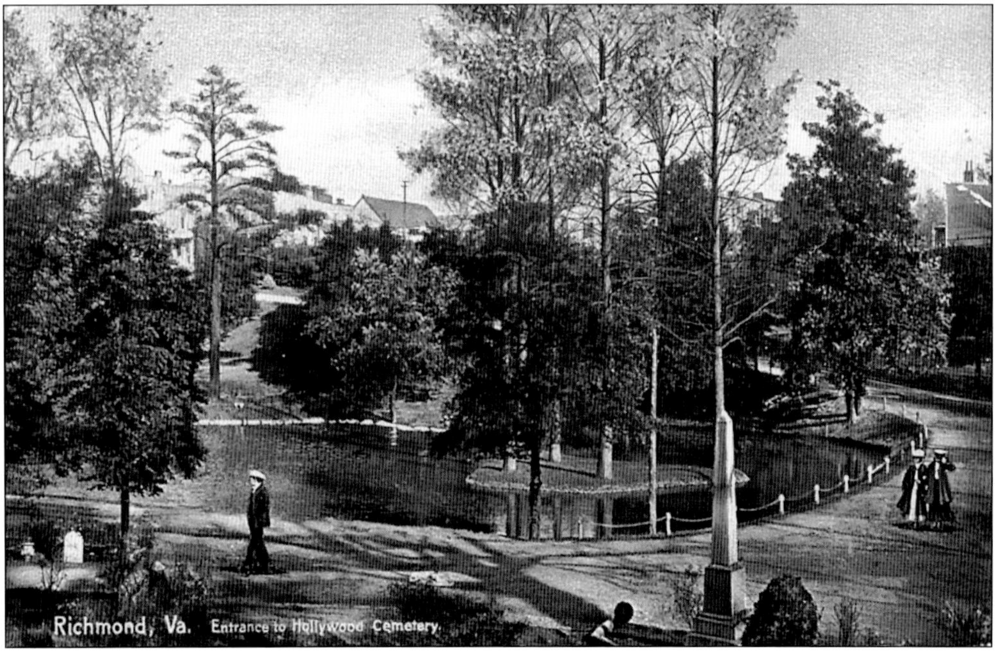

Just beyond the mortuary chapel and office the terrain drops. In an effort to maintain the natural setting, John Notman incorporated ponds in his landscaping design.

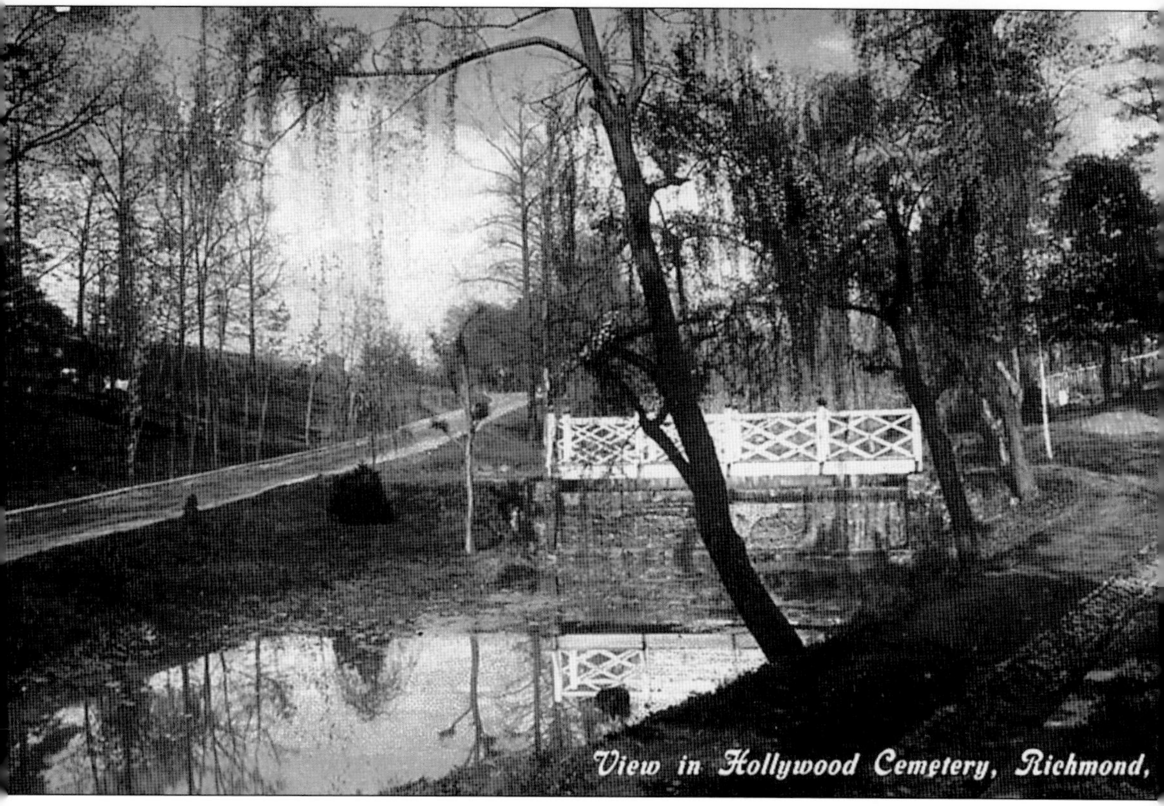

John Notman also incorporated at least five bridges in his design of the cemetery. He stressed that the bridges were to be made of straight timbers resting on stone abutments of dry stone walling on each side of the stream.

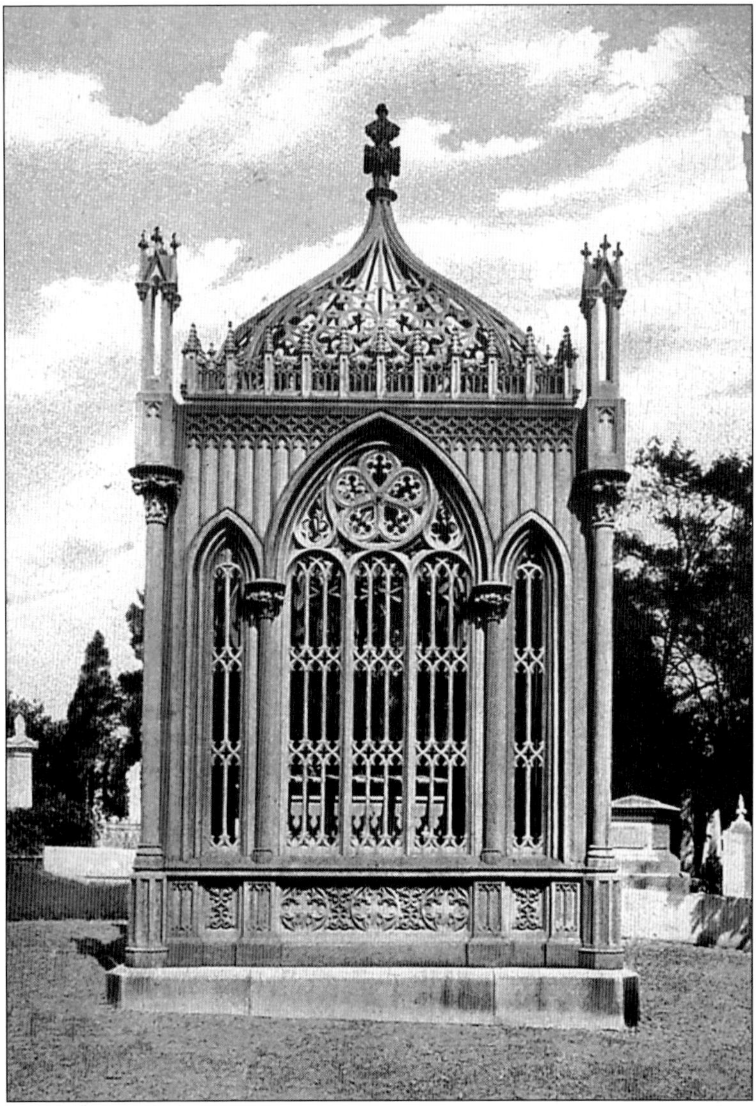

President James Monroe died in New York on July 4, 1831, and his remains were buried in a vault in Marble Cemetery in that city. In 1858 efforts were undertaken to remove Monroe's remains to Hollywood Cemetery. With the concurrence of his descendants, the General Assembly of Virginia, and the City of New York, Monroe's remains were returned to Virginia on July 3 and escorted by the 7th Regiment New York Volunteers. Arriving at Rockett's wharf around 8 a.m., July 5, 1858, Monroe's remains were placed in an open hearse drawn by six white horses. Local military companies lined Main Street as the hearse moved up that street toward Hollywood Cemetery. There, after remarks by Gov. Henry A. Wise and a prayer by Dr. C.H. Read of the United Presbyterian Church, the author of the "Monroe Doctrine" was laid to rest on Virginia soil. Monroe's reburial brought recognition and prestige to Hollywood Cemetery and to the city.

Gov. Henry A. Wise chose Albert Lybrock's design for the Monroe Monument. Lybrock, an Alsatian by birth, was a Richmond architect who had prepared architectural drawings of the State Capitol. Lybrock's Gothic Revival design, dubbed the "bird cage," was cast by Wood and Perot of Philadelphia. The 12-foot structure was erected over Monroe's grave in 1859.

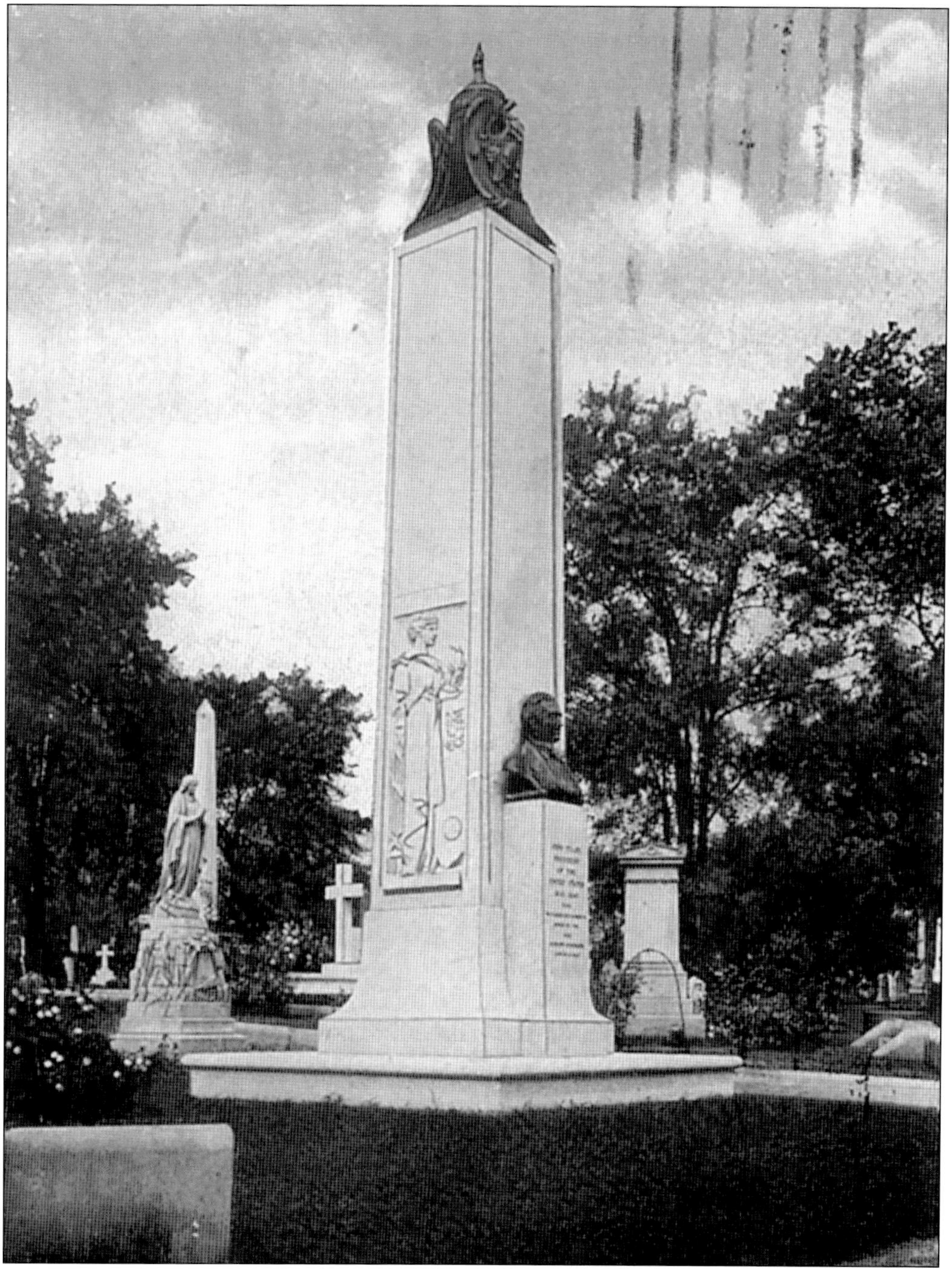

President John Tyler died in Richmond on January 18, 1862, while serving as a member of the Confederate House of Representatives. The tenth president of the United States was interred in Hollywood Cemetery near Monroe's Monument. His grave was marked with a simple plaque until 1915 when, by act of Congress, funds were appropriated for a suitable monument. T.F. McGann and Sons of Boston fabricated the granite column and the bronze bust and cap and sent it to Richmond in pieces. The U.S. Corps of Engineers assembled the monument, and it was dedicated on October 12, 1915.

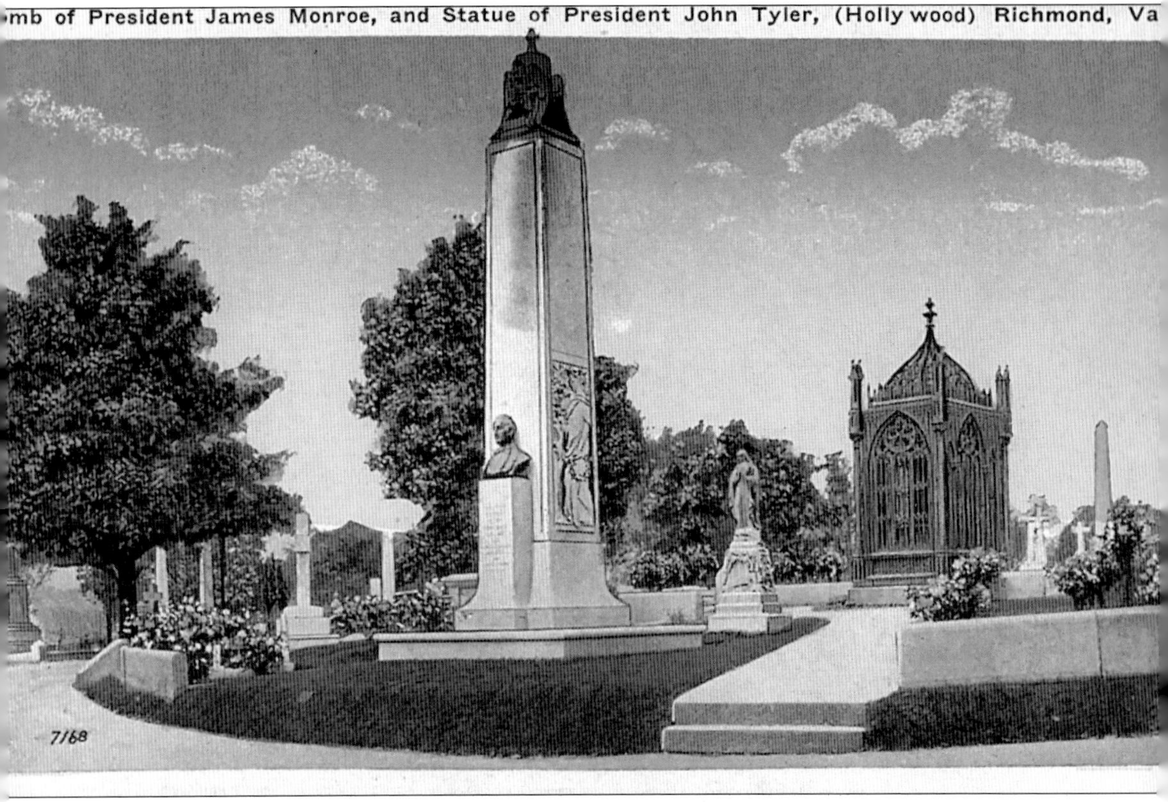

Hollywood's Mount Circle became Presidents Circle, and over the years, members of the Monroe and Tyler families were interred in the circle. Julia Gardiner Tyler, the president's widow reserved the lot next to his and she was buried in it on July 12, 1889, two days after her death. In November 1903 the General Assembly appropriated funds to remove the remains of Monroe's wife, Elizabeth Kortright Monroe, and daughter Maria Hester Monroe Gouveneur from Oak Hill, Loudon County, to Hollywood. The caskets reached Richmond on November 18, 1903, and they were immediately taken to Hollywood where they were buried near Monroe's grave. Bishop Robert A. Gibson conducted the religious service and Sen. John W. Daniel addressed the assembled crowd.

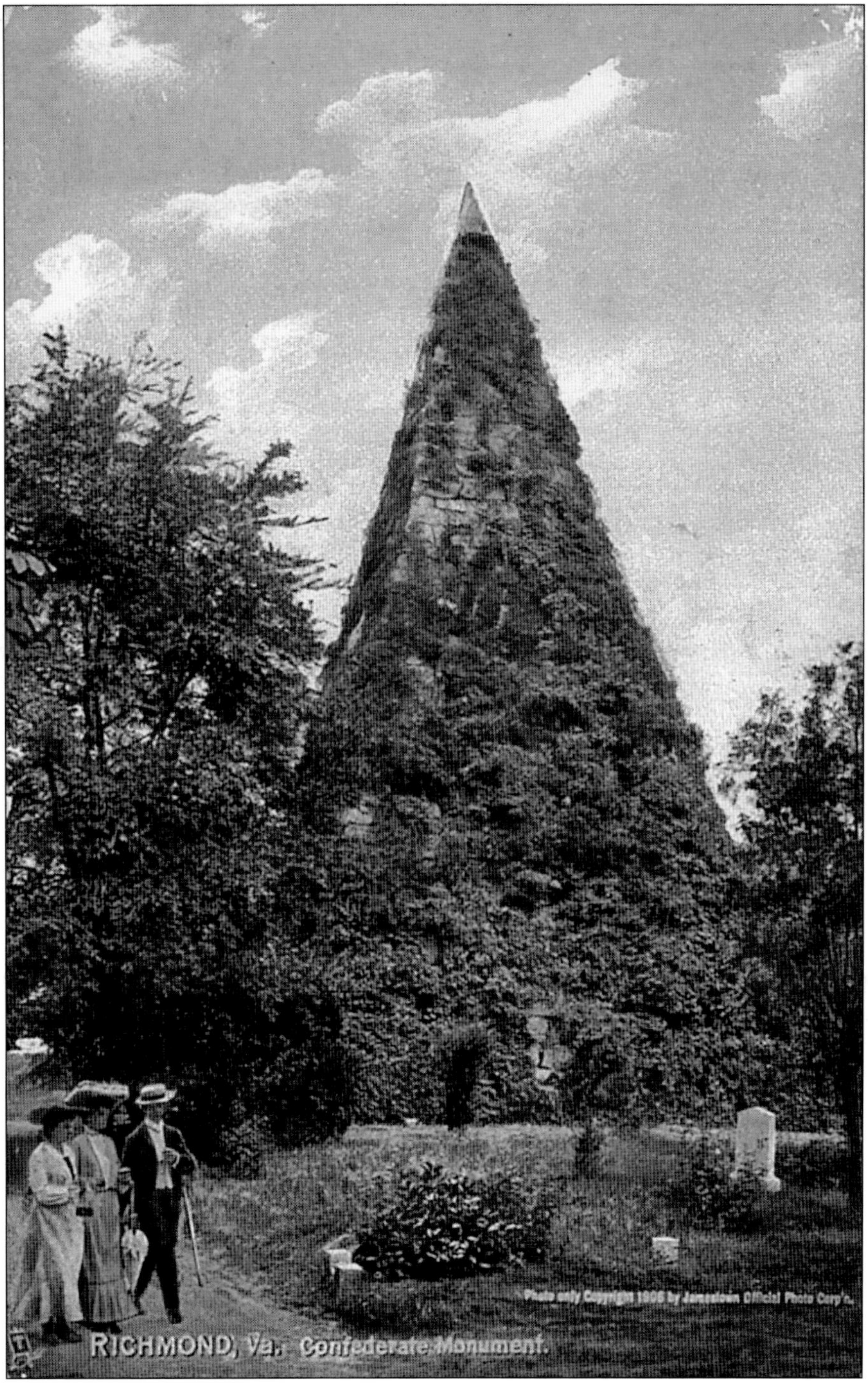

The memorial pyramid pictured above was dedicated on May 31, 1869. Made of undressed James River granite, it stands 90 feet high and was designed by Charles H. Dimmock, city engineer. On November 6, 1869, the capstone was put into position. The granite pyramid stands in the Confederate Soldiers section where some 12,000 Confederates are buried. It became the symbol of the Hollywood Memorial Association.

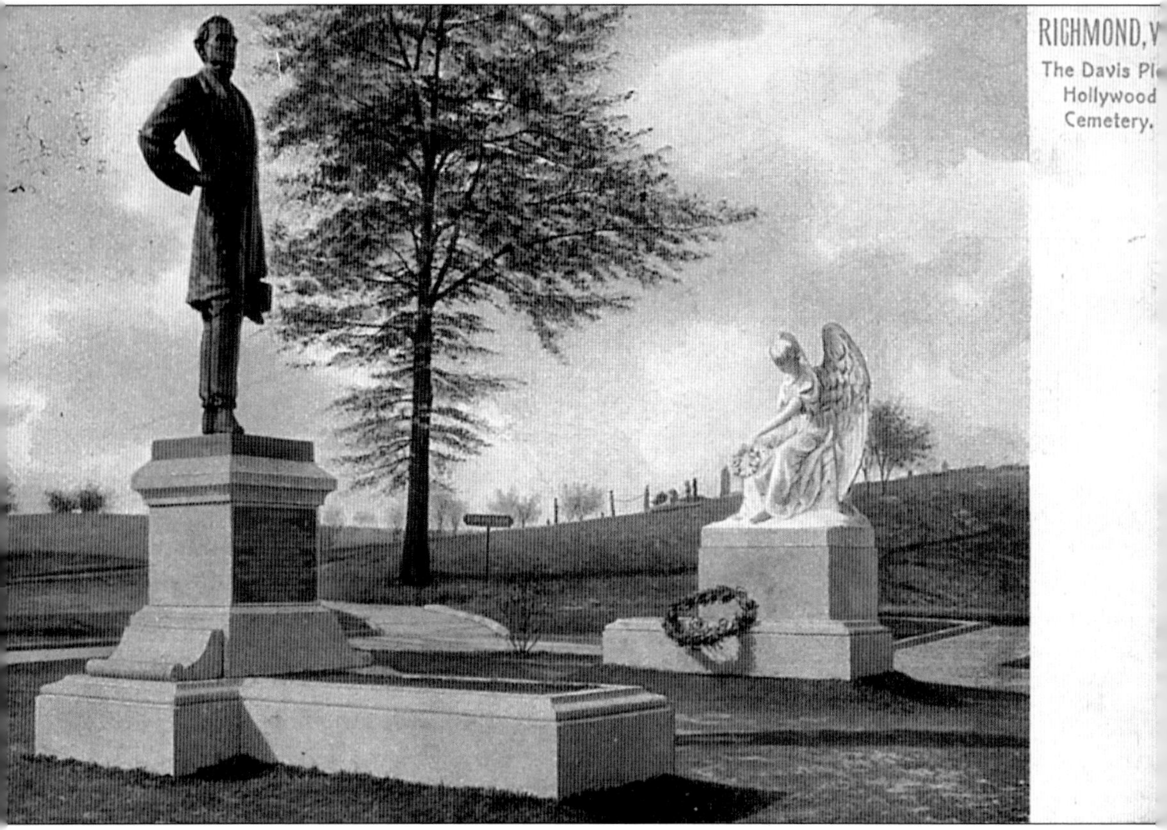

When Jefferson Davis died on December 6, 1889, Hollywood directors offered his widow her choice of any section she desired. She selected an imposing circular lot. Temporarily interred in Metairie Cemetery in New Orleans, Davis's remains were re-interred in Hollywood on May 31, 1893. Three of Davis's sons were re-interred beside their father on June 3, 1893, and a fourth was re-interred on November 27, 1895. Davis's daughter Varina Anne "Winnie" Davis died September 18, 1898, and she was also interred in the family circle. The Hollywood Company contracted with George Julian Zolnay to prepare a statue of Davis, which was unveiled on November 9, 1899. Zolnay also designed a seven-foot angel of grief in memory of Winnie, and it, too, was unveiled at that time. A third monument executed by Andrew J. Wray, a broken column, was unveiled in memory of Jefferson Davis Jr. Mrs. Jefferson Davis died in New York City on October 16, 1906, and she was moved from St. Paul's on October 19 and interred next to her husband. The ashes of Davis's other daughter Margaret Howell Davis Hayes were buried in Davis Circle on October 29, 1909. Zolnay sculpted an angel within the pages of a Bible to mark her grave.

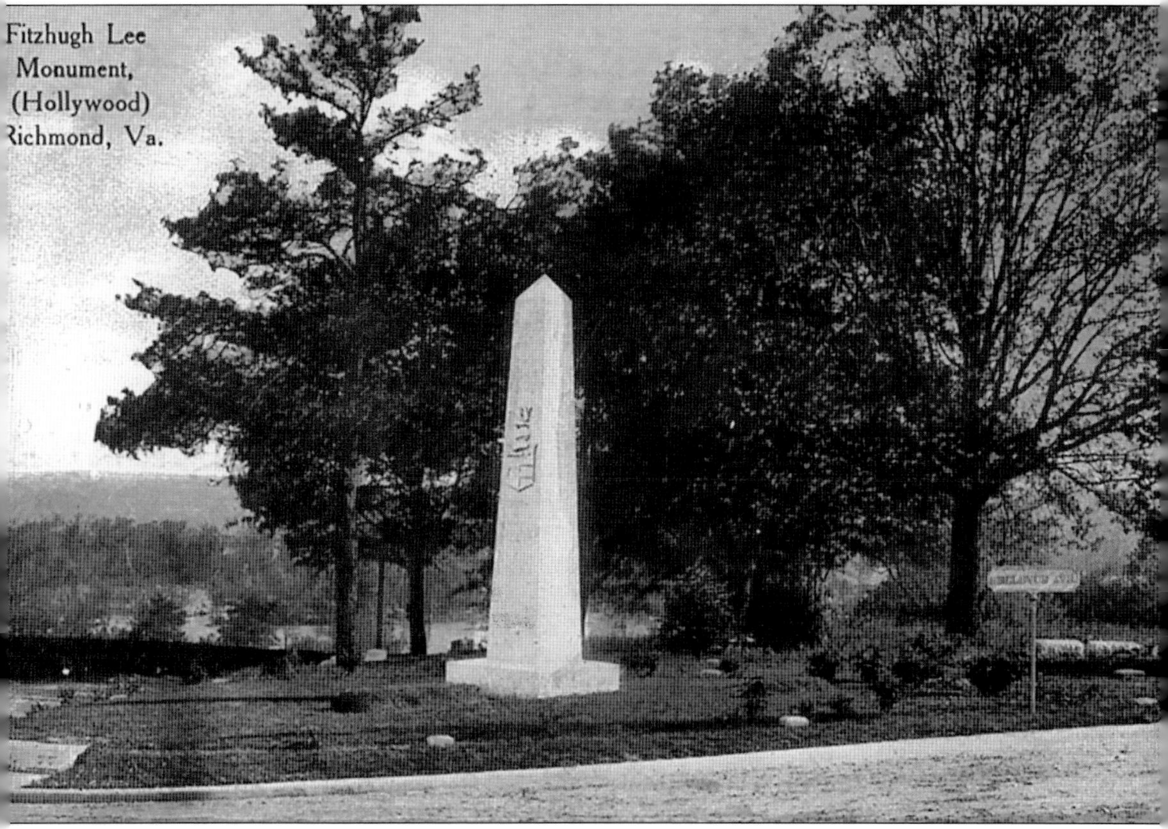

Fitzhugh Lee, a nephew of Robert E. Lee, died in Washington, D.C. on April 28, 1905. His body was brought to Richmond where it lay in state in City Hall until May 4, and then it was taken to |St. Paul's for funeral services. Following the services his remains were buried near the Davis Circle. The inscription on the monument reads, "Fitzhugh Lee, of Virginia, Nov. 1835–1905. Faithful Unto Death. Major General C.S.A. 1862–1865. Commanding Cavalry Corps A.N.V. 1864–1865. Governor of Virginia 1886–1890. Consul-General to Cuba 1896–1898. Major-General Commanding 7th Army Corps U.S.V. 1898. Brigadier General U.S.A. Retired 1901."

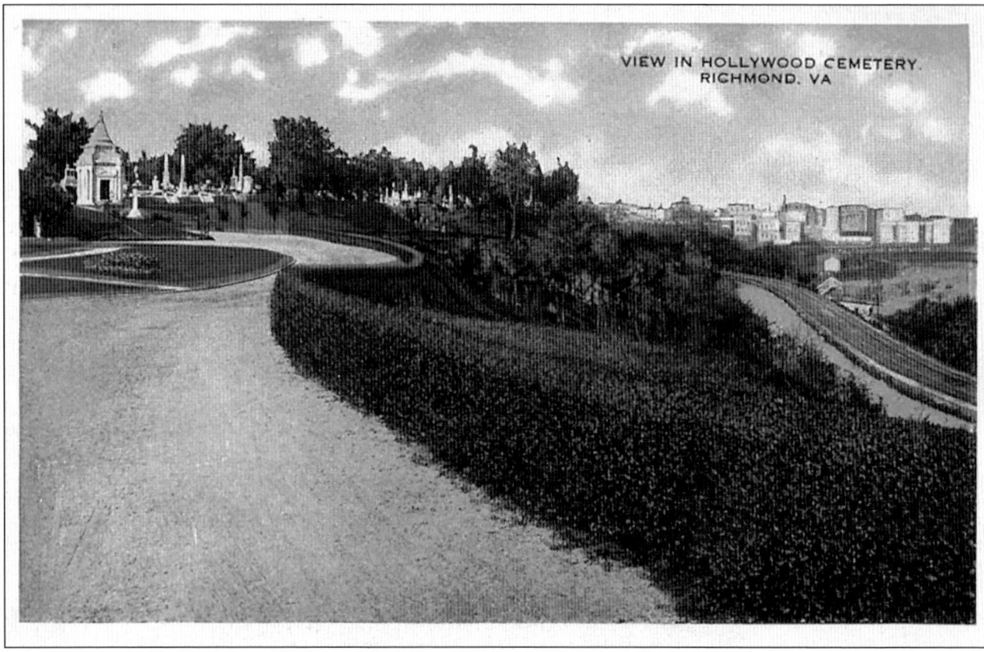

Hollywood Cemetery provides a view of the both the city and the river as it overlooks the falls of the James. The large mausoleum to the left in these views is the tomb of Lewis Ginter, a native of New York who made Richmond his home. Ginter had been successful in the tobacco business and in land development. Charles E. Taylor of New York designed the mausoleum. Each corner has two Corinthian columns and the bronze doors have glass plates designed by Louis Tiffany. In addition, the tomb has three Tiffany windows.

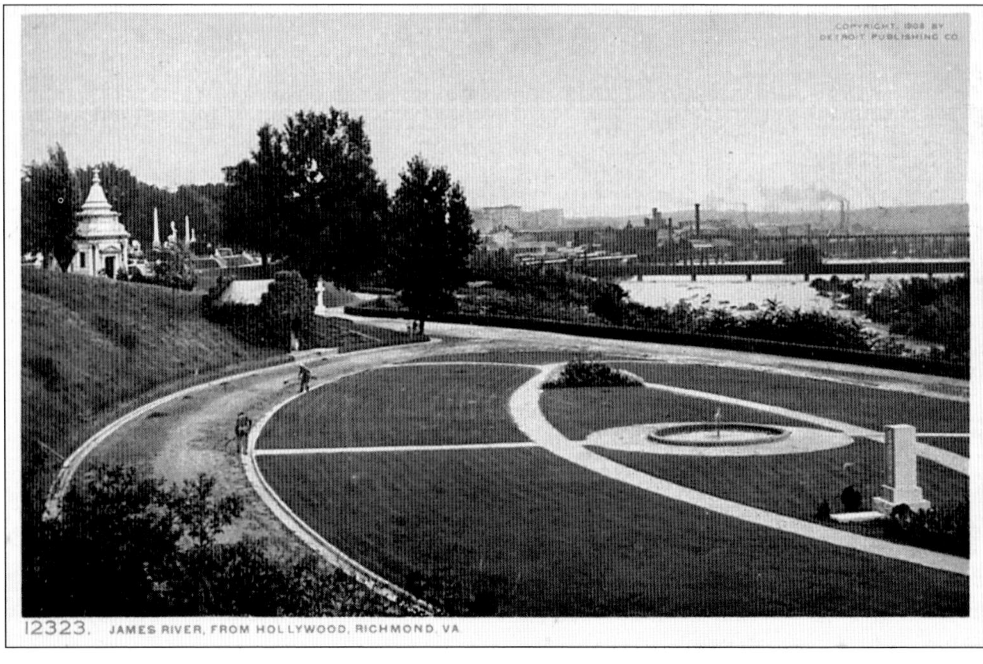

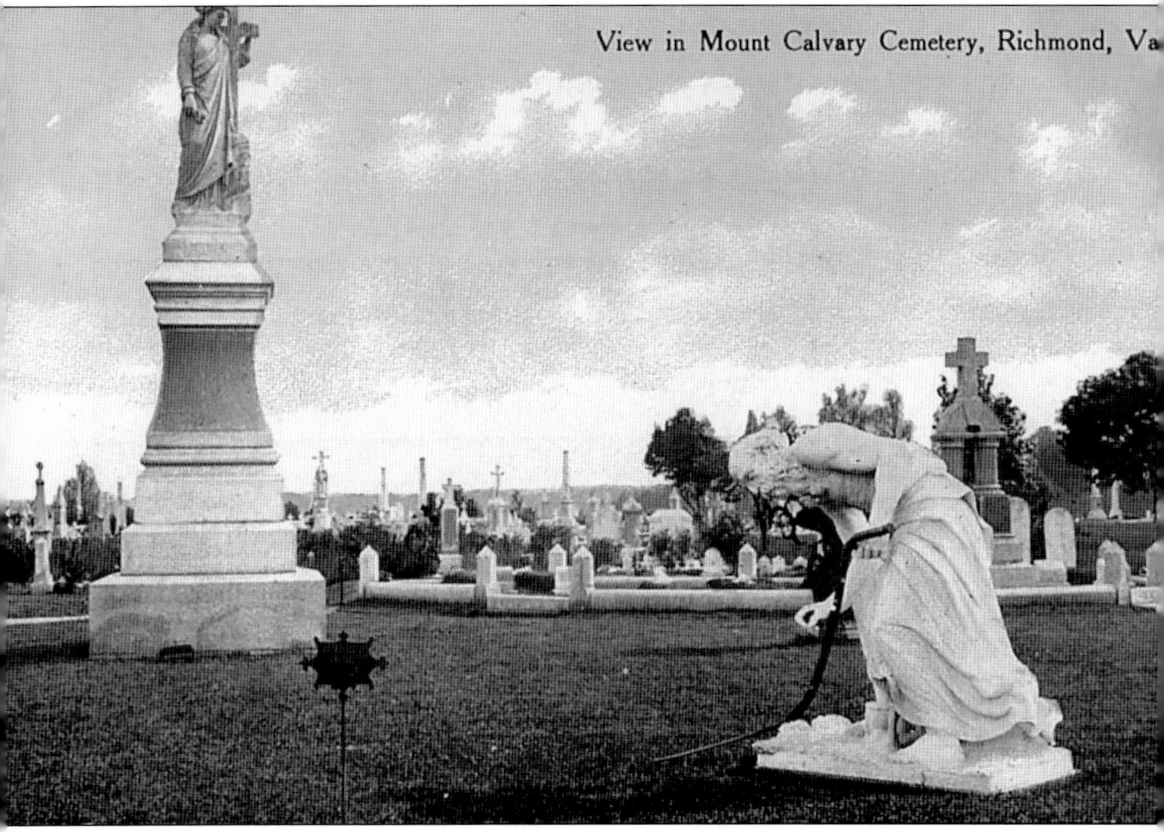

Mt. Calvary was laid out by Colonel C.P.E. Burgwyn; it was officially dedicated and opened on November 2, 1887. This view of Mt. Calvary captures the statue of the grim reaper.

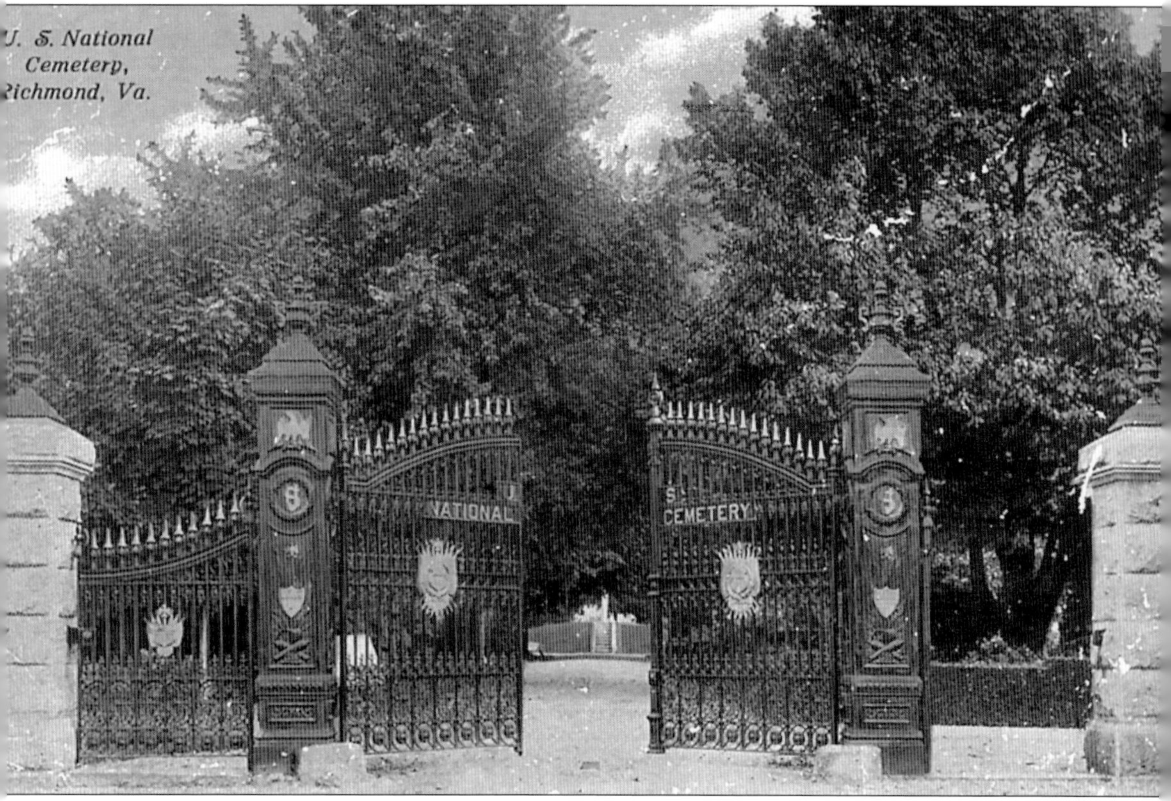

The Richmond National Cemetery on Williamsburg Road was established September 1, 1866. Re-interments of Union soldiers were made from Oakwood and Hollywood Cemeteries, the prisoner of war cemetery on Belle Island, and from battlefields in Chesterfield, Hanover, and Henrico Counties. Over 5,665 unknown Union soldiers were re-interred by July 1871. The cemetery was closed during the fiscal year 1963. As of September 30, 1999, there were 9,142 interments.

Selected Bibliography

Christian, W. Asbury. *Richmond: Her Past and Present.* Richmond: L.H. Jenkins, 1912.

Claiborne, Virginia Mc K., comp. *Fifty Years in Richmond 1898–1948 A Photographic Review.* Richmond: Whittet & Shepperson, 1948.

Clinger, David M. *The Ghosts and Glories of Monroe Park: A Sesquicentennial History.* Richmond: The Dietz Press, 1998.

Dabney, Virginius. *Richmond: The Story of a City.* New York: Doubleday & Company, 1976.

Dodson, E. Griffith. *The Capitol at Richmond, Virginia.* Richmond: Whittet & Shepperson, 1938.

Dulaney, Paul S. *The Architecture of Historic Richmond.* Charlottesville: The University Press of Virginia, 1968.

DuPriest, James E. Jr. *Hollywood Cemetery A Tour.* Richmond: Waterman Press, 1985.

Eckenrode, H.T., ed. *Richmond Capital of Virginia Approaches to Its History.* Richmond: Whittet & Shepperson, 1938.

Hale, Thomas F., and Louis H. Manarin. *Richmond A Pictorial History from the Valentine Museum and Dementi Collections.* Richmond: Whittet & Shepperson, 1974.

Kimball, Fiske. *The Capitol of Virginia.* Richmond: Virginia State Library and Archives, 1989.

Lutz, Earle. *A Richmond Album.* Richmond: Garrett & Massie, 1937.

Manarin, Louis H., ed. *Richmond at War The Minutes of the City Council 1861–1865.* Chapel Hill: The University of North Carolina Press, 1966.

Manarin, Louis H., and Clifford Dowdey. *The History of Henrico County.* Charlottesville: University of Virginia Press, 1984.

Mitchell, Mary H. *Hollywood Cemetery: The History of a Southern Shrine.* Richmond: Virginia State Library, 1985.

Ryan, David D., and Wayland W. Rennie. *Lewis Ginter's Richmond.* Richmond: Whittet & Shepperson, 1991.

Sanford, James K., comp. and ed. *Richmond Her Triumphs, Tragedies & Growth.* Richmond: Whittet & Shepperson, 1975.

Scott, Mary Wingfield. *Old Richmond Neighborhoods.* Richmond: Whittet & Shepperson, 1950.

Scott, Mary Wingfield, and Louise F. Catterall. *Virginia's Capitol Square: Its Buildings & Its Monuments.* Richmond: The Valentine Museum, 1957.

Stanard, Mary Newton. *Richmond: Its People and Its Story.* Philadelphia: J.B. Lippincott Company, 1923.

Ward, Harry M. *Richmond An Illustrated History.* Northridge: Windsor Publications, Inc., 1985.

Zehmer, John G. *Old Richmond Today.* Richmond: Historic Richmond Foundation, 1988.

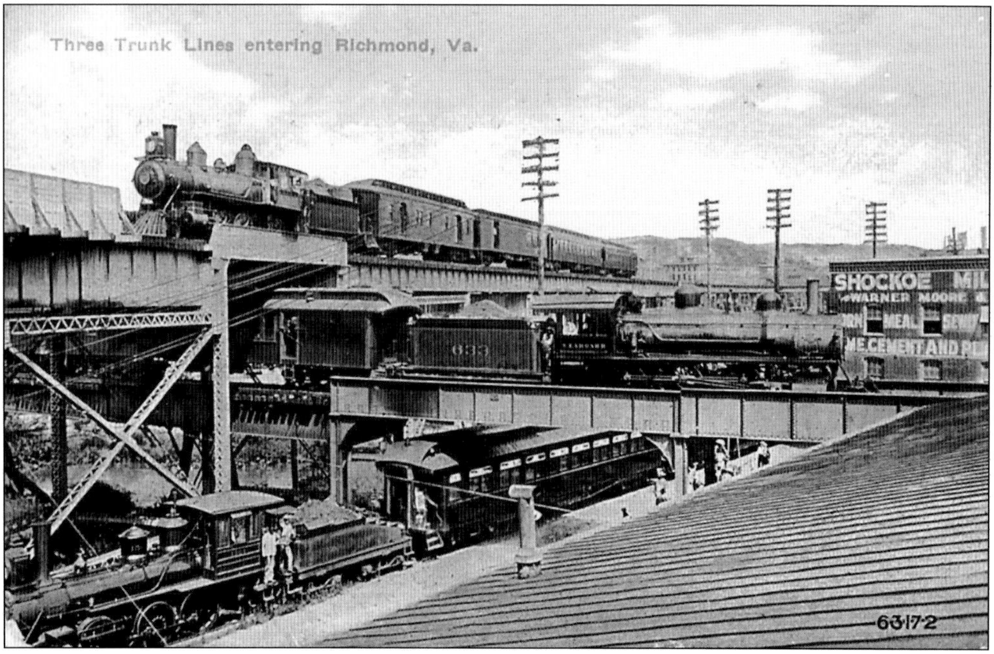

This three-deck track crossing was constructed in 1900 at Seventeenth and Dock Streets in conjunction with the Main Street Station project. The top level contains the Chesapeake & Ohio track. The Seaboard Air Line track is in the middle, and the Southern Railway line appears on the ground level. Passenger trains from each line were aligned on the crossing for a photograph, and this postcard was printed using the photo.